Everything In Its Own Time

A mother's memoir about adopting five children and the ones that got away

Rebecca Patton Falco

Honey Locust Press

EVERYTHING IN ITS OWN TIME

A mother's memoir about adopting five children and the ones that got away

ISBN-13 978-1-60364-025-1

Library of Congress Control Number: 2010931538

For information, contact:
info@honeylocustpress.com
or
Honey Locust Press
238 Park Drive NE
Ranger, GA 30734

Falco, Rebecca Patton.
Everything in its own time: a mother's memoir about adopting five children and the ones that got away / Rebecca Patton Falco.

p. cm.

1. Adoption—Personal narratives. 2. Adopted children—Family relationships. I. Title.

ISBN-13 978-1-60364-025-1

HV875.F35 2010
362.7'34—dc22 2010931538

A lesson learned, a loving God,
And things in their own time,
In nothing more do I trust.
We own nothing. Nothing is ours.
Not even love so fierce, it burns like baby stars.
But this poverty is our greatest gift
The weightlessness of us
As things around begin to shift.

Remember everything I told you.
Keep it in your heart like a stone.
And when the winds have blown things
Round and back again,
What was once your pain, will be your home.
Everything in its own time.
Everything in its own time.

-Emily Saliers

Dedication

To John, my amazing husband, who has taken this eventful journey with me, to Sherry, our children's *third* mother, without whom I would have had neither the time nor the temperament to write this story, and to my mother, Helen, the strongest, kindest woman I have ever known.

What others say...

As our culture explores new and more inclusive forms of connection, along come the Falco's. Rebecca and John's commitment to expanding the idea of family began with their marriage vows and now includes seven different birth families with all the attendant drama, heartbreak and profound joy. Read this book to be moved, to be inspired, to witness an astonishing open-heartedness that has the power to be contagious.

Martha Abshire Simmons, *Founding Director of the Duke University Women's Center*

§ § §

I know firsthand the love Rebecca Falco has for her family and her passionate concern for issues around adoption from the time her family was active in a church where I was the Senior Pastor. All persons concerned about or interested in adoption will benefit from reading her book. Readers will gain a clearer understanding of the legal issues around adoption, but more importantly will experience the personal side of adoption, the emotions and struggles of parents who are wanting to adopt. Falco writes with fearless honesty and a deep understanding of the subject, allowing the reader to experience the frustration, fear, joy and excitement of her journey. This book is a gift.

Rev. Jimmy Moor
Senior Pastor
Tucker United Methodist Church

§ § §

I've known Rebecca since 2003 when she came to Special Link seeking guidance and assistance in the adoption of her 5th child. I was instantly warmed by her compassion toward birthmothers (and their families) and her desire to make all of her adoptions "open" adoptions.

The adoption process has a way of pulling us along in what can sometimes be a frightening road fraught with unexpected twists and turns with prospective parents not knowing where it will lead or when it will stop. These parents can feel as if they are groping in the dark, not sure of how to respond to the roller coaster they find themselves on. Those who find this process the most successful are those who are able to flow with it and allow God to sit in the driver's seat. This goes against the grain of our human nature because we want to control it's every bend and curve, even though that may not lead us to the destination God has prepared for us.

It was so refreshing to witness that, even though Rebecca and her husband had some specific ideas about where they wanted to go on their journey (and how they planned to get there), they ultimately chose to let go and they relinquished the wheel. Soon, they "took off" and God carried them to *His* perfect provision for them. The Falco family brought home their new son, Becton. I wonder how many families miss their own "Bectons" because they're unwilling to flow along with this wonderful and God-breathed process.

It has been a joy to watch the Falco family revel in the blessedness of their infertility—and how God used that for a greater good and to bring infinite joy. Because of their infertility, they have witnessed the miracle of adoption. Not just once, but five times. He turned their ashes into gold… just as He promised.

Carri Uram, Executive Director
Special Link, Inc. Adoptions

§ § §

Everything In Its Own Time is a story of adoption, one woman's journey to answer her call to be a mother and to have a family. Rebecca Falco chronicles her experience creating a family through adoption and provides first hand knowledge of the complex process to adopt and the varied forms it can take. "Everything in its own time" is so much more than a memoir about adoption. It is about recovery, from trauma and the pain of infertility. It is about exploration, allowing life to unfold and braving the unknown paths ahead. It is about mothering, in the deepest, most pure sense of the word. It is a love story about a marriage, two people who open their lives and hearts to five beautiful, unique children. "Everything in its own time" will make you believe in open adoption and in the wisdom of the women who chose Rebecca and John to parent their children.

Sonya Green, adoptive parent

§ § §

For years Rebecca has shared vignettes of her family life with select friends. Her writing always draws me in. These are moments or events told not only with setting and conversation, but thoughtful reflection and analysis, which is what sets her writing apart. Her heart is always about the big picture of parenting, guiding through resistance, trying to expose her children to the real world, and how you personally go about making it better. I encouraged her to put the collection in a book, but she's done more than that. She's told the whole story.

Sherry Warner, adoptive parent

§ § §

Everything In Its Own Time is an honest reflection of one family's quest to complete itself. Part memoir, raw and reflective; part guidebook for potential adoptive parents and birth parents alike; part tale of courage, love, divinity and direction.

Ms. Falco does not leave any stone unturned in her detailed description of their family-forming odyssey. Humorous, gut-wrenching and informative. In context, the whole Falco family makes perfect sense.

Leslie Foge, MA, MFT
Adoption specialist and Co-Author of
The Third Choice: A Woman's Guide To
Placing a Child for Adoption

§ § §

This book is a valuable resource for prospective adoptive families and adoption professionals. It provides thorough information for individuals seeking to learn about the general adoption process and adoption options. The book is written in a warm, sensitive manner with a sense of humor. Rebecca has personal as well as professional experience in this area and has contributed to the available adoption literature.

Ronnie Fishbein, MA, JD
Fellow, American Academy of Adoption Attorneys
Adoptive parent
Founder and director, Adoption Planning, Inc

§ § §

Rebecca was instrumental in orchestrating the adoption of both of our children. We will always be forever grateful to her for what she has done for us. Without her, we wouldn't have the two beautiful children that were brought to us through open adoption.

The Murphys, adoptive parents

§ § §

I have always enjoyed Rebecca's emails about her family's life. She has shared incidents, insights, and thoughts, and always left me thinking about what she had written long after I'd read the email. I am someone whom she helped through an adoption, as part of a birth family. Rebecca's love and support during that time were invaluable. Her book reflects her thoughtfulness and caring, while her practical, open-minded approach to adoption is a model for everyone to follow.

Barbara Martin, birth-grandmother

§ § §

Rebecca and I share a love for families, adoption, and the Indigo Girls. Her writing clearly and powerfully conveys the many emotions of family building - the fears, joys, sorrows and surprises. Her words read like helpful friends to anyone feeling isolated or daunted along the path. Her candid, warm voice and variety of experiences during her own family's growth provide support for the journey."

Lori M. Surmay, Adoption Attorney, Atlanta, GA

§ § §

The U.S. Census tells us that the current generation of American children is spectacularly diverse, the most varied by race, ethnicity, religion, language, and country of origin of any generation in American history, or in global history. Here is a story of an Atlanta family that reflects the diversity of America's children. The author-mother, Rebecca Falco, bridges, with love and resilience, her children's varied pasts, challenges, and far-flung relations. In these pages she describes the creation, with her husband, of their larger-than-usual family, and the struggle to knit them all together into one loving, noisy, happy, and precious group.

Melissa Fay Greene, author of
Praying for Sheetrock and
There Is No Me Without You

Preface

This is the story of the creation of our family through adoption. It is written for my children: Emily, K.J., Skye, Journey, and Becton. It is also written for those who are interested in our particular family and for those who want to learn, anecdotally, about domestic adoption in this country from 1993 to 2004, and beyond. It is my hope that sharing my experiences will help others navigate their own family creation more successfully.

In all honesty, I am also writing this book out of a need to justify my existence. I have felt guilty for a long time that I am not the professional working mother and role model that I envisioned I would be. I have more formal education than most people and little to show for it–other than my children.

It's ironic. When my mother married my father in 1956, she said that her choices were to become a teacher, a secretary, or a wife and future mother. She chose the latter. By the time I was making a similar decision about my future, the possibilities were endless. I was a capable student, so educational requirements for various professions were not a stumbling block. Still, I never found a lasting passion for any of my chosen work until infertility propelled me into the world of adoption. Becoming Emily's mother through open adoption was the best thing that had ever happened to me. I wanted others to have that kind of top-of-the-mountain experience. I wanted to repeat it myself. Becoming the mother of my five children and helping others to become parents through adoption has been my "work" and my passion now for many years.

Parenting is not easy for me. Every day is challenging in one way or another. I am not who I thought I would be when I imagined being a *different* kind of mother than my own because I had choices and opportunities she didn't have. "Everything in its own time" speaks volumes to me about my own journey. A mother of five is who I have become because I loved my husband John, because we could not conceive children on our own, and because those circumstances led us to Emily and then to K.J., to Skye, to Journey, and to Becton. "What was once *[my]* pain"–the pain of infertility–"will be *[my]* home"–a family created through adoption.

The contents of this book, my story, are more than the compilation of five separate adoption events. As I was collecting documents related to the adoptions, I realized that I needed to include some of the in-between times: the adoption attempts that failed and a few of the highs and lows with our particular children. The stories didn't make any sense without the in-between times. Perhaps most couples plan how many children to have and then go about creating that result. Not so in our case. As you will read, each adoption situation we considered influenced our evolving family plan.

Emily asked me not to include anything "too embarrassing," but I cannot promise that I have lived up to her standards. I decided it was more important to be honest than to cleanse these pages of our mistakes and shortcomings. However, I did decide to use fictitious names for many of the characters, including birth family members, to protect their privacy.

After all, adoption exists because life is not perfect. If it were, all women who give birth would be able to raise their children. If it were, the women who wanted to become pregnant and bear children would be able to. If it were, children would live with their original parents and have all of their needs met. But life is not always easy or pleasant. We try to make the best of it. And, if we are lucky, as I have been, it turns out better than we ever could have imagined.

If it is any consolation to Emily, I believe the most "embarrassing" moments revealed in this account belong to *me*. Years from now, I hope my children will be able to say that I painted an accurate portrait of myself as I experienced these events.

I wanted to capture the thoughts and emotions I was feeling at the time of these events, so I have used some of my original emails, letters, and journal entries to piece together my story. When quoting sources written at an earlier time, I have dated them. When quoting from materials written by others, I have either disguised them or gained their permission to use the source.

Table of Contents

Before the Adoptions

"You're not pregnant after all."

The phone had rung in my office, and I had picked it up. The nurse from the Fertility Clinic identified herself.

"The HCG from your fertility medication was responsible for the incorrect result."

"W-what?"

I couldn't believe what I was hearing. Was this an apology? A joke?

Three hours ago, before coming to work at the law firm where I was a first-year litigation associate, I had been to the clinic for a pregnancy test. To my amazement, this time the result was positive. Finally, after four months of Clomid treatments to increase my egg production, followed by inseminations of my husband, John's washed sperm, I was pregnant! I went to work feeling like I was walking on air.

Having children together had been an acknowledged goal of our marriage. My husband and I had begun trying to make a baby from Day One. In fact, I had calculated that I was ovulating on our wedding day. I fully expected it to happen. No pregnancy. After trying unsuccessfully for six months, I made an appointment with a fertility specialist. John and I engaged in all the routine medical tests and were coached on charting my ovulations. The doctor found no obvious reasons for my inability to conceive.

After more months without conceiving, I underwent an exploratory laparoscopy, with the thought being that I might have endometriosis or some other abnormality that could not be detected without looking inside me. Nothing of any significance was discovered. I received the label: "unexplained infertility."

A month later, in August 1992, John received his M.B.A. degree and we resigned from our jobs in Durham, North Carolina. In

September, we began a much anticipated and well-planned month-long, zigzag trip across the United States, covering 7000 miles. The trip ended in Palo Alto where I began work in October as a lawyer. We found an apartment, walking distance from my office, and John began his job search. After a few months, he secured a job with a real estate research and consulting firm in San Francisco.

Now that we were settled, we began to focus on baby-making again. I soon located another fertility clinic close by. We began treatments *again* in earnest.

The phone call from the nurse announcing my barren womb sent me tumbling into a deep, dark abyss. I was not at all sure I could climb out as the walls were closing in.

There is a roller coaster of emotions associated with infertility. My story of treatments, pills, shots, procedures, highs and lows, is probably very similar to the stories of others who have asked medicine to do what their own bodies could not do alone. But, in my case, the emotional pain I felt was intensified by my history as a rape survivor.

On June 24, 1982, when I was twenty-four, while delivering newspapers at 4 a.m. in Midtown Atlanta, a stranger who needed help with his broken-down car approached me. The Good Samaritan that I was, I agreed to drive him to help. The stranger raped me. I reported the crime. He was found, arrested, and later convicted and sentenced to 20 years in prison. My clarity about who and what I could trust had been destroyed.

In rape, the victim's sense of control over her (or his) life is taken by the assailant through the act of forced sexual contact. For the assailant, it isn't about the sex. It is about taking *power*. The resulting powerlessness I felt affected all aspects of my life but particularly in areas that related to my sexuality. Over the next three years, I was raped two more times–first by one of my employers and then by a date. I did not report these crimes. I knew too much about how difficult rape prosecutions were from my first experience with the criminal justice system. I thought I could live with the pain.

During this same time period, I was also "romantically" involved with a man who was emotionally and sexually abusive to me. I didn't have the strength to leave him.

In 1988, at age thirty, I left Atlanta, my home for most of my life, to attend Duke University Law School in Durham, North Carolina. I saw this move, even then, as a new beginning–a new chance to take control of my life. Though I had been offered a full scholarship to attend Emory University Law School, my desperation to gain geographical distance from my negative entanglements in Atlanta prompted me to turn down the financial security and move to Durham. I also reasoned that with the prestige of a Duke Law degree, I could find a job anywhere in the country. I would not need a man. If I chose to remain single, if I chose to have a child on my own, I would be in a good position to do so. I felt both courageous and reckless. I packed my belongings and left with my dog, Adagio, in my pick-up truck.

In my first year of law school, I worked hard. I made friends. I sought therapy to deal with the sexual violence and abuse in my twenties, and I did a lot of healing.

I was in a joint-degree program, at the end of which I would earn both a Juris Doctor from the Law School and a Master of Arts in history from the Graduate School of Arts and Sciences. It was through this latter program that I met the woman who would become the first Director of the new Duke Women's Center. In my second year of school, she hired me as the Safety Programming Coordinator for the Women's Center. I was also a member of the Rape and Sexual Assault Task Force. Along with the Director of the Women's Center, I oversaw an intensive educational campaign, which included major advertising and weekly panels or other programs related to date rape and other forms of sexual violence. The highlight of the campaign for me was a play I wrote based on Duke students' experiences with the keg scene and date rape, titled "Date Rape on Trial."

At the law school, I was elected co-chair of the Forum for Legal Alternatives, a public interest club. We planned and sponsored a conference focused on critical race theory and feminist legal thought. Through all of these activities at Duke, I was regaining a sense of my self, my power, and my worthiness.

However, a few years later, when I relinquished control over my body to medical intervention with the understanding that pregnancy would result, the rape-related feelings resurfaced when I received the false pregnancy report. My body had been manipulated and controlled by outside forces. I felt an intense sense of betrayal. I hated my body. I hated myself. My feelings of inadequacy and brokenness progressed to the point that I no longer considered myself worthy to be John's partner. Being with him only reminded me of my failure.

But John would not let me go. He said he loved me and wanted to be with me whether or not we *ever* had children. His love buoyed me just enough to get me into individual counseling. I found a pastoral counselor near our home who diagnosed me with depression and encouraged me to get anti-depressant medication. The medicine helped.

Soon John joined me in counseling. Within a few weeks, it became clear to both of us that we still wanted to be parents together, but that our quest for a biologically similar child had been tearing us apart. Coming to terms with our infertility meant accepting ourselves and letting go of feelings of failure, remorse, and anger. Once we dealt with our grief, we could make a new commitment to becoming parents through other means. Our wonderful therapist said that he didn't usually advise couples to have a child to save a marriage. But, in this case, that was exactly the thing we needed to do.

§ § §

I met John in the midst of my personal and professional growth during the second year of law and graduate school. He was the roommate of one of my law school classmates. He asked me out three times before I said "yes" because my focus was firmly directed toward self-improvement, not romance. But the offer of tickets to the *Duke v. Arizona* men's basketball game on my birthday was more than I could resist.

I warned John that I was "much older" than he–six and a half years, to be exact. That did not deter him. I put John through a rigorous two-prong test: First, Adagio–my best friend–had to approve of him. She did. Second, I asked John to watch an Indigo Girls music video while I observed him for his reaction. John loved their music too! Why the Indigo Girls? My patchwork educational, work, and social history had led me to them.

I had graduated from Emory University in Atlanta, Georgia, with a B.A. in history and psychology in 1980, with no clear idea of what I wanted to do next. After a year of bookkeeping and selling building materials, I decided that I my future might lie in following in my father's footsteps. He was a United Methodist minister and pastoral counselor. Accordingly, I enrolled in theology school. Though I completed my Master of Theological Studies in 1984, by the end of the first year of schooling, I had decided that ordination was not for me. Instead, I discovered a love of teaching and completed the educational requirements to become a certified high school social studies teacher. I taught in public school and in private psychiatric hospitals. I also took a job as a Minster to Youth.

It was through my work at the church that I was introduced to Jenna, a young woman who became a supportive and loving friend for years to come. She introduced me to a music group who played in local Atlanta bars: the Indigo Girls. Through the power of their music and the circle of women who made up their following, I found a safe haven during those years when I was suffering the effects of three rapes and an abusive relationship. It was empowering to be in the company of women.

Coincidentally, I was also exposed, for the first time that I recognized, to lesbians. Although I did not count myself among them, I accepted that women loving women was no better or worse than men and women loving each other. It was my belief that this diversity of human being was all a reflection of "the image of God." I did not know it then, but these positive experiences with same-sex couples would set the stage for my choice of work and community in the future.

Though teaching and ministry were compelling, they were not fulfilling. I was still searching for my calling. Through work with troubled teenagers and my experiences with sexual violence, I began to form the idea that I wanted to be an attorney. I would fix social problems, such as racial and gender inequality and violence against women and children, through legal means.

Fast forward to my second year at Duke. After my first date with John, we grew closer and closer. He was so different from the other men I had dated. He carried little baggage from past relationships or early family life. He had a positive outlook. He felt good about himself. He saw opportunity and beauty around him. He serenaded me with music that he wrote. We took trips together; and we shared our histories and values with each other.

At the end of May 1990, I left for summer law clerk jobs in Palo Alto, California, and Phoenix, Arizona. John agreed to store my furniture in his apartment while I was away. I remember saying to my mother as she, Adagio, and I made the long drive in my pick-up truck to California: "If it doesn't work out, at least I had a place to store my stuff for the summer." John seemed too good to be true. Surely, I thought, this could not last.

During the summer, John flew out to California to visit me; and our time together was wonderful. A few weeks later, on the drive to Arizona with my sister and Adagio for my second summer job, we stopped in Hollywood and found Emily Saliers and Amy Ray: the Indigo Girls, in the recording studio. During casual conversation with Emily, I told her about John and asked: "Will you sing at our wedding if we decide to get married?" At the time, my question was idle talk, only half-serious. But, a few weeks later, when John came to visit me in Arizona, he came with a ring and a proposal of marriage. In utter shock and disbelief, I said, "Yes."

There is so much more I could say about our courtship, our months of wedding planning while we lived in an old farmhouse in Bahama, North Carolina, the coming together of an Italian, New York mostly-Catholic family with a Scots-Irish, Southern Protestant one, our pursuit of graduate degrees and the forging of professional identities. These things are all background to the events that came after and would resurface, consciously or unconsciously, as we moved forward as a couple. For now, it is important to know that in the months before our wedding, we were discovering that we were a good team in terms of supporting each other's individual pursuits: social, athletic, and economic; and that our commitment to be lifelong partners included the promise and hope that we would be parents together. In one conversation, I confided to John, "You know, I may not make a lot of money. My goal is to 'do good'."

He responded, "That's fine. Is it okay if I make a lot of money?"

On March 9, 1991, my father walked me down the aisle as father of the bride and then pulled on his robe to preside over our wedding ceremony. I had spent countless hours crafting *my part* of the service and selecting the persons who would utter the chosen words.

In the end, our statement to the persons who were witnessing our formal commitment included excerpts from speeches, lyrics, and poetry that affirmed our families of origin, asked God to be with us through the good and bad times, expressed our opposition to the current war: Desert Storm, voiced our concerns for the health of the planet, the rights of children and animals, racial equality, and gay rights. We would not be bystanders. We hoped to be part of the solutions. We saw ourselves as members of a worldwide community whose culture and religion was no better or worse than any other nation. Were we naïve? Perhaps. But these were our ideals. These were our guideposts.

In the homily that my father preached later in the service, he noted our commitment to "care for the creation." I thought I understood that statement on March 9, 1991. But in the years to come, it would take on additional meanings as we journeyed to create a family of our own.

And, yes, Emily Saliers and the Indigo Girls sang at our wedding and reception.

I was 33 years old when John and I married. We knew we wanted to have children right away. In my written responses to our premarital counseling questionnaire, I had written: "Family is very important. Before I met John, I was prepared to attempt childrearing on my own. Now I wouldn't want to do it without him. But I'm also scared. I have wanted to have children for so long. I don't know how I'll react if I can't."

We hoped for two or three children. We had names picked out for a first boy and first girl. A boy would be named "Kevin" after John's best friend, Kevin Elden. A girl would be named "Emily" after my friend Emily Saliers.

After our honeymoon, we returned to Durham where I completed my final year at Duke, graduating in May 1991 with a J.D. and a M.A. Over the summer, I studied for and passed the California Bar Exam. Meanwhile, John needed an additional year to complete his Executive M.B.A. program at UNC-Chapel Hill. He would continue to work for a real estate developer in Durham, and I would become the first Coordinator of Sexual Assault Services at the Women's Center at Duke for the school year, 1991 to 1992.

As I reflected on the first year of marriage in a letter to a friend dated May 28, 1992, I wrote: "…I don't know why we 'work' so well together. I know we pay attention to each other. We listen for the feelings behind the words each of us speaks. There are back rubs and morning runs and workouts together. We safeguard Friday nights for videos and pizza. But I can't help but believe that I am most of all extremely *lucky* that John and I wandered into each other's lives. No one could be more supportive or kind than John is to me–without my even asking."

Once John and I confirmed through counseling that we still wanted to be parents, we began to research our alternatives. We attended "Resolve" meetings. Resolve is the national infertility association that provides support, education, and advocacy to the millions of Americans who suffer with infertility. The meetings helped us identify questions which, when answered, would enable us to determine our path to parenthood:

- How much time were we willing to give to infertility treatments?
- How much time were we willing to take away from work?
- How long were we willing to wait for a pregnancy?
- How optimistic were we that infertility treatments would work?

- How much stress could we handle?
- How much money were we willing to spend?
- How much physical pain or discomfort was I willing to endure?
- Could our faith sustain us?
- How important was it to have a child bearing our own DNA?
- How important was it to me, to us, to experience pregnancy?

I would like to say that we took our time and rationally analyzed our responses to each of these questions. That was not the case. Primarily, it came down to two factors: money and personality. Our next step in the infertility treatment process was to be in vitro fertilization ("IVF") at a cost of $10,000 per cycle. The doctors could provide no assurance that IVF would work since they had been unable to figure out why I was not conceiving. On the other hand, we had heard that we could adopt a child for that amount of money or less. I was (and am) an impatient person. I was ready to be a mother. I wanted a child right away.

Learning the Process of Adoption

September to December 1993

Our sights turned toward adoption. John and I attended information sessions at a number of adoption agencies, both domestic and international. We were lucky enough to meet a couple who had adopted a baby girl, domestically, after meeting her biological mother. They shared their story and research with us, and it piqued our interest.

In October 1993, we decided to attend an information session offered by Open Adoption Now, a facilitator specializing in fully open adoption. "Open adoption," as our presenter defined it, referred to open channels of communication between birth parents and adoptive parents. In open adoption, the adoptive parents meet the birth parents, share full identifying information, and engage in ongoing contact over the years, either through correspondence or in person, based on the mutual needs of everyone involved.

Our presenter stated that Open Adoption Now ("OAN") would provide the birth parents and us with educational resources and counseling to prepare for the problems and issues that usually arise in open adoption and to help us deal with any emotional complications or conflicts. Although we initially feared, as many prospective adoptive parents do, that birth parents who knew us might take back our baby or interfere in our parenting, this honest and humane approach to adoption appealed to us. Moreover, one of the real advantages of open adoption, it seemed to us, was that birth parents *preferred* it. They were choosing open adoption over more closed forms in greater numbers each year. As a consequence, we were more likely to get a baby sooner with this approach. John and I decided to sign up.

Adoption is complicated, both emotionally and legally. As we were to learn, there are distinctions between the kinds of services that adoption *agencies*, adoption *facilitators*, and adoption *attorneys* provide. Though there are many exceptions and nuances to the following statements when applied to different states in this country, these are some general rules.

Adoption *agencies* are licensed by their state. They are required to comply with government regulations and receive regular oversight. Their services tend to be comprehensive. Adoption *facilitators* are brokers who bring birth parents and adoptive parents together. They may be individuals or companies. The range of their services is varied, and they receive little oversight other then word of mouth by customers. Agencies and facilitators may charge a fee for each service provided or a flat fee for a group of services. Adoption *attorneys* are licensed professionals with ethical obligations who charge by the hour. They are often restricted by law from advertising for birth parents, but their legal services are necessary to finalize an adoption in court.

OAN, an adoption facilitator, provided a group of services and charged a flat fee on a sliding scale based on the income of the adoptive parents. OAN provided direct education to adoptive parents (in the form of workshops, written materials, and meetings with adoption professionals), counseling services to the adoptive parents and the birth parents, a 24/7 birth parent intake service, ongoing advertising to attract birth parents in the Yellow Pages, periodic ads, magazines, and newspapers, administrative services to maintain our file and distribute our marketing letter to birth parents, as well as community outreach to promote the public's understanding of open adoption.

In addition to the services provided by OAN, in order for us to adopt, we needed a "Home Study" completed and approved. A Home Study, sometimes called an "adoption study," is a written report containing the findings of the caseworker who has met, on several occasions, with the prospective adoptive parents, has visited their home, and who has investigated the health, medical, criminal, family and individual backgrounds of the adoptive parents. The purpose of the home study is to help the Court determine whether the adoptive parents are qualified to adopt a child, based on the criteria that have been established by state law. For any interstate adoption–that is, an adoption where the child and the adoptive parent(s) are from different states–a home study is required and reviewed by an official in the sending state before the child can be brought home.

Home studies can only be completed by licensed adoption *agencies* (in most states). Because OAN was not a licensed adoption agency, we had to contact the Department of Family and Children Services, a governmental entity, to complete our home study. We would also need to contact one or more attorneys–depending on the number of states involved in the adoption–to terminate the parental rights of the birth parents and to finalize our adoption in the county of our residence. I intended to do the finalization myself as a member of the California Bar.

At our first meeting, after we signed our contract with OAN, John and I were given a notebook that outlined the likely steps in the process of adopting and a list of documents needed for our file. The long list of documents included: a confidential questionnaire, a preference form, verifications of employment, health history forms, letters of recommendation, a phone calling card number (so that calls placed on our behalf could be charged to us), an approved "Dear Birthmother" letter, and a number of other worksheets and documents related to liability and grievances. While this list appeared to be a set of objective and administrative forms, our tasks were intensely subjective and personal.

The "Preference Form" would indicate the types of birthmothers we wanted our profile letter sent to. The first category was race and/or ethnic background. The form allowed us to choose:

___ both birth parents White
___ both birth parents Hispanic
___ both birth parents Asian
___ both birth parents Black
___ one birth parent White and the other Hispanic

___ one birth parent White and the other Asian
___ one birth parent White and the other Black
___ both birth parents Non-White but of different racial backgrounds
___ one or both birth parents American Indian
___ specify "other"

We could select as many categories as we wanted. And we were told that the more categories we selected, the quicker we might adopt. However, we were also told to ask ourselves: "If I were to get a call next week about a birthmother whose baby is of this racial background, could I truly be excited without reservation?" If the answer was "no," we were directed not to select the category. OAN gave us reading materials to help us with our decision, as well as resources if we selected to adopt outside our race.

John and I discussed the "race issue," but it wasn't much of a discussion. We would have given birth to a Caucasian child, so why wouldn't we want to *adopt* a Caucasian child? It wasn't that we wanted to hide the fact that our child would be adopted. We just wanted a child that looked like us. Almost as an afterthought, we decided to include Hispanic, half Hispanic/half Caucasian, and American Indian. Why? John is part Italian, with dark eyes and hair. We thought a Hispanic or Native American child might look more like John. At this point in time, we were not thinking deeply about our obligation to incorporate Hispanic or Native American culture into our lives–our child's life–if we adopted a child who was not White.

At the time, we also still believed that I might someday become pregnant. We wanted our child by adoption to blend in with any biological children we might have. We excluded Black as being too different. *I* rejected Asian on the basis of a height prejudice. I'm not kidding. I thought about all the short Asian adults I knew. As a tall woman, I was hoping I would get a tall-*ish* child.

Over the years I have come to realize that those unfamiliar with adoption sometimes believe that "beggars can't be choosers" when it comes to adoptive parents. Or, they hold the opinion that adoptees are "unwanted children," meaning "undesirable children." Neither statement is true. Yes, adoptive parents are dependent on others to become parents in a way that biological parents are not. But adoptive parents do have choices. And children placed for adoption are no less desirable than children conceived and raised by their biological parents.

People adopt children for a variety of reasons. Some have a humanitarian desire to give a family, stability, and a home to a child without parents. Prospective parents may have a connection to or affinity with a particular culture or country, and that helps them decide where to direct their efforts to adopt. Some couples or individuals have one or more biological children and then suffer secondary infertilty. Some couples seek a child of a particular sex. Some adoptions happen almost by accident–parents die, a parent has a drug problem, the daughter of a friend is pregnant, and so forth. A person is in the right place at the right time to fulfill a need.

Other prospective adoptive parents, like John and me, seek to adopt as a *replacement* for their inability to conceive or carry a pregnancy to term. Though we acknowledge differences between biological and adoptive parenting, our desire is still to parent a child who would be similar, in certain ways, to one we might have produced.

Anyone who considers adoption must face some difficult questions. What if the adoption fails? How much will I know about the genetic/biological components of my adopted child? Of course, there are no guarantees of a physically and mentally *perfect* baby when creating one's own offspring. But most of the people I have talked to about this issue believe they have more control over the health of a baby when they can control their own diet and exercise during pregnancy.

Ultimately, someone considering adoption is likely to ask: What will the adopted child *look* like? Will s/he *act* like me and/or my partner? The fantasized child of the infertile couple can become an *idealized* child. S/he has the beautiful eyes of one spouse, the cute nose of the other, an aptitude for competitive sports, is gifted in areas of math and science, has a great sense of humor, and so forth. It's logical to want our children to look and act like us. After all, most of us choose a partner or spouse at least partially based on our personal attractiveness criteria.

I recently received a birth announcement from a new father who began his good news with the words: "*[Our baby]* is absolutely beautiful." He *didn't* say: she has a great set of lungs or, from the size of her head, we are sure she will be brilliant. He is a typical parent. And at the beginning of our journey to parenthood, John and I were much the same. We were not ready or able to concede that we might parent a child through adoption who was not both beautiful and healthy in ways that were familiar to us.

At a Resolve conference, I heard a speaker talk about her journey to adopting one child and then, miraculously, giving birth to another. She laughed at herself because the reality was that the adopted child had beautiful hair and perfect skin, while the biological child inherited her frizzy hair and acne. I laughed too. The example helped me realize that there are no guarantees of a hoped-for outcome for biological parents.

Most of us are vain. By that I mean: if we were not satisfied with ourselves, whether it be looks, brains, talents, or other criteria, we would not intentionally reproduce ourselves. If we are selecting donor eggs or sperm, we don't just close our eyes and grab some. Instead, we are selective based on some subjective criteria about what is *attractive* in a child or human being. The races and ethnicities of the people who populate the communities we grow up in, or live and work in may also affect who is attractive to us.

Our analysis of the child we wanted to adopt would change over time as we changed. Each time we began the process, we were asked to declare our expectations about our hoped-for child, instead of simply accepting any child who came to us as we would if we conceived on our own.

Our desire for a child who was more like than different from us was part of the reason that open adoption seemed so promising. We would *see and know* at least one of the child's birth parents. If we didn't like what we saw, heard, or experienced, we could back out. Oh, we were warned that being chosen and then rejecting a birthmother could be devastating to her. But, I felt pretty confident about the safeguards.

That is, a birthmother would initially choose us based on our profile. If she was attracted to us, I suspected the attraction would be mutual. As we talked on the phone, our attraction to each other would be further tested. If all went well there, we would meet and test our physical attraction to each other. The mutuality of the process was reassuring. Moreover, we were told: if it didn't feel right, we didn't have to do it. There was always a back-up exit strategy.

Years later, when I was working for an adoption agency, I saw these principles painfully put into action. We were working with an extremely poor birthmother. She had not received proper dental care as a child. Consequently, her front teeth stuck straight out. She was otherwise healthy, seemingly intelligent, and extremely kind. On several occasions she selected adoptive parents for her baby and established good relationships with them by phone. However, upon meeting the birthmother, each of these couples, in turn, decided not to work with her. None of them ever said it had to do with her looks. But I could see the shock in their eyes. And I experienced them, mentally and emotionally, closing the door on her. It was heartbreaking. In the end, this particular birthmother chose a husband and wife who had been waiting a long time to be chosen. The appearance of this birthmother did not affect their decision to move forward.

Returning to the "preference form," the next category concerned the age of the child. We could select:

____ newborn up to 6 months

____ 6 to 12 months

____ 1-2 years

____ age 2 and over.

John and I wanted to experience parenting from birth, so we selected the youngest category.

Would we be interested in twins? Siblings? Yes. Yes. We had no idea what we were getting into, so the more the merrier, it seemed.

We were asked if we were open to *discussing* working with birth parents who had a mental health history or a possible genetic problem. Yes. Yes. We figured that there was a range of genetic abnormalities and mental health problems, including the depression I had been experiencing because of my infertility. "Discussion" was not commitment. We would cross that bridge if and when the time came.

We were also asked to choose one or more descriptions of a birthmother's use of drugs:

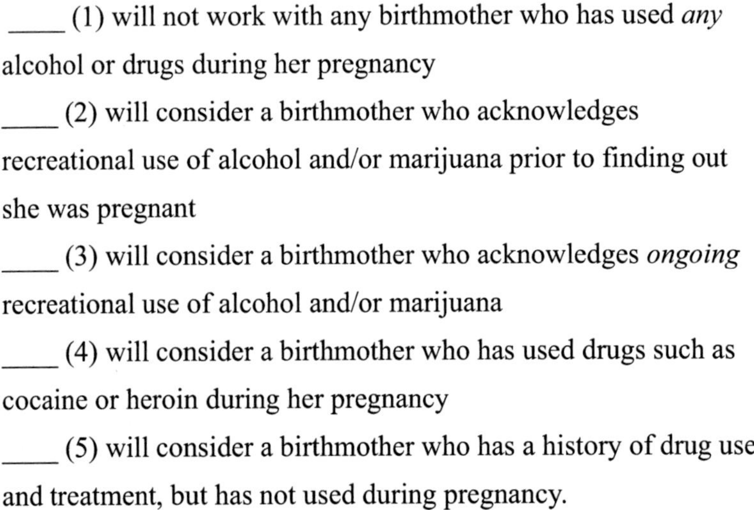

____ (1) will not work with any birthmother who has used *any* alcohol or drugs during her pregnancy

____ (2) will consider a birthmother who acknowledges recreational use of alcohol and/or marijuana prior to finding out she was pregnant

____ (3) will consider a birthmother who acknowledges *ongoing* recreational use of alcohol and/or marijuana

____ (4) will consider a birthmother who has used drugs such as cocaine or heroin during her pregnancy

____ (5) will consider a birthmother who has a history of drug use and treatment, but has not used during pregnancy.

John and I selected (2) and (5). Although we knew that I would not partake of alcohol and marijuana if I became pregnant, both of us had known women who used drugs recreationally and delivered healthy babies. We thought we were willing to take that risk. This choosing of "preferences" was a balancing act. We prayed for a healthy child, but we wanted to make ourselves as open as possible to attract as many birthmothers as possible. How much waiting could we tolerate? How much risk were we willing to take?

Finally, we were asked about HIV and AIDS. Would we adopt a child whose mother was dying from AIDS but who tested negative for the HIV virus? Yes. Would we consider a birthmother who was pregnant and HIV positive, but no determination had been made about the baby's HIV status? No. That seemed too potentially painful.

How would the pregnant women who wished to place their babies for adoption know about our existence and interest? This is where the "Dear Birthmother" letter came in. OAN provided very specific instructions about what the letter should look like. Too much variation from the formula, and our letter would not be approved. The letter had to be one-page, two-sided, with a 4"x6" photo of the adoptive family on the front and additional smaller photos. The content of the letter included a greeting, talk about our relationship, our employment, our home and community, our leisure time, extended family, and thoughts about parenting. Other acceptable topics were spiritual life and values, education, travel, and pets. We were asked to address the birthmother with encouraging and comforting words, and to consider what she must be feeling, thinking, and looking for in adoptive parents. This was our primary marketing tool. This was what a birthmother would see before we received a phone call or made any direct contact with her. A birthmother who contacted OAN would receive *all* the letters from prospective adoptive parents who were interested in parenting the baby she was carrying. She would read the letters and make a choice.

It was a most difficult letter to write! For several days, we did not know how to begin. Here we were: two highly educated individuals who made our living, in part, by the written word, and we could not come up with a thing to say. So much was at stake! Then, one morning, John had a brainstorm. He started writing about *me*–about meeting me, about my attributes, about the kind of mother he thought I would be, and so forth. Suddenly, the juices were flowing again and the rest of the letter came together quickly.

Though OAN placed advertisements and did other forms of outreach for us, we were also required to do networking on our own.

We sent cover letters and copies of our Dear Birthmother letter to friends and family, telling them about open adoption and asking them to pass on the enclosed letter and brochure about OAN to anyone who might be considering placing her child for adoption.

Our Dear Birthmother letter included a head-to-shoulders photo of John and me, as well as a smaller photo of us in wedding attire at our reception. The front side of the letter read:

Greetings,

As we write this letter, we are full of excitement and joy at the thought that we might yet become parents. We hope you learn enough about us here to choose us as the adoptive parents for your baby.

John: When I met Rebecca, we were on opposite sides of the net in a game of volleyball. I thought she was beautiful and athletic, and I hoped to get to know her better. Little did I know, I would have to be approved by Adagio, the dog Rebecca had adopted from an animal shelter eight years earlier. Adagio's snuggle of approval signaled the beginning of a wondrous romance (with Rebecca).

When I met Rebecca's friends, one of the things that struck me was the continuing bond between her and several young adults who were once members of the church youth group Rebecca had led in Atlanta, Georgia. These young adults still thought of Rebecca as a friend and mentor, and they talked about how well she listened to them when they were teenagers struggling with the problems of teenage life. They said Rebecca was always there to listen and never made their problems seem smaller or unimportant just because they were younger. I felt then and still feel lucky to have found Rebecca: not only is she the woman I had dreamed of and thought I would never find, but I also learned early on that she would be a wonderful mother to the children we hope to have.

Rebecca: I am still amazed that John Falco wanted to date me. At the time we met, I was in law school at Duke University because I wanted to learn the skills necessary to make life better for children and others who had been hurt or abused. John was different than anyone I had ever met before. Not only was he handsome and playful, smart and talented, he was (and is) the most sensitive man I've ever met. I am biased, of course. But from the beginning he understood me like no one else. He knows how to make me laugh and provides a shoulder to lean on when I need to cry. He is going to make the best father in the world!

Us: There are at least three qualities that we feel make us a special couple: (1) we are equal partners; (2) we respect and take pride in each other's talents, interests, and abilities: and (3) our strengths complement each other. We both want to make the world a better place for ourselves and future generations – Rebecca, through her education as an attorney, teacher, and crisis counselor, and John, through his experience and aptitude for business and his entrepreneurial spirit. Toward that end, we have promised to support each other in our individual and collective dreams.

Infertility has been our greatest sadness, but this letter symbolizes our hope that you will give us the chance to change fate. If you bless us with a child, we promise to nurture and love that child, and to teach him or her to treat all living things with compassion and respect. We will encourage a child to be true to him/herself and to move to an inner voice rather than to the persuasive or threatening voices outside. Just as our families have supported us as individuals and as a couple, so will we always be there for a child who comes into our lives.

We have friends with birth children and adopted children and we long to experience the joys they have. We'd love to hear about you and tell you more about us. You can call us collect at *[personal and OAN phone numbers given]*. We hope to hear from you soon. Our thoughts and prayers are with you.

[Signed] Rebecca and John Falco

§ § §

The back side of the letter included four small photos: (1) Rebecca singing with church youth group members; (2) Coach John giving an inspirational talk to little league players; (3) John with his sister, Gina, and niece Adrianna; and (4) Rebecca with mother Helen. The back side of the letter read:

Since the beginning of our relationship we have wanted children. We dream about how we will include a child in most of our activities. When we run together each morning before work, we will share the job of pushing the baby jogger (of course we'll try to avoid the hills). When we go cycling on the weekends, one of us will pull the bike trailer that will hold baby and Adagio; the other will carry the picnic. When we camp, and our child is old enough to help out, s/he will learn to cook turkey in a pit and bake Bisquick pies on a stick. We will climb mountains together and learn the names of the plants and animals we see (and all the dinosaur names as well). When we sit at our computers as a family, we will click on computer games and educational software like encyclopedias and interactive learning programs. When we read, we will embark on adventures with an array of Disney characters, Winnie-the-Pooh and friends, Barney, and others. Our keyboard and guitars will welcome new fingers (and toes?) on their keys and strings. We will learn and sing new songs together (in harmony, of course). And, as players and coaches of children's sports, we know the satisfaction of being part of a team, and we look forward to helping a son or daughter discover the sports that bring him/her happiness.

We chose open adoption because we like the idea that the birth parents and adoptive parents select each other. We meet in person and share full identifying information. We also like the idea that we have the option of ongoing contact over the years, either in person or through correspondence that is based on the mutual needs of the birth parents, adopting parents, and the child.

A child we adopt will become a member of a close and growing family that spans the country. We live in Menlo Park, California. Rebecca's two brothers and sister, as well as her parents, live in Atlanta. John's mother, father, and younger sister live in New York. His older sister, her husband and their two children live outside Chicago. Among the members of this extended family are educators, artists, ministers, administrators, nurses, and musicians. Fortunately, between vacations, holidays, and travel for work, we get numerous opportunities to visit with family. Every member of our family is as excited as we are about the prospect of our adopting a baby.

§ § §

Our file was completed and our letter officially approved and available to birthmothers in December 1993. I kept lists of who we sent letters to and created new ones, almost daily. It kept me busy. Otherwise, all there was to do now was *wait*....

The Perfect Birthmother and Open Adoption

January to December 1994

On January 4, 1994, I received a letter from a young woman and dear friend who had been a colleague at Duke University. She wrote: "I have felt that very strange urge/feeling, almost a calling of sorts, to tell you that I would be willing to be a surrogate for you and John if that is an option you so desire…" I was stunned. Although we declined the offer because our focus was set on adoption, the fact that this friend was willing to offer the use of her body to bring a child into the world for us felt so affirming. By sharing our struggle to become parents and asking for help, we had given our friends an opening to reach in and hug us. I had not realized how isolating and lonely our quest for a child had become until the love started pouring in. It continued to flow in the form of letters, cards, and calls.

Another supporter wrote: "As I read and stared at your letter, I found myself praying that at this very moment your child is growing in its birthmother's womb…."

Three weeks after our letter had been approved, we received a call. Close to the time of the events described below, I recorded these edited journal entries:

Friday, January 14, 1994

When we arrived home from work, there were several messages on our answering machine from someone who identified herself as a birthmother named Michelle. We were very excited, but calmed down enough to make a call to her. We could tell she was nervous too. But the longer we talked, the more comfortable it became. We learned that she was a young mother of three daughters and was now pregnant by a man, not her husband. Michelle and her husband, Dan, had separated in June and dated others. In December, they had decided to try and make their marriage work, but Michelle was pregnant with another man's child. They had decided to give Michelle's unborn child to a couple that could not have children.

We learned that Michelle lived in Columbus, Nebraska, and had found us by calling the OAN 1-800 number in the yellow pages of the telephone book after talking with several other adoption agencies that made her uncomfortable. The counselor she spoke with at OAN sent her 160 birthmother letters, including our own. She selected our letter along with 4 or 5 others and began making calls. Michelle said she felt most comfortable with us. We decided we were interested in meeting each other, but didn't know what the next step was. We agreed to check with our respective counselors when OAN opened again after the MLK, Jr. holiday, and to talk again that night.

Tuesday, January 18, 1994

John spoke with our counselor about Michelle and she referred us on to Eileen, a "match counselor." Eileen told us that the next stop would be to fly Michelle to the Bay Area for a "match meeting." She would speak with each of us separately and then lead us in a discussion of some of the issues we needed to address in order to decide if we wanted to continue to work with each other toward adoption.

We called Michelle that evening. She would fly out with her sister-in-law, Mary (who was also pregnant), on Thursday, Jan. 27, and stay until Sunday, Jan. 30, so that we could get better acquainted and make our decision. How would we recognize them? Michelle said that Mary would be wearing a shirt with a baby on it.

§ § §

Most adoption agencies or facilitators would not have sent so many profile letters to a birthmother. It could be overwhelming to read the pleas of so many deserving and desperate couples and individuals. In fact, Michelle later told us that she got help from relatives to weed through her letters. But OAN took the position that a birthmother was *entitled* to make the initial selection from *all* the possibilities. It was her right. Through our education at OAN, John and I learned about the lack of respect historically afforded birth parents. This lack of respect was rooted in the assumption that conceiving and giving birth *naturally* mandated daily parental responsibility. In the past, social workers had selected adoptive parents for a birthmother's child based on their own criteria because of this prejudice against birth parents.

Moreover, adoptive parents, who desperately wanted children, found it difficult to understand the act of *giving away* a baby. Historically, this adoptive parent prejudice made it easier to dismiss or punish a birthmother by denying her information about her child.

The reality, as we learned at OAN, is that birth parents make adoption plans for a variety of reasons, including a sense of responsibility. They know they are not in a position to parent their child; but they feel a parental sense of duty to find the best people to give their child what they can't. They want mature, emotionally and financially secure parents who are ready for a baby. Denial of information about the adoptive parents prevents birth parents from ever being sure that their decision was right.

For the child–the adoptee–secrecy may rob her/him of the right to reach her/his full potential. Instead of her/his psychological energy being directed to the normal process of growth, the adoptee may spend time dwelling on dreams of abandonment, distorted fantasies about her/his birth parents, and the unanswered questions: Who are my birth parents? Who do I look like? How could someone give me away? In *open* adoption, these central questions are answered by the person (or persons) most capable of providing answers: the birth parents. It became clear to John and me that a child's curiosity about and interest in her/his past and future lineage ought to be encouraged and celebrated as a sign that s/he is a healthy individual. My journal continued:

Thursday, January 27, 1994

Michelle and Mary were to arrive from Omaha via Denver at 10:13 a.m. We waited anxiously at the arrival gate as the passengers on the plane from Denver entered the terminal. No pregnant young women, no Michelle. Then the door closed. Could she have changed her mind? Wouldn't she have called us? Did she miss the flight? John began to investigate. He discovered that many of the passengers scheduled for the flight from Omaha to Denver had been rerouted through Houston to San Francisco because of bad weather. John called Eileen to tell her we might be late for our appointment.

We waited anxiously again as passengers came off the flight from Houston. There they were. What a relief! When I first laid eyes on Michelle and her sister-in-law, I forgot to look for the baby t-shirt. Which one was she? Suddenly, I remembered my instructions. I looked again and breathed a sigh of relief. Michelle was not tall or thin or particularly athletic-looking, like me. But there was something about her that I intuitively found comforting, approachable, genuine, and lovely. Before any words had been spoken between us face-to-face, before any counseling or paperwork, before the nitty-gritty working out of the details of adoption, Michelle had passed my attractiveness test. I felt the ground shifting. Attractiveness was not about descriptors like height, weight, eye and hair color. It was more complicated than that....

The flight had been turbulent, but they were in pretty good spirits. After retrieving their luggage, we had a good conversation on the ride to our meetings with Eileen and OAN's attorney. The most exciting moment was when Michelle handed us the ultrasound picture of her baby at 14 ½ weeks for our baby book.

That afternoon went very smoothly and all of us got our most important questions about each other and the law answered. I would be doing the legal representation for John and myself, and we would hire a Nebraska lawyer for Michelle. At the end of a long day, we drove home to Menlo Park, ate dinner, and delivered our guests to their hotel for much needed sleep.

I was impressed that the match meeting was conducted in an egalitarian fashion. For example, after Michelle shared information about her use of alcohol, tobacco, or other drugs, we too shared our experiences with these drugs. At the close of the meeting, our counselor instructed us to wait until after our weekend together was over before expressing our desire regarding the "match." Secretly, John and I agreed that Michelle was the perfect birthmother for us. We liked her, and we believed she would carry out her commitment.

Friday, January 28, 1994

John left early for work while I waited for Michelle and Mary to call me. When they did, Adagio and I went over to the hotel to pick them up. Much to my surprise, Michelle handed me a "tummy talk" t-shirt that read: "My heart belongs to Mommy." Michelle said she was giving it to me so I would know she was really going to give us her baby.

We spent the morning sightseeing. We toured Stanford University, downtown Palo Alto, and my law firm. At noon, we drove to San Francisco to pick-up John, and then shopped at Pier 39, ate pizza, watched the sea lions, and walked up the famous hills to the crooked-est road. We went to Ghirardelli Square for chocolate and ice cream before boarding a cable car headed for Union Square and F.A.O. Schwarz. We picked up Chinese food and returned to the apartment where John conducted a tour of our modest apartment. I flipped through photo albums to show Michelle pictures of our extended family.

Our counselor had assigned us the task of discussing a cooperative agreement that detailed what we tentatively expected from each other at the hospital and after the birth. We responded to written questions such as: Will the adoptive parents be at the hospital with the birthmother/parents? What kind of special time does the birthmother want with the baby in the hospital? What kind of contact–letters, pictures, phone calls, and/or visits–with the adoptive family will the birth parents have in the future?

We decided that I would be in the delivery room with Michelle and that John would be in the hospital waiting room until after the child was born. During her hospital stay, Michelle could ask to see the baby at any time. We would send pictures to her every month for the first year of the baby's life. We would continue to call each other after the baby came to our home. And we would visit at everyone's convenience. We also decided that John and I would begin talking to the baby about his or her birthmother and the adoption in the early childhood years. At the end of our meeting, I gave Michelle a Stanford cow stuffed animal to take home.

Saturday, January 29, 1994

The four of us went out to breakfast before heading to the coast at Half Moon Bay so that Michelle could get her first up-close look at a real ocean. Next we drove back to San Francisco and over to the wharf to catch a ferry to the island of Alcatraz for the tour. Afterwards, we picked up a quick meal and drove through Chinatown and back down the Peninsula.

Michelle needed maternity clothes. John excused himself from the process. I gave Michelle one of my old duffle bags to hold all her new clothes, the cow, and a pair of teddy bear slippers.

§ § §

Michelle and Mary left the following day. Michelle would have her doctor's appointment on Monday and planned to discuss when I should come to Nebraska for the ultrasound that would show us her baby's sex.

Following OAN protocol, we reported to our counselor that we wanted to be "matched" with Michelle. Michelle made her call to the counselor and it was official. As the weeks passed, we continued to have conversations with Michelle by phone. We broadcast the news of our adoption plan to everyone. Notes of encouragement and support arrived and kept our spirits high as the days passed ever so slowly.

Back at the law firm in Palo Alto, I knew I was ill suited to my job. But, what choice did I have? I kept applying for public interest law jobs, but I was not successful in finding different work. And, now, there was a baby on the way…

My edited journal continues:

Friday, April 22, 1994

With great excitement, I boarded a plane for Chicago and on to Omaha, Nebraska at 3 p.m. When I finally arrived in Omaha at 11 p.m., Michelle, her husband Dan, and a friend were waiting for me. Dan drove us the 85 miles to Columbus, NE where we talked of the weekend ahead and got reacquainted with each other. I was taken to my hotel in Columbus for a good night's sleep.

On Saturday, April 23rd and Sunday, April 24th, I met dozens of people who supported Michelle in her adoption plan. These folks included the grandmother and grandfather who had raised her, her mother and younger sister, aunts, uncles, and cousins. Of particular interest to me were Michelle's three daughters: Sarah (age 6), Teresa (age 4) and Bella (age 2). They were beautiful! I got to spend a number of hours playing with them and taking their pictures.

Michelle was driving us around town when she spotted Kaitlyn, the biological father's sister. Michelle asked her to stop and meet me. Although Kaitlyn's brother, Jason, denied paternity, Kaitlyn brought me pictures of Jason, her mother (who also denied that Jason was the father of Michelle's baby), another brother, a sister, and Jason's children, who were our unborn baby's biological half sisters and brother. Kaitlyn agreed to fill out some medical background information about her family. She told us she thought Jason had moved to North Dakota, but she did not know how to contact him.

Monday, April 25, 1994

Michelle picked me up for her doctor's appointment at 9 a.m. The nurse drew blood and checked her for diabetes, as well as other conditions. Everything was fine. The doctor came in to listen to the baby's heartbeat and do the ultrasound. He said the heartbeat was strong. He turned the machine on and almost immediately found the baby's genital area. It was a GIRL! Michelle and I were both happy. John and I were going to become the parents of Emily Rebecca Falco.

Michelle told me on the ride home that she had decided to give the baby a name too so that her daughter would know she cared enough about her to name her. The name she had chosen was Destinie Rian. She said it was our "destiny" to adopt her baby. Emily's adoptive daddy-to-be was thrilled when he heard the good news. Emily was real now, a little girl waiting to be born to parents who would always love her, and a birthmother that loved her enough to give her the opportunity to be part of our family.

I had already packed my bags and checked out of the hotel, so Michelle and I drove on to Omaha. I bought more maternity clothes for Michelle and we ate lunch. Afterward, we drove downtown and met with the attorney that we had hired to represent Michelle's interests. She made an appointment to meet Michelle to do paperwork in a couple of weeks. I was taken to the airport to catch my airplane to Dallas and then home. It was a great trip!

§ § §

Back in Menlo Park, we spread the news about Emily Rebecca and waited some more. John and I could see nothing but blue skies ahead. Unlike some other prospective parents, we had never experienced disappointment in the arena of adoption. The fact that our counselor worried about Michelle not taking advantage of phone counseling did not faze us. We trusted Michelle when she said her counseling and support needs were being met by relatives and friends in Nebraska. We were so confident about this adoption that we allowed our family and friends in Atlanta and in California to throw us baby showers.

The education we received from OAN helped us begin to educate our families of origin about the kind of family formation we would all experience through open adoption. My mother was the first to reach out to Michelle. On Mother's Day, May 8, 1994, she wrote to Michelle:

> I woke up today thinking of you and wanting to send you my Mother's Day greeting. Rebecca and John are here in Atlanta this weekend, full of excitement over the prospect of being parents at last–thanks to you. All of us in Rebecca's family are excited about having a new member of our family.
>
> Rebecca shared a glowing report of her trip to Nebraska last month and pictures of your three precious daughters... Rebecca talks about what a good and loving mother you are to them.
>
> But what I am thinking about today is what a very special kind of mother love you must have to be able to bring the baby you are now carrying into the world and share her with the Falcos. I expect that you have gotten to know Rebecca and John well enough to believe that they not only are very anxious to have a child, but that they also are going to be wonderful parents to your baby. I'm sure that helps, but I realize it can't completely take away the sense of loss that you will feel.
>
> As Rebecca's mother, I want you to know what a brave and loving thing I think you are doing, and how very grateful all of us are to you.

§ § §

My law firm allowed me to leave two weeks before the expected arrival date of the baby to travel the 1800 miles to Nebraska in my pick-up truck with Adagio. On Friday, June 17, 1994, I met with colleagues at a local restaurant in Palo Alto for a send-off party. On the TV screen above the bar, we watched a white SUV driven by O.J. Simpson travel for miles and miles down the road....

The next day, June 18th, I began my own travels and arrived in Columbus, Nebraska on June 22nd. As luck would have it, the baby was late, and the motel became my home for three and a half weeks. I spent some portion of each day with Michelle and her family. The long wait gave us unhurried time to know each other better, to build trust, and to build memories I could share with our child. John arrived in time to spend the July 4th holiday at Michelle's uncle's lake house and to play in the water with at least a dozen relatives. My brother Timothy and his fiancé flew out to Nebraska to retrieve my truck and Adagio, and to drive both back to California.

Michelle's doctor decided to induce labor on July 7, 1994. Michelle went into the hospital early, but her dilation proceeded slowly. As I recall, she was calm and reassuring to me. Although I was the older one, I relied on Michelle's experience with childbirth to guide me through this exciting but emotionally volatile time. As evening approached, Michelle decided to stand in a warm shower. This seemed to relax her body enough that her labor began to intensify. With her aunt on one side and Kaitlyn on the other, Michelle pushed baby Emily into the world at 5:45 p.m. as I watched in wonder. "It's okay, Rebecca. You can cry," declared Michelle, turning the attention of everyone else in the room toward me. Michelle's words brought me out of a dreamlike state and released the tears trapped in the corners of my eyes. I ran down the hall to get John to meet his new eight pound, three ounce, healthy baby girl. The pictures taken of us at the time, holding baby Emily, reveal our complete happiness and amazement.

Michelle and her baby spent two days in the hospital and received many visitors. She and the nurses taught us how to feed, burp, change, and bathe the baby. Michelle told us that at 2 a.m., on the second night, she asked the nurse to bring the baby to her. She spent several hours talking to Destinie about why she made her plan for adoption.

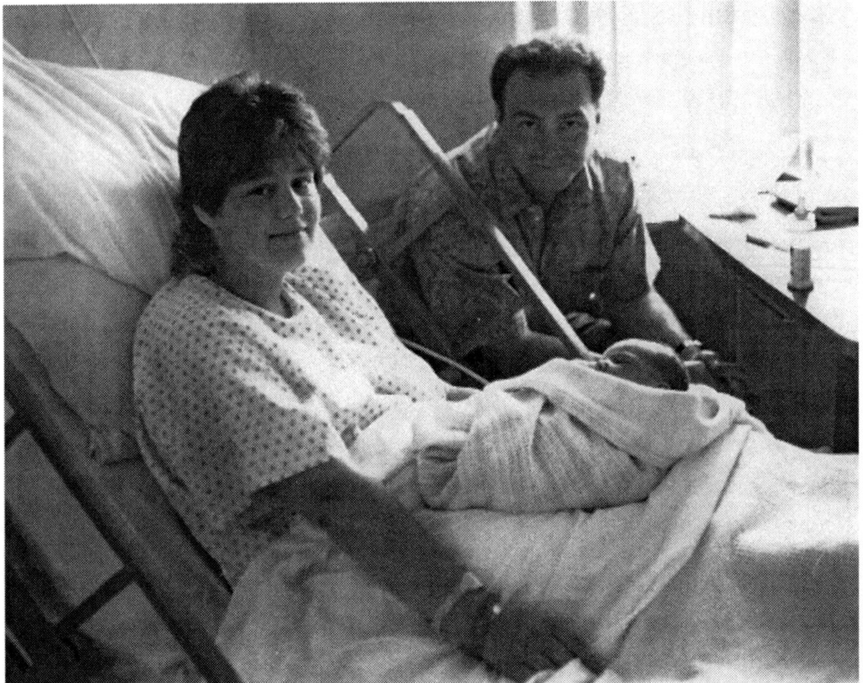

The most bittersweet moment came when Michelle and Destinie checked out of the hospital, and Michelle helped John put the baby in the car seat. As she turned away after saying goodbye, her tears began to fall. I wanted to run to her, but knew I couldn't. At this moment, we had different roles to play. She needed to return to her family, and John and I needed to begin parenting this beautiful gift of a child. We would meet again soon, but this was a moment none of us would ever forget.

We were in Nebraska for a few more days, living at our motel, while the requirements of the Interstate Compact on the Placement of Children ("ICPC") were complied with. The Nebraska attorney drove to Columbus and brought documents for Michelle and Dan to sign that would relinquish their parental rights to the baby. We all met at our motel room. Michelle signed; but Dan refused to do so–claiming he was not the baby's father. He worried that if the adoption fell through, he would become responsible for the child. Michelle was clearly upset. She begged him to sign. Though he was not the biological father of the baby, the law deemed him to be the legal father because he was married to Michelle when she conceived. It was a tense few moments. But, in the end, Dan signed the documents. The interests of the actual father, Jason, would be terminated involuntarily over the next months. The ICPC office in Nebraska had to review the Surrender(s) of Parental Rights, our home study, the baby's medical papers, and other documents prepared by the attorney before giving its approval and sending the package to the California ICPC office. Once California gave its approval, we could return home.

We had borrowed a bassinet, electric cooler, and microwave oven for the motel room. We jumped at every sound the baby made. We checked her breathing every few minutes. But, mostly, we stared and marveled at the mystery and magnificence of her, our daughter.

Before we left Nebraska, Michelle's daughters each had the opportunity to hold the baby. I captured those moments on film. The pictures hung over Emily's crib and were given in a photo album to Michelle. On the day we left town, Michelle gave us a letter that read, in part:

> I know deep down inside this is all for the best, but still it is very hard for all of us. I could not have chosen a better couple to love and care for Destinie. You will be great parents I see that a whole lot and so do the rest of my family. I love you two wonderful people for loving my little girl. Well, our little girl. I have no fear of your not keeping our openness open.

Arriving home, we called Michelle immediately to let her know that we were safe and sound. Timothy had left a letter for us. It read, in part:

> Welcome home Falco Family. Emily, I am disappointed that I didn't get to meet you this trip, but I know I will soon. You are a very lucky little girl to have been blessed with two people I know will be wonderful parents. I know this in part because they are a better brother and sister than I could ever dream of or pray for. You see, I too have been very lucky with family. It's not

something you can work for or earn, but a gift from God you can only be thankful for.

Whether or not John and I would be good parents remained to be seen; but Timothy's expressed love and admiration represented the kind of support that buoyed me, that buoyed us, as we ventured into parenthood 3000 miles away from our families of origin.

Our birth announcement read: *Emily Rebecca Falco was born in love to her birthmother, Michelle [last name], and given in love to her adoptive parents, Rebecca and John Falco*. A picture of baby Emily with Adagio accompanied the announcement.

I had leave from my job at the law firm until the end of September. I knew that most new mothers stayed home with their infants to bond, to recover from the delivery, to sleep when they could, and to protect their child from infections. But I could not contain myself. Within the first week, Emily and I were all over town. I just had to show her off. We walked or strollered everywhere: to the grocery store, to the coffee shop, to the pediatrician's office, and beyond.

On one of these trips, I saw a notice about a "Mommies and Babies" group meeting at Stanford University Hospital and decided that Emily and I would attend. It was a large group with a leader who offered practical advice to new mothers about getting their babies to eat or sleep, among other things. New members to the group told their birth story as their introduction, while other mothers responded with knowing *ooohs* and *aaahs*. I felt the old jealousy and sadness that plagues infertile women. But I told myself: *Remember how happy and proud you are. You are one of the lucky ones. You know things they will never know....* I pushed the jealousy and sadness aside and told my adoption story in all its glory.

One day, at the group meeting, a young mother, Liesl, announced that she was looking for a family with whom to share a nanny when she started back to work in October. Liesl, her husband, Rob, and her son, Nate, lived less than a mile from our home. It was the perfect solution to our own childcare dilemma.

Liesl later created a scrapbook for Emily that included a remembrance of our first meeting. She wrote to Emily:

> Your mother was in awe of you. In awe of finally being a mother. In awe of the little life that she was given to raise, to be responsible for, to nurture and nourish. She was a little unsure of herself, as we all were....

In October, I returned to work as a three-quarter-time employee. I would leave work in the late afternoon each day to go to Liesl's house where the children's nanny would report on Emily's full day of naps, meals, walks, and playtime. As I lounged on the overstuffed couches, cuddling my baby, and talking with Liesl, a new and profound friendship was formed. It was my first adult friendship formed by virtue of our children. But for Nate and Emily, Liesl and I would not have met. Oh, what a loss that would have been!

I found that being a first-time mother leveled the playing field. No matter what one's education, profession, or worldly experience, the responsibility for an infant brought us all to our knees and made us question our competency. I was all too aware of my inadequacies. Which baby foods were best? What formula and how much? How much holding and soothing to do versus letting the child comfort herself? Was she reaching the milestones pronounced in the baby books in the correct time frame? Which were the most appropriate educational toys? The questions were endless.

Emily's nanny stressed the importance of routines. At first, she rolled her eyes after every weekend because we had been so bad at keeping the schedule. We eventually caught on. Part of our ritual with Emily was singing a special lullaby each night. Hers was an adaptation of "Edelweiss" from *The Sound of Music.*

Emily's birth brought a stream of visitors. First came Nanna and Papa, my parents, to meet their first grandchild. My sister, Joanna, and her fiancé followed them. John's study group from business school made a visit. We also made a trip to Chicago, to see John's sister, Gina, and her family.

In September, we traveled to Atlanta for Emily's baptism. My father, always the minister and educator, gave me an article that he had written years ago on the meaning of baptism for United Methodists. He wanted me to understand that infant Baptism was not something parents did for their child, like buying a new pair of shoes. It was "something done for us, not deserved, but given by God in spite of our unworthiness." The church claimed responsibility for the child because s/he belonged to God. I both understood and failed to understand. I would spend many more years wrestling with what it means to be a member of a church family, to be accepted by God and to be accepting of other people as God's children.

At this point in time, I was more interested in educating everyone else about my passion for open adoption and how I conceived of it intersecting with my faith in a higher power. I got special permission from the senior pastor at my home church in Atlanta to make a post-baptism speech to the congregation. I reflected:

"During the homily at our wedding, my father commented, 'In your own way, you have managed to say one of the things that is important in the Judeo-Christian tradition… Marriage is far from a private affair… Marriage is about a personal relationship, but it is about a lot more. It is about two persons committed to working out their calling in the world together. In the Genesis text, God blesses man and woman and charges them with the vocation of caring for the world around them… Your marriage commitment affirms that you have chosen not only to love and cherish each other, but to make it possible for each of you separately and together to love and cherish the world in which we live.'

"At the time, neither John nor I knew the extent to which our commitment to this ideal would be tested in our efforts to enlarge our family of two. But God works in mysterious ways – and somehow we were enabled to move from the sadness and bitterness we felt about infertility to the adoption–the *open* adoption–of Emily and a whole new set of relationships with her extended birth family. Through our acts of parenting *this* child, God reminds us of our commitment to 'love and cherish the world in which we live'."

I also recognized Emily's godparents, Emily Saliers, and my sister, Joanna. Liesl had defined a godparent for me as "someone who is there to remind you that your child is a gift, and that she doesn't belong to you–she belongs to the world and to God."

§ § §

During the remainder of 1994, we traveled to North Carolina, to Atlanta twice for Timothy's and Joanna's weddings, and to New York at Christmas. Emily was becoming a seasoned traveler. We knew just when to feed and nap her to make the plane rides tolerable.

Back in Nebraska, Michelle received letters and pictures from us regularly. Although I took the lead on this correspondence, John also wrote, in October, to express his gratitude:

I wanted to write to you to tell you what fatherhood has meant to

> me. I did not and could not have realized how much this child would affect my life. Watching her each day, seeing her smile, or cry, and watching her grow, is simply amazing. I know she will try my patience as she gets older and all thru the years, but I will never forget how special this beautiful child is to me, to us. Emily alone has the ability to make each moment more precious than time itself. Bedtime is our special time together. Each night she falls asleep to the sound of my voice and the feel of my arms holding her. That alone can brighten any day, no matter how stressful it's been....

Michelle studied for and received her G.E.D. She got a full-time job. She also kept putting subtle pressure on Emily's paternal side of the family to acknowledge their relationship. Kaitlyn wrote to tell us that her mother still didn't believe Emily was her son's child, but she would keep trying to persuade her.

In the latter months of 1994, I came to the conclusion that my future lay in promoting open adoption AND that our family needed to be back on the East Coast. John concurred. I went to the Executive Director of OAN and made my case for opening a branch office in Atlanta. The timing must have been right, because he agreed with me. John was just as fortunate. His company was ready to open a new office in mid-1995 as well. Everything was falling into place.

Opening an Office & Looking for Number Two

January to December 1995

January 31, 1995 was my last day of work at the law firm in Palo Alto. On February 1st, I began a five-month, unpaid internship with OAN to learn all the details about running a branch office. I was trained in the areas of administration, birth parent intake, adoptive parent intake, adoptive parent and birth parent outreach, and membership services. Although I would be hiring a counselor with a Masters degree in social work to prepare home studies and do open adoption counseling, OAN's counselors also trained me in their responsibilities. I observed match meetings and the taking of birth parent relinquishments.

I worked on the Georgia office proposal for the OAN Board of Directors. Having researched Georgia law and regulations at the request of the Executive Director [*to whom I will refer by title only*], I was concerned that we would not be able to advertise our services in Georgia without first becoming a licensed adoption agency. The Executive Director dismissed my concern. In March, the Board approved the opening of the office and salaries for three employees: a counselor, an administrative assistant, and the branch director.

The winter and spring of 1995 was a happy time of experiencing our baby's *firsts* and of cherishing time spent with California friends, knowing our time together would soon come to an end. Emily's adoption became final with a trip to court on February 16, 1995. For a celebration, we spent the day at the San Francisco Zoo with Emily's buddy, Nate, Liesl, and the children's nanny. John and I later created a video entitled: "The Story of Emily's Adoption," for Michelle. It told the adoption story from the day we joined OAN and Michelle's first call through our day at the zoo.

We also looked ahead to life in Atlanta. We would finally be able to buy a home of our own. Even with my reduced salary, houses in the Atlanta area were much more affordable than in California.

On June 16, 1995, we began a cross-country trip that took us through Columbus, Nebraska so that Emily's biological relatives could see her again after almost a year. We were greeted with warmth and affection. It felt much like seeing extended family after a long absence. They belonged to us and we belonged to them. This kind of reunion was part of what made open adoption so special.

We arrived at our new home in Decatur, Georgia on June 25th. The summer was spent getting settled in our new house, finding office locations for our two new offices, outfitting the offices, hiring staff, and securing childcare for Emily for the Fall. We celebrated Emily's first birthday with a gathering of family members, friends, and new neighbors on July 7, 1995. My sister and her husband were moving around the block from us. They were expecting their first child in November. She would be named Kylie Christine Breazeale.

My branch office of OAN officially opened on September 14, 1995, though I had been marketing for clients for a month or more. Two weeks later, anonymous complaints were filed with the Department of Human Resources ("DHR"), Child-Care Licensing Division regarding OAN. The complaints stated that we were performing functions, such as advertising for birthmothers, that could only be performed by licensed adoption agencies.

Non-compliance with Georgia laws and regulations is what I had warned the Executive Director about. I was privately kicking myself because I had not been more insistent, so eager was I to open the office in Atlanta for my own personal reasons. Though I attended meetings with DHR personnel and made proposals to keep the office open, we were asked, in October, to cease operations until we were duly licensed.

My current clients were formally transferred to the Central Office of OAN in California.

The Executive Director was not pleased. He blamed me for the inconvenience and cost. While we worked diligently to complete all the requirements for licensing, I also did extensive outreach in surrounding southeastern states where it was legal to do so, and made monthly membership calls to all clients in all the offices. Nevertheless, the Executive Director fired my administrative assistant, and I was on the receiving end of many angry outbursts from him regarding issues over which I had no control.

The most contentious issues concerned responsibilities assigned to me that I considered illegal. The Executive Director wanted me to fly to New Hampshire to conduct a recruiting seminar for new clients though I had researched the issue and determined that it was unlawful for OAN to do so. Ultimately, I refused to go. But to save my job, I did spend many hours on the phone contacting New Hampshire residents about attending the seminar that the Executive Director intended to conduct himself.

The Executive Director also asked me to extract an additional fee from existing Georgia office clients who had already signed binding contracts. The threat was always that he would close my office if the additional money was not forthcoming. I did as I was told, sending letters to ask clients to sign new contracts and pay more money, but I was very unhappy about it. After receiving my letter, one client called my request "morally indefensible and extortionist," amounting to a "breach of contract." The Executive Director told me to forget that client, but to collect the money from the other clients.

In the midst of all this professional strife, John and I had decided to adopt again. We loved parenting Emily. There had never been any doubt in our minds that we wanted more than one child. We wanted our children to be close in age; but we knew it could take as much as a year to 18 months to find another birthmother. Moreover, as an employee of

OAN, I was entitled to a significant discount of our fee. For these reasons, it made sense to begin our search sooner rather than later.

Our new Dear Birthmother letter was approved to send to pregnant women who contacted OAN in late November 1995. It included some of the old material about our relationship, extended families, and values from our previous letter. But we could now write even more exuberantly about parenting and our belief in open adoption. We were living proof that it worked!

New sections of our letter described our life as parents:

> Rebecca: ... For example, John makes great chicken quesadillas and homemade mashed potatoes. He also vacuums and does most of the yard-work and odd jobs around the house–like building Emily's changing table or adding lights to a room.
>
> John: Rebecca makes vegetarian quiche and lasagna (along with the requisite peanut butter sandwiches for Emily). She does the laundry, dusting, and decorates our house with photographs she has taken of beautiful places we have seen together and of people who are important to us...
>
> Rebecca: Together we care for Emily by playing with her, teaching her new words and skills, bathing her, reading stories, and singing lullabies before bedtime. On weekends, we jog with Emily who reclines in her baby jogger.
>
> Someday we will teach her to shoot a basketball, throw a baseball, strum a guitar, build a shelf and sew a new outfit for herself....
>
> John: Emily loves four things most of all: animals, music, the outdoors, and playing with other children. She gives great hugs, and she has the best laugh in the world. She is going to make a wonderful big sister.
>
> Us: We truly believe that love for our child–for our children–is a

commitment to raise them with whole identities that include knowing the people who gave them life.

We live in Atlanta, Georgia in a neighborhood with big shade trees and sidewalks for strollers, skates, and running feet. Our four-bedroom house, with two big family rooms and a large backyard, provides ample room for another child. Our hours at home together are precious to us. John's office, where he manages a branch of a commercial real estate consulting firm, is only a fifteen-minute drive from home. Rebecca, who is Director of the Georgia Branch of OAN, works less than a mile from home.

§ § §

When John and I were first dating, I was working on a manuscript about being raped and my recovery. When we moved to Atlanta, I offered my manuscript to our county rape crisis center to see if it would be useful to them. On December 19, 1995, I called the center to follow-up regarding the manuscript. In the course of my conversation with the crisis counselor, she told me about a young woman who had been raped the previous Spring and had become pregnant as a result of that rape. Her family was now looking into adoption. I offered to assist the family if they were interested.

The next day, Cindy Brown, the mother of 18-year-old Mary Brown, called me at my office. She told me her daughter's story; and I told her about open adoption, the choices her daughter could have, and the process Mary would go through if she chose this kind of adoption. Cindy had just learned about the rape and pregnancy in early December, and was obviously still reeling from her daughter's recent revelation. But she was very interested in exploring this "solution" to the family's dilemma. We set up a meeting for January 9th, after the Christmas and New Year holidays, because, according to a recent visit to the doctor, Mary was not due until February 29, 1996.

Two days before Christmas, John's mother, Barbara Falco, came to stay with us for the holidays. The next day, John's younger sister, Julie, and her boyfriend arrived. We hosted a Christmas Eve party at our house after the evening church service. We spent Christmas morning with the Falco family and then descended on the Patton relatives for more gift opening and feasting.

On Tuesday, December 26th, I went back to work and Cindy called me. She sounded frantic. She had taken Mary to the doctor again and discovered via ultrasound that Mary was having twins! Mary's due date had been moved up to February 15th, and Cindy wanted to know if our appointment could be changed to January 2nd so that the process of finding parents could begin sooner. We decided to meet two days later, after some more discussion about the urgency the Browns felt.

Cindy had indicated that the biological father of the pregnancy was "unknown," which meant–in this case–that his race was also "unknown." Mary, I had learned, was Caucasian. In preparation for our meeting on the 28th, I went through our OAN files searching for every potential adoptive couple or individual who was open to adopting a racially-mixed child, that is: Caucasian and any other race, *and* open to adopting twins. There were only 9 or 10 clients whose preferences matched Mary's babies.

When John and I had filled out our "Preference Form" for the second adoption, we had selected the same racial categories we had selected with the first adoption: Caucasian, Hispanic, and Native American. Mary's babies might be any of those racial categories, but they might also have African or Asian ancestry. I liked this family from what I knew about them. The idea of adopting twins was very exciting to me. I also thought the Falcos could handle the twins' conception story as well as any parents could given our knowledge about and my experience with sexual assault. What if John and I added our letter to the pile?

I went home and made this proposal to John. He trusted my judgment. He, too, found the idea of raising twins enticing.

In retrospect, I am sure that our decision to add our letter to the pile of others was not a reasoned one so much as "seizing the opportunity" that was right in front of us. The funny thing about categories such as race and ethnicity–or, for purposes of adoption planning: amount of prenatal care, use of alcohol and drugs, family medical history, and so forth–is that specific situations or individuals can sometimes convince you to change a reasoned opinion. I had thought I wanted a baby from a tall, athletic woman like me. Emily's mother was not that. But when I met her, those imagined criteria didn't matter. Something similar was happening here. I felt positive about my interactions with the Browns thus far. They just might be the perfect birth family for our second *and third* children.

On December 28th, I met with Bob and Cindy, Mary's parents, and Mary for an in-person discussion about open adoption through OAN and also to gather pertinent information for the would-be adoptive family. Mary sat quietly between her parents who did most of the talking and asked all of the questions. Mary seemed comfortable with this arrangement, but responded when I spoke to her directly.

When asked about the incident that led to her pregnancy, Mary told me that several months earlier, in May, when she was a senior in high school, she left her classroom trailer to go to the restroom. To get to the nearest restroom, she had to walk through an empty gymnasium and make her way down to the girls' locker room area. She remembered walking into the restroom. The next thing she remembered was waking up on the bathroom floor, becoming aware of a sore place on the back of her head, pain in her vaginal area, and her pants down around her ankles. She sat on the floor for a while trying to collect herself, and then she returned to class. Her friend told her she looked ill. Mary said she didn't tell anyone about the rape. In June, she graduated from high school, got a job, and bought a car. In July, she realized she was pregnant, but kept it a secret. It was not until her mother's birthday, on December 3rd, that Mary finally told her family what had happened.

Cindy interjected that Mary seemed like a different person during those months. She was quiet and stayed in her room a lot. Cindy had attributed the changes to post-high school adjustment. Bob said the family had not noticed Mary was pregnant because she wore baggy clothes. It wasn't until Cindy confronted Mary about her behavioral changes that she told her story. Cindy was tearful. She was concerned that no one would want to parent these babies because of the rape history, an unknown birth father, and because there would be two babies involved. More than anything else she wanted the babies to have a good home to go to when they left the hospital. The idea that a social worker from the state would come and whisk them away to an unknown destination was unthinkable. I tried to reassure her that her nightmare could be avoided with an open adoption plan.

Bob said he was angry and had consulted an attorney. He had wanted to report the rape to the high school, but ultimately decided that reporting would not be in his daughter's best interest and might jeopardize her anonymity. He was primarily concerned about the financial consequences of this pregnancy to the family. Mary lived at home and he supported her while she went to school. Mary was covered on his insurance, but the babies would not be. I assured him that the adoptive parents Mary selected would take financial responsibility for the twins. Bob was also concerned about the effect parenting would have on Mary's chance to complete a college education. Both parents agreed that Mary was not mature enough to handle parenting.

The family agreed that they wanted to move forward and select parents for the twins. I gave them the letters, warned them that the Falco letter was included, and asked them to make the best decision for Mary and the children. I assured them that my feelings would not be hurt if the Falcos were not selected. In fact, if they were primarily interested in putting the incident behind them after the births, a family in California or another far away place might make the most sense. They were to call me with their first, second, and third choices as soon as they could so that I could contact the couples to see if they were interested.

Two days later, Cindy Brown called my home and said that they had poured over the letters, let other relatives read them, and the Falcos were definitely their first choice! They wanted a family that was close so they could see how the children were doing as they grew up.

The Browns' choice of a geographically close adoptive family might seem strange to those unfamiliar with the emotions associated with adoption. My education about birthmothers had helped me understand that many women start with the assumption that getting the baby as far away as possible is the best solution to their unwanted pregnancy. There is so much pain associated with their dilemma, and the baby seems to be the source of it. Once a birthmother begins to realize that her baby is a "gift" to someone else, the baby's geographical location usually becomes less important. She can, instead, focus on finding the kind of parents she wants to raise her child.

I told Cindy that I wanted them to meet John as soon as possible; and we arranged to get together at their house the following afternoon. John and I drove out to meet Cindy, Bob, Mary, and Mary's older sister, Beth, who also lived at home. We talked for two and a half hours about our family origins, jobs, interests, cars, and lots of other things. As we drove home, I asked John for his impressions of the family. He said he felt very good about them. He just wished we could have some time alone with Mary to get to know her better as an individual. We also discussed some questions we would like a counselor to ask Mary when her parents did not accompany her.

Then Came Twins

January 1996

On Monday, January 1, 1996, before we went to the Pattons' house for New Year's Day festivities, Michelle called to say "Happy New Year" and to tell us that her cousin Kyle's girlfriend, Tessa, was two months pregnant and would consider placing her child with us for adoption. Tessa was sixteen and Kyle was eighteen. Michelle knew Tessa as a baby-sitter for her three other children. I spoke with Tessa briefly. I told Michelle that we were terribly flattered. This child would be Emily's second cousin!

I tried to remember Kyle. Was he that rambunctious teenage boy at the lake on July 4, 1994, where we celebrated with extended birth family and awaited Emily's birth? I could not clearly see him in my mind's eye. Surely, if he was Michelle's cousin, he must be okay. I wondered what Tessa looked like. This was an amazing opportunity.

For the rest of the day, John and our extended families contemplated what we should do. Could we pass up the chance of adopting twins? Could we pass up the opportunity of adopting one of Emily's biological relatives from a family we already loved and respected? Could we adopt them all?

The next day, I told our OAN counselor, Phoebe, about our situation with both birthmothers. Phoebe was willing to call each one to explore certain issues with them that would provide the Falcos with additional information. Phoebe asked Mary her reasons for selecting open adoption. She said, "It isn't my fault or the babies' fault what happened to me. I feel love for them and want to know they are okay." Mary said she wanted phone contact and pictures of the children, but she didn't want to interfere in our lives. She said she didn't want to be selfish. Adoption was a way she could "contribute to society."

John and I wanted to rule out the possibility that Mary had become pregnant by a known male without challenging her assertion that she had been raped by an unknown stranger. Phoebe decided to ask Mary about her dating life. She told Phoebe that she was a virgin before she was raped. She was not dating anyone at that time of the rape. She had been to the prom three weeks earlier with someone who was only a friend. During the preceding winter months, she had dated a graduate of her high school and they had parted amicably. When asked about interracial dating, Mary said that her parents preferred their daughters "date within your race," and she had always done so. When asked if she had noticed anyone stalking her, hanging around the bathroom, or otherwise being particularly interested in her, she said "no."

Phoebe also called Tessa and did a routine intake with her. OAN's Birthmother Intake form requested identifying information: name, age, date of birth, address, phone numbers, race, and marital status. Similar information was requested about the biological father, if known. Other, more open-ended questions asked of a birthmother included discussion of the father's awareness of the pregnancy and adoption plan. The intake counselor asked about the birthmother's support system, living and financial situation, and reasons for considering adoption. Did this birthmother have insurance or Medicaid? Prenatal care? Prior counseling, psychiatric treatment, or medication? Did this birthmother use drugs or alcohol during the pregnancy? Had she experienced other pregnancies? Were there medical problems?

As far as Phoebe could determine, Tessa was a healthy teenage girl, living at home with her mother and younger sister, on her mother's health insurance. Kyle was the only possible father. The information gathered by Phoebe from both birthmothers was helpful, but it did not provide us any reason to choose one birthmother over another. I sent Tessa a packet of information about OAN and a copy of our Dear Birthmother letter.

I then called an adoption attorney regarding the unknown biological father of Mary's babies. He said Mary would need to state the circumstances regarding her conception under oath. A notice to the unknown birth father would be published in a legal newspaper once a week for three weeks after the babies were born stating the date of their births and Mary's name. Mary might also be asked to explain her situation in court. As long as the adoptive parents operated in good faith and "exercised reasonable efforts to obtain the truth," we would be in good shape. The Georgia Legislature had recently passed a statute that gave biological fathers only six months after an adoption was finalized to come forward and challenge it.

On January 3rd, I left at 5:30 a.m. to drive to south Alabama (Dothan and the surrounding area) to give two presentations at pregnancy crisis centers about open adoption and how to get past a shutdown response from counselees. On the ride down and back, I scanned baby name books and made a list of all the names I liked and their meanings. I returned home after dinner that night.

On January 4th, I met Mary, her mother, and her father at the doctor's office for an ultrasound. The pictures showed that the babies were both girls and indicated that there appeared to be no medical problems despite Mary's lack of prenatal care. The doctor also suggested the babies might be born in two to three weeks instead of mid-February!

That evening, the Falcos and Browns met with Phoebe for a match meeting at our house. John's mother, my mother, and Emily all came in briefly to meet the Browns. The only new information we learned concerned the Browns' membership in a Primitive Baptist Church. We ate dinner at the house and parted about 8 p.m. We had 24 hours to decide whether or not we wanted to be officially matched.

Later that evening, John's older sister's family, the LaRussos: Craig, Gina, Adrianna, and Marina, arrived from Chicago to stay with us until January 9th.

On the morning of January 5th, I was running when a sudden panic pierced through me: What if the babies looked some way that reminded me of the men who had raped me years ago? What if I couldn't love the twins as much as I loved Emily? Until now, I had been thinking that adopting twins who were the product of rape was a fitting response to the fact that I had been raped, and that sexual assaults were perhaps the cause of my infertility. Suddenly, I was feeling just the opposite–the potential for disaster.

I told John about my fears and he suggested I find someone professional to talk to. I went to work at 9 a.m. feeling a little desperate. We had to decide about being matched *today* and I was stuck with my fears. I called the senior minister of our church, and he told me to come over. I gave him a thumbnail sketch of my rape history and the current situation we were facing. He didn't have any specific suggestions to offer, but he was sympathetic and very supportive. He hoped we could manage to get more time to make the decision. I then went to see my friend Jenna at her workplace. She already knew my history, so I hoped she could help me sort out this current situation. She too was supportive and loving, but my fears persisted.

I had to get back to work. When I arrived about 12:30 p.m., Phoebe was on the phone trying to locate me. My pager was not working. Phoebe told me that Mary had gone into premature labor that morning. She was currently being wheeled into the operating room at Rockdale County Hospital for a C-section because the babies were in breech position. According to recent calculations, the babies were only 31 or 32 gestational weeks old. I called John and told him I would be at his office shortly to pick him up. I called Mom to relate what was going on and to ask her to pick up Emily from daycare. I called Mary's sister, Beth, at the hospital and told her we were coming. On the drive to the hospital, John and I wondered what we were going to do and what the Browns would expect of us.

Bob and Cindy were in the waiting area when we arrived at the hospital. They said Mary was okay and resting in her room. They ushered us down the hall to see the babies. They were so tiny. The first one born, Baby A, was 3 pounds, 14 ounces. The second one born,

Baby B, was larger at 4 pounds, 6 ounces, but her breathing was labored. At first, I was relieved to see them because my worst fears did not surface. They did not scare me. They were beautiful. When we made phone calls later, I told the senior pastor my initial feelings, and he tearfully hoped this would turn out to be the best day of our lives.

When the LaRussos arrived at the hospital, my brother-in-law, Craig, a pediatric ICU nurse in Chicago, helped us understand the medical situation with the twins. He knew how to read the numbers on the machines that were hooked up to the babies. He told us that the lungs in a baby are one of the last things to fully develop and it looked like Baby B was having difficulty breathing. Later that day, she was put on a ventilator to breath for her. The plan was to move her to a different hospital that specialized in caring for premature babies with medical problems.

Meanwhile, it was clear that the Browns *assumed* John and I were adopting the babies. We did not do or say anything to dissuade them of that notion. John's family, my parents, and Emily had arrived. We observed the babies and wondered about their racial heritage. We thought they might be part Hispanic or part African-American.

That evening, Bob Brown approached us with his concern that the transfer team wanted him to ride to Crawford Long Hospital with Baby B to sign financial papers for her care. He told John he couldn't do that. John reassured him that the Falcos would take responsibility once the surrender documents had been signed. In the meantime, Craig assured us the hospital could not refuse to treat her because no one signed papers. He was concerned, however, that the team could delay if it looked like no one was going to pay. Fortunately, we did not have to wait too much longer to find out that Baby B had safely arrived at Crawford Long. That day, we began a long series of discussions about medical issues for premature infants with Craig and Gina that would consume many of our waking hours over the next few days.

Once we left the hospital, Gina and Craig volunteered to keep Emily so that we could have a few minutes alone to process everything that was happening. John and I drove to a restaurant to eat and talk. How did we feel? We did not know. For sure, it wasn't the same as our first adoption when there had been time to really get to know Emily's birthmother and family, to establish a relationship built on trust and to feel like we had a good deal of understanding about each other's needs and desires. I remembered loving Emily from the beginning, from the first moment I saw her–or maybe even before that because I loved Michelle first. John and I realized that we weren't *bonded* to these new babies. We had not touched them. We had no connection. We resolved to make a concerted effort to spend time with each of them, time that involved touching and holding–at least as much as was possible given the tubes and machines that were controlling their lives.

John also wanted to make sure his insurance would pick up the tab on the babies. We went to my sister's house where there was a little more peace and quiet than at our full house, and called the adoption attorney. The attorney was willing to make any statement to the insurance company that would insure coverage. He also said he was willing to go out to the hospital on Sunday to take Mary's surrender of parental rights before her discharge. At this point, we felt there were too many medical issues involved to make a decision about *when* the surrender should be signed. We said we'd be back in touch with him soon.

We went home. I called Phoebe and asked her if she would be willing to go to the hospital tomorrow and discuss the content and meaning of the surrender documents with Mary. This is something that might have been covered with the counselor prior to birth but for the twins' early arrival. I didn't want Mary to see the documents for the first time when the attorney showed up to ask her to sign them.

There was also the issue of names. We had not completely decided about both girls' names. That night the names tentatively became Kelly Michaela and Elinor Helen. I thought the sick baby should have my mother's name Helen as a source of strength from which to draw.

On Saturday, January 6th, we confirmed that Mary would be checking out of the hospital on Sunday. John, Craig and I spoke with the doctor at Crawford Long to find out how Baby B was doing. She was on the ventilator, but they were gradually bringing down the percent of oxygen and the rate the machine was breathing for her. At this point in time, no one could be sure how she would do or the possible long-term consequences, although there was no real reason to think she would not be fine. John spoke at length with the hospital social worker about financial issues. The social worker suggested Mary apply for Medicaid to cover the infants' expenses in the event the Falcos did not adopt.

My brothers and sister met us at Rockdale County Hospital to see the baby who remained there. We took our family members to Mary's room to meet her and her family. Other members of the extended Brown family were milling around the nursery area and Mary's room just as they had been the day before. Everyone was pleasant to us and seemed to know about the adoption plan.

After my family stepped outside, John and I started a difficult discussion with Bob, Cindy, and a drowsy Mary. Their conversation with Phoebe earlier in the day had been hard on them because they had learned for the first time that Mary's name and the birth of the twins to an unknown birthfather would need to be published in a newspaper for three weeks to comply with legal requirements. We brought another unpleasant topic to the table. We knew Bob wanted the question of financial responsibility for the twins resolved. We had to tell the Browns that, although we wanted everything to work out and we didn't want to hurt them, we really needed to wait until the doctors at Crawford Long could give us some reassurance about the other baby's health. Apparently, there was a brain scan that would be done that would rule out brain damage. We wanted to wait until after that test to take Mary's surrender. They could understand that, couldn't they? John suggested Bob contact his insurance company to see if there was a way to add the twins. He also told the Browns what the social worker at

Crawford Long had said to us: Mary should apply for Medicaid. Bob and Cindy acknowledged our position, but Cindy cried and Bob did not look happy.

Later that day, Bob called to ask for the names of the babies. They needed names for the birth certificates before Mary could check out of the hospital the next day. We gave him the names we had decided on the night before.

On Sunday, we awoke to find our yard and city blanketed with snow. Although certain roads were passable, many were not, and there were ice patches on passable roads. I needed to get out, clear my head, and run in the snow. The name Elinor wasn't right. The twins would be "Kel and El." John had said we should remember his family in the naming process. How about a name that started with "J" like the sound of Gina, John, and Julie? After I returned home, John and I went through the list of names again. This time we settled on Jessica–Jessica Helen Falco.

We called the hospitals to check on the babies and change one of the names. Kelly was fine. She was small but breathing well. However, Jessica was a different story. She had had a bad spell and been put on 100% oxygen and a high rate for a period during the night. They were coming down slower with her this time. Craig told us the potential negative consequences of a baby spending too much time on 100% oxygen or too many days on a ventilator.

The Falcos and LaRussos went to church. It was a small crowd because of the snow, but there were a number of people there who knew about our situation. We provided an update and stated that we anticipated adopting once we had reassurances from the doctors that there were no major medical problems.

We all went over to the Patton parents' house for lunch. John ate quickly and went back to the church to coach a boys' basketball game. The rest of us stayed to visit at the Pattons' house while the three cousins played. When John was done with his game, he and I went to visit Jessica at Crawford Long.

The visit to the NICU (Neonatal Intensive Care Unit) was scary the first time. We removed all jewelry and scrubbed thoroughly. The babies were hooked to monitors and machines by many wires and tubes. We could not hold Jessica in her current condition without dislodging some vital equipment; but we touched and patted her. She was beautiful but seemed frail. They said it might be weeks before she was home.

That night, after the girls were in bed, Gina and Craig sat down with us and described what our life might be like with two babies on apnea monitors for many months. The monitors were likely to go off several times during the night and would be very loud. The babies probably would not sleep and eat on the same schedule, so we could look forward to many sleepless nights.

On Monday, January 8th, schools were closed because of the snow. We had promised to do some sightseeing with the LaRussos, and this had to be the day because they were leaving on Tuesday. We had phone conversations with medical and social work personnel about the babies that day, but otherwise we spent time with our guests on the train, in Underground Atlanta, and at the World of Coca Cola.

On Tuesday, the schools were closed again. John and I had to split our workdays to take care of Emily. John went to Crawford Long to see Jessica after he took the LaRussos to the airport. He didn't get to hold her, but he talked with her and later said he felt more bonded.

I went to work early and then took care of Emily in the afternoon. Kelly would be eating from a bottle at 5 p.m. I told the nurse at her hospital that I would like to come and feed her. She said Mary was coming then too. I asked my mother's assistance in carrying out the plan. She came along to watch Emily while I was with the baby.

When we arrived at the hospital, I scrubbed and went into the nursery to hold Kelly. At first Mom held Emily outside the window, but she was screaming and crying with jealously because I was holding another baby. Then Mary arrived and I offered to let her feed Kelly. She took the baby without a word. We sat together in silence while the baby ate. Eventually I struck up a conversation with the nurse about Kelly's progress and the likelihood of monitors or other equipment. The nurse said Kelly needed to gain weight and keep her weight at or above 4 lbs. before being discharged. That could take a week or two. After Kelly finished eating, I got up to check on Emily and Mary said, "Would you ask my mother to come in here?" I told her I would.

Mary and Cindy stayed in the nursery a very long time, never making eye contact with me or saying a word. They looked deathly serious. I wondered if they were having second thoughts. I wondered if they hated us because we had wanted to wait for some reassurance about Jessica's health. Finally, I wrote Mary an upbeat note for the nurse to give to her, and I left. As Mom, Emily and I were pulling out of the hospital parking lot, Bob drove up to the front door of the hospital to speak to Cindy who had suddenly appeared there. I felt sick. Why were they avoiding me? What was going on?

When I got home, I told John what had happened and we immediately called the Browns. Cindy answered the phone and said, "I can't talk now. We'll call you back in an hour." The next hour was torture, but we stayed busy feeding Emily and getting her ready for bed.

A little more than an hour later, Cindy called and said Mary was *very* depressed. John asked if we could speak to her. Mary expressed some of her fears–primarily the fear that she would not see her children again. We tried to reassure her that we wanted her in our lives and the lives of the girls very much. She didn't say that she had changed her mind, although it sounded like Bob had spent the last hour firming up the family's commitment to follow through with the adoption plan. The conversation ended with our request to Mary that she talk with her parents about a good time to sign her surrender documents. The brain scan on Jessica was scheduled for the next day. Assuming nothing wrong was found, we were prepared to go forward. Cindy called back later and said, "The sooner the better..."

We also talked with Phoebe that night. She said she had learned that Bob was angry with us because, in his words, "They were supposed to adopt the babies unconditionally."

On Wednesday, we learned that the cranial ultrasound was normal. Jessica's doctor was pleased with her lungs and didn't see any long-term health issues. But the doctor also said she didn't believe Mary's story about conception because the baby acted older than 32 gestational weeks. She warned us that lack of a family history made it difficult to predict Jessica's future.

Jessica was off the ventilator now, and Kelly was feeding exclusively by bottle. The results of the brain scan came too late in the day for our attorney to get out to Mary's house to take her surrender. The Browns and the attorney scheduled that event for the following afternoon.

I reported the latest news to my parents, stating that we had promised the Browns to adopt the twins if the brain scan was normal. Dad, knowing I could be persuasive when I wanted something bad enough, wanted to hear John's perspective directly. Dad also worried that we were taking care of the Browns to our detriment. While I got Emily ready for bed, John spoke to my parents, reporting all the data and our logical reasons for moving forward. Dad was satisfied that this was a joint decision.

Suddenly, a mutual panic set in. John said, "I know what I told your father–but are we doing the right thing?!" I said, "I don't know; and I don't know how to know. What else can we do?" What would happen to the babies if we didn't adopt them? Would Cindy's nightmare about DFCS come true? Had we ever really made a decision to adopt, or were we just moving? Could we love the twins? Certainly, we would eventually, right? This was so different than Emily's adoption. It had happened so fast. But maybe we were trying to compare apples to oranges. Oranges were just as tasty; but they were clearly different than apples.

John wanted to know how I felt. I said, "Numb." John said, "You can't stay numb. You have to help me decide." I was too tired. I couldn't think. We went to bed.

The next morning, John ran and then I ran. He asked me how I felt. I said I was still numb. *He* would have to decide. John took a shower. When he was done, he came to me and said, "Are you ready for the ride of your life?" We were going forward…. For the next few days, John and I juggled work responsibilities, Emily and home responsibilities, and visits to two different hospitals 50 miles apart.

I went to see Jessica who was at 4 pounds and 1 ounce, breathing room air, and feeding from a tube. John visited with Kelly at Rockdale. She was 3 pounds, 11 ounces and eating well from a bottle. The nurses and doctor said Kelly would be able to go home when she reached 4 lbs., which might be in 4 to 7 days. We had a lot to do to get prepared for the arrival of the babies.

On Friday, January 12th, Jessica moved to intermediate care. The nurses told John on his visit that she could be home in 2 to 3 weeks. At Rockdale, I was told that Kelly could be home in a week. We began making calls to round up baby items we could use for a nursery.

On Saturday, January 13th, I left Emily with John in the morning to attend and speak at a Resolve Symposium. I practiced talking about the recent adoption of twins. In the afternoon, we went shopping for nursery items.

On Sunday, January 14th, the family went to church and created a stir when we announced "officially" in Sunday School and after the service that we were adopting the twins. The surrender had been signed on Thursday, and one twin was coming home probably this week. At Disciple Bible Study that night, I made a similar announcement.

Emily stayed with her grandparents while John coached a basketball game and I visited Jessica at Crawford Long. I discovered that she was already eating from a bottle. The nurses predicted she could be discharged on Wednesday, Thursday, or Friday of *this* week. I signed John and myself up for infant CPR class. John's visit to Kelly was less eventful. The nurses said it would still be a few days before she was ready to go home.

The rest of our free time that day was spent preparing the nursery. I told our next-door neighbor, Sherry, about the twins. She was very excited for us and spread the news to the neighborhood. My mother provided essential items such as blankets and inserts for car seats. John found a rug that would work in the room.

On Monday, January 15th, the schools were closed again for the Martin Luther King, Jr. Holiday. Emily and I drove out to the Baby Superstore to find a changing table pad and covers. Then we went straight to my parents' house to pick up some chests and a rocker for the babies' room.

John was trying to reach me. Rockdale County Hospital was ready to discharge Kelly! We needed to get over there as soon as possible. Emily and Mom would be at our house when we returned from the hospital with a new sister. Mary, her mother, and other relatives were already at the hospital to say good-bye to Kelly. John and I arrived about 2:15, took pictures of Mary holding Kelly and pictures of the rest of the birth family present at the hospital. We received discharge plans from the nurse. The nurse noted that this baby was "stinky" even after they bathed her. Mary seemed to be in good spirits. She and her family left before our attorney walked out of the hospital with the baby and handed her to us.

When we arrived home, Sherry appeared with preemie baby clothes and an offer to make dinner for us. We had to feed Kelly every three hours. I knew I wouldn't get much sleep. What was I going to do about work? This event, this homecoming, had happened so fast. I was the only full-time employee at OAN. We were waiting to hear if we had received our agency license. When we did, the office would become very busy again. My sister-in-law had agreed to be our nanny, but we still had no definite plans or a start date for her. It was too much to think about. Right now, Emily was upset and hungry.

§ § §

On Tuesday, January 16th, in the wee morning hours, Kelly was fussy, so I stayed in her room to comfort and feed her on schedule. I felt sick. I didn't sleep much. Kelly's smell reminded me of the man who had raped me in 1982. I remembered being trapped under him in my Chevy Vega. I remembered the stench of sweat, the windows fogged, and the fear that I might not live. I could not help thinking: How can I love Kelly or Jessica as much as Emily if they remind me of rape? Something was very wrong.

In the morning, I went to John right away and said, "We have to talk. I don't know if I can do this. We have to figure this out *now*." He looked horrified and relieved at the same time. We got Emily ready and took her to the daycare center. We called the senior minister at our church. He wasn't available, but the associate minister, Donn Ann, was. She said she could come over right away.

John started at the beginning, giving Donn Ann as much detail as he could remember about what we'd been through the past two weeks. It was helpful just hearing aloud the long list of events and crises packed into a few short days. It helped us realize at least two things. First, we had *not* had time to make a decision. Second, we *were* guilty of trying to take care of the Browns, just as my father had warned. Indeed, I had spent the time before Donn Ann arrived researching families I could call who might want to adopt the twins in the event we decided we could not. John pointed out that we had no idea how the Browns would respond yet. Donn Ann tried to refocus us. We needed to decide whether we were going to adopt before we tried to figure out how to deal with a hypothetical response from the Browns.

I said it first: "We cannot go on. We have to undo the adoption. Others can love these babies better than we can. They deserve better...."

Donn Ann had been wonderful. When she left, John and I held onto each other, sobbing from our depths. When we were empty, we straightened ourselves. John made calls to the attorney, family members, and Cindy Brown. To the latter he said, "We need to come over and talk to all of you tonight. It's about the adoption."

The ride to the Browns' house was torture. I felt guilt beyond measure. I was a horrible person, a weak person, a coward. I would not be able to speak. I begged John to *please* do the speaking for us. He said he didn't know what he would say. He trusted the words would come.

At 6 p.m., we arrived at the Browns' house. We sat in the living room and John began slowly. Not more than one or two sentences into John's speech, Bob said, "Relax, John. Go ahead and get to the point. It's okay." John's announcement that we didn't think we could go through with the adoption was quickly interrupted by Bob's announcement that the Browns wanted to raise the babies themselves. Bob said he had been pushing the rest of the family to see the financial hardship this would cause; but that today all he could think about at work was the babies. They were family. They should be with them. He could tell Cindy was heart-broken from the moment of their birth. Mary had been very depressed. The extended family had volunteered to help in ways such as paying off the loan on Mary's car or baby-sitting. This was a sign. This was the way it was meant to be. John and I were unbelievably relieved at this response and told the family so. We agreed to bring Kelly to them the following evening.

That night Kelly was fussy until I held her in my arms. I slept curled up around her through the night. She didn't seem as smelly anymore. She was small and dependent and as innocent as she could be. I was going to miss her.

Kelly spent the next day with me at work. She was easy to take care of. I wondered what taking care of two of them would have been like.

At 5 p.m., I went home to gather new and used items of clothing and equipment to take to the Browns for the babies. We knew they didn't have much, if anything, for the children when we saw them the day before. At the last minute, I dressed Kelly in Emily's pink knit cap, the one she had been given at birth in Columbus, Nebraska, as a good omen and a sign of our connection to her.

My friend Jenna drove us to the Browns' house since John was in Washington, D.C. The family greeted us at the door. Mary was quiet, as usual. Bob led the chit-chat. Cindy was beaming. They showed me the new crib a grandmother had bought for the twins. I showed them the books, baby paraphernalia, clothes, formula, diapers, and bottles I brought. There was a silence. I said good-bye to Kelly, hugged Mary, and we were gone.

Jenna seemed more distressed than I felt. I knew that she and her husband were trying to have a baby. I tried to imagine what this must look like from her perspective. I just *gave away* a baby. That wasn't normal behavior. It probably didn't even seem humane. Who rejects a baby because of an imperfect situation or a lack of guarantees? Such behavior is only an option in adoption. But, in this case, given *all* the circumstances, it seemed like the right thing to do. It felt like the best conclusion to the story.

On Thursday, January 18th, to the best of my knowledge, Jessica was discharged from Crawford Long Hospital to her mother, Mary Brown.

On Friday, John called the Browns to see how things were going. Cindy told John, "We are in heaven." The church had heard of their situation and many members had brought items for the babies. They were no longer in need, she said. The babies were identical, except for a birthmark on Kelly's thigh.

During our meeting with Donn Ann on January 16th, she had said something that stuck with me. She said, "You helped the Browns to heal." At first, I wasn't sure what that meant. But, as I had some time to think about it and reflect on our days together, I began to believe Donn Ann was right. When I first talked with Cindy on December 19th, she wanted a closed adoption–a way to make the babies and any reminder of the rape of her daughter go away. By our first meeting together, she had already moved from wanting a closed adoption to wanting an open adoption. She wanted a "good home" for the babies. They were beginning to care about the children.

When the Browns chose the Falcos, they chose the adoptive family that was closest to them. They had shifted again from simply a desire for a "good home" to a desire for actual visits and ongoing contact. The reality of the babies came quickly, but our willingness to take them (after certain medical assurances) gave the Browns time to experience these little people as their own flesh and blood, and as innocent and beautiful creations. We thought *we* had little time to make a decision about adoption–but look at what the *Browns* faced: December 3rd was the first time Mary acknowledged that she had been raped and that she was pregnant. The family was still in shock when they approached the idea of adoption.

We didn't know Mary very well. We never saw her alone. We were never really sure how she, as an individual, felt. We didn't know whether to believe what she said about the babies' conception given the doctor's assessment of Jessica's age. Whether Mary was raped by an unknown stranger or not mattered to us as *adoptive* parents in several ways: (1) it mattered whether there was a birth father out there who could come forward and claim rights to the children; (2) it mattered to us as parents who would someday tell this story to their children, knowing the pain it would cause them; and (3) it mattered to us as parents who would not have complete medical histories on their children.

For the Browns, who were conservative Christians and wanted their daughters to date Caucasian men, Mary's story would have been disturbing whether she was raped or not because it involved sex and pregnancy before marriage with a man who was probably not of their race. Whatever the true story, the Falcos gave the Browns a chance to live with the reality of all these difficult ideas long enough to realize none of them mattered in a way that made adoption the right solution for them. Their family works together as a team; and they could work together as a team to raise these babies too.

In this process, John and I also learned about ourselves. We learned more about our compassion for others in difficult positions. We learned again how good we were at making those in crisis feel reassured even when those reassurances cost us. John was magnificent at handling the dozens of phone calls and numerous parties involved in these proceedings. John said he learned that he needed to take time to listen to his instincts, to listen to that little voice inside him. I learned I could stop a runaway train before it wrecked. We were both reminded of how blessed we were to belong to our extended Falco and Patton families, and to be members of our neighborhood, church, and work communities.

Teenagers In Love & A Baby Boy

February to December 1996

My focus returned to work at the adoption agency. After a number of delays, OAN's application was reviewed by DHR and we were notified that our temporary agency license would become effective February 1, 1996. At that time, we could begin doing all our previous functions *plus* home studies and post-placement supervision. This was good news. However, we had lost valuable time recruiting adoptive parents and their financial contribution to the new business. The Executive Director was still trying to cut costs. On February 27th, he announced that I would become a part-time employee in two weeks.

As conditions worsened with the Executive Director, I decided I needed a back-up plan. I would study for and take the Georgia Bar Exam so that I would be licensed to practice law in Georgia. Now, I just had to find the time.

By March, Phoebe, and I were both part-time employees. Eventually, I was allowed to hire another part-time employee, an administrative assistant. At least, the Executive Director understood that it was critical to have our files and other paperwork in order when DHR came to review us for our permanent agency license in June.

The Executive Director asked me to prepare a memo regarding our "Objectives for June-December 1996." In part of the memo I stated:

> To adequately respond to the many responsibilities assigned to us, Phoebe and I often work some part of seven days a week. We do this because we are committed to our clients, our birth parents and to open adoption. We also work additional time because it is the only way to get the work done. Often, we are

> working in territory unfamiliar to OAN–for instance, facilitating an interstate adoption between two Southeastern states or between a Southern state and a New England state. Blazing new trails can be time consuming. *[The administrative assistant]*, Phoebe, and I are a good team. We want to continue to work together in spite of our uncompensated time. However, financial necessity will probably force Phoebe and/or me to resign if some assurances and a date certain regarding full-time employment are not given soon.
>
> I have been asked on several occasions to do legal research and to render an opinion because of my legal background. My opinion has been ignored; and I have been put in the precarious position of being asked to take certain actions as a requirement of my job that contradicted my assessment of what was legally permissible. In the future, I will only perform those actions that, in my educated opinion, are morally and legally defensible.

§ § §

Our clients loved us. We loved the work. But the support from California was less than ideal. In the meantime, John and I were still trying to grow our family.

After the twins were returned to their mother, we turned our attention to the offer that had been made to us on January 1st. We made plans for Tessa, Kyle, and Tessa's mother, Kate, to visit us in Atlanta and to meet with Phoebe to begin the adoption process. The best time for Tessa to visit was during her Spring Break because she was a sophomore in high school.

On Wednesday, March 20, 1996, we borrowed our neighbors' van and went to the airport to pick up our guests. Kyle and Tessa were on their first airplane trip; and Kate had not flown in 20 years. Everyone arrived safely–although we were disappointed that Michelle, who was originally scheduled to fly to Atlanta with the others, could not make the trip at the last minute.

When Tessa and Kyle walked off the plane with Tessa's mother, we knew immediately who they were. There was something very Midwestern-looking about them–the haircuts, the clothes, and their apparent wide-eyed innocence. Just as I had with Michelle, I breathed a sigh of relief when I saw Tessa. She was adorable. I would love to have a child who looked like her. Both teenagers were taller than average, healthy and athletic-looking to me. Tessa had dark hair and eyes like John. Kyle had light brown hair and green or blue eyes, like me. I chuckled to myself: Maybe there would be a basketball player in our future.

That evening I made dinner at home. We spent time getting to know one another. We learned that Tessa was Kate's second child. Tessa had a 21-year-old brother by a different father and a sister who was 15 years old. Kate agreed to provide us with an extended list of family members before she left.

We had previously met most of Kyle's family. He had an older sister. His mother, Ginger, was the younger sister of Michelle's mother. Ginger and Kyle's father were both remarried. We also learned that Tessa and Kyle liked to fish and to watch professional wrestling. Tessa was a huge fan of both the Dallas Cowboys and Mustang automobiles. Tessa's due date was July 13th.

On Thursday, March 21st, we had our match meeting at OAN, and then took a train downtown to do some sightseeing. On Friday, I took our guests back to OAN for a counseling session with Phoebe. Then we drove to Stone Mountain and a number of other tourist sights. That night we went through the hospital and open adoption agreements and made some preliminary decisions about what would happen at the hospital and afterward.

On Saturday, we headed for Shoney's breakfast bar and gorged ourselves. Our plan was to spend most of the day at the Atlanta Zoo. But before we went to the zoo, John drove us to a Ford dealership and expressed interest in checking out the new Mustangs so that Tessa could have her picture taken in the car of her dreams. She had been counting Mustangs on the road since she arrived in Atlanta and was up to 173. That evening, many family and friends came over to meet our Nebraska guests and help them know a little more about the Falcos.

On Sunday, John took Kate to catch her 6 a.m. flight and returned to make pancakes for everyone else. We took Tessa for a walk to show her where our children would go to school one day. Kyle remained at home watching cartoons. After lunch, we took Tessa and Kyle to the airport to return home.

Time passed and we continued our daily routines….

On May 21, 1996, Tessa called and said that on the preceding Thursday, May 16th, she had started having contractions. She had stayed in the hospital overnight to be treated for a bacterial infection that could have caused the contractions. The doctor also started her on Brethine™, a drug designed to relax her uterus. She told her to limit her activity–no gym for the last week of school. Tessa's weight had also dropped from 171 to 165 in a week. Tessa said that she had been to the doctor for a routine check-up that day, and everything seemed fine. But she was warned that if the contractions resumed, she would have to go on bed rest.

We continued to be in contact with Tessa by phone. Honestly, I was not all that worried. I knew Tessa and Kyle had a great support system through Michelle and the extended families in Nebraska. I trusted that if there was a medical emergency, Kate would insure that Tessa received the appropriate treatment. Moreover, this was a second adoption, so parenting our first child, as well as our paid employment, distracted us.

As the baby's due date in July approached, we received more frequent phone calls from the birth parents and their families. They sounded increasingly more anxious and stressed about the impending birth. On Tuesday, July 2nd, we decided it would give everyone in Columbus more peace of mind if Emily, my mother, and I went ahead and flew to Nebraska. My mother went to meet Emily's and the baby's birth families. She was also going to help me with Emily so that I could continue to study for the Bar Exam. Tessa's doctor had told her that she would induce delivery of the baby on July 9th, if Tessa did not go into labor sooner. That was only a week away.

Our first stop in Nebraska was at the apartment Tessa shared with her mother and younger sister. Then we crossed town to Kyle's mother and stepfather's house, which was only three blocks from the hospital. Ginger had offered to let us stay in her home while we were in Nebraska. She was clearly glad to see us. She showed us her two extra upstairs bedrooms, and we settled in.

That evening, we went to a diner with Tessa, Kyle, and members of both families. Emily had begun to cry and could not be consoled. She was pulling at her ears. When I gave her decongestant medicine, she tried to pour it in her ear. Michelle's mother gave the family pediatrician a call. The doctor could see us in 5 minutes! This was small town living, I thought. Sure enough–both ears were infected. The doctor prescribed medicine and some drops for immediate comfort. Emily slept soundly that night.

On Wednesday, July 3rd, I went with Tessa and her mother to Tessa's weekly doctor's appointment. She reminded Tessa to be at the hospital on Tuesday, July 9th at 6:30 a.m. to begin inducing labor.

Emily and I were drawing chalk pictures on the sidewalk when Michelle drove up. She wanted to know what our plans were because Emily's grandmother *on her birth father's side* wanted to meet Emily sometime during our trip. Two years after Emily's birth, her paternal grandmother was finally convinced that Emily was her relative. I told Michelle we were free that day and she said she would pick us up in an hour.

Michelle drove us out to Vera 's farm where she and her husband raised pigs. As we approached the house and went inside, there were children everywhere. Michelle pointed out the three that were also Jason's children: two by one mother, and another by Jason's ex-wife.

The house and yard were full of animals. In the house were birds, a squirrel, an iguana, and fish. Outside there was a pet pig and a dog, as well as other pigs and piglets, horses, and a new colt. Vera asked her husband to saddle a horse so that we could ride. Emily was frightened and wanted "Mama" to hold her way off the ground. However, after Nanna (as Emily had begun calling her grandmother Helen) willingly rode the horse, Emily agreed to ride with me. She loved it and wanted more. Vera took a turn riding with Emily and so did Kaitlyn, Emily's paternal aunt, who arrived an hour or so after we did.

Some of the children took Emily back to see the newest piglets. Afterward, we went inside the house. Vera showed us her baby pictures and told us how much she thought Emily looked like her. Emily played with Vera's collection of toy horses and a baby doll and bed while the adults drank tea and talked.

Suddenly remembering it was Tessa's 17th birthday, my mother, Emily, and I went to Wal-mart to buy presents. We got her a denim jumper, a purse, and an Indigo Girls' CD. I also bought some videos for Emily's upcoming birthday on July 7th.

That evening, Kate took us to a family "Pop and Fireworks" event at one of her brother's houses outside of town. Emily learned about Snaps and had a great time stomping on them. We met most of Kate's extended family there. However, I confess that the biggest excitement for me came when Emily took me to the back of the warehouse, asked to use the potty, and actually did!

On July 4th, Kyle's extended family and friends were invited to his father and stepmother's lake house for a Fourth of July celebration with swimming, food and fireworks–just as we had done on the Fourth before Emily's birth two years ago. We left when the fireworks started getting too loud for Emily. John arrived at Ginger's house about 9 p.m. that evening.

My original journal from these days in Nebraska describes in detail every meal we ate, each person we saw, each activity and conversation we engaged in, and each place we visited. In sum, these events gave us a feel for the culture, values, and lifestyle of our children's original parents and their families.

On Sunday, July 7th, my mother left to return to Atlanta. We received a call from Phoebe, who had just spoken with Tessa. She said that Tessa was frightened about the actual birth process. Michelle made a call for us; and we proceeded over to the hospital, pre-registered Tessa, got a tour of the labor and delivery area, and borrowed a videotape of three births and a C-section. We went back to Ginger's house to watch the video together. However, Tessa didn't see much. She was in and out of the room chasing her nephew, probably avoiding what seemed too painful to watch.

It was Emily's birthday; and Michelle and I had planned her party. I was beaming inside. Wasn't this a testimony about the healthiness of open adoption? Here was my child and her two mothers, working together for the good of Emily, surrounded by so many people who loved her.

Michelle brought over matching outfits for her four daughters to wear. The birthday party was held at a park where we ate birthday cake and watermelon. Emily received presents from both sides of her birth family. I took lots of pictures of the four girls in their outfits, as well as pictures of the other guests. Tessa, at nine months pregnant, was still limber enough to slide with the younger children.

On Tuesday, July 9, 1996, Michelle and her girls picked up Emily to spend the day at Vera's farm while John and I waited at the hospital for the baby to be born. Tessa had arrived at 6:30 a.m. and been given her first dose of medicinal cream to induce labor. By the time we arrived between 9 and 10, she had received another dose and was not at all happy about the pain she was experiencing. She wanted to go home! The nurse advised that Tessa should have only one visitor in the room at a time to keep her from getting tired out.

Over the course of the day, Tessa had many visitors, including the Children's Home Society social worker who would be taking her surrender of parental rights in a day or so. John was particularly thrilled when Tessa told him that she wanted him to be at the delivery to "see your son being born." By afternoon, Tessa had only progressed to three centimeters dilated, though her water had already broken. She had been given several doses of a painkiller and would eventually get an epidural. But what she kept telling everyone was that she was hungry and wanted pizza.

A little after 5 p.m., I went in the room where the nurse was checking Tessa again. She was at 10 centimeters and ready to push! I suddenly became one of Tessa's coaches. She pushed well but was crying and kept saying she couldn't do it. At about 5:45 p.m. the top of the baby's head was visible and the doctor called the fathers in. The doctor injected Tessa with a long needle and Kyle exclaimed about its size, causing the doctor to remark that Kyle could either "show some maturity or leave as fast as *[he]* came in." Kyle got mad, kicked a stool, and left. With a final push, the baby's head popped out in a gush of fluid. The doctor then worked at removing the umbilical cord from the baby's neck. It was wrapped around twice. She said, "That's one. That's two," as she pulled the cord over his head. Tessa exclaimed, "I had twins!?" We all laughed.

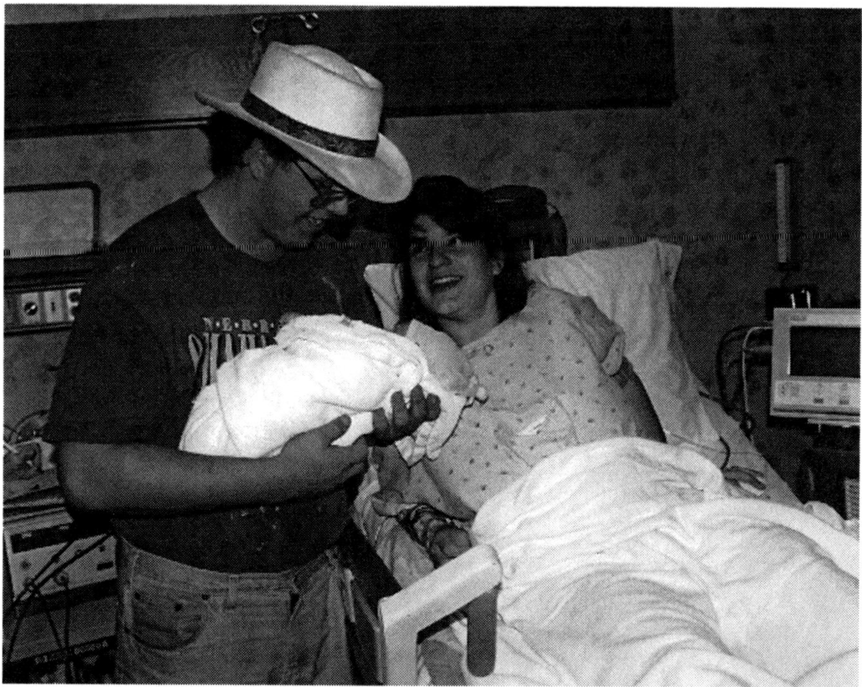

As the baby was inspected and wiped off, Kyle came back in the room and pictures were taken of baby and parents. Tessa had decided to name him Shawn Michael after a world class professional wrestler, but we all knew he would be known as Kevin John Falco–"K.J."

Phone calls were made to family to announce the birth, and we promised to buy pizza for Tessa and Kyle. Vera had continued to care for Emily after Michelle went to work; and she was called to return our daughter to the hospital. Vera's eyes were red from crying as she told us how grateful she was that we trusted her to have this time with her grandchild. I was again beaming inside at the testimony to the value of openness. If Emily's adoption had been closed at birth, she might never have known Vera and vice versa.... We delivered the pizza to the young parents and visited in the solarium before returning "home" to Ginger's house from an exciting but exhausting day.

The next morning, Emily went to the hospital with us to see the baby and hold him. In fact, we could hardly get him away from her as she smothered him with kisses and exclaimed, "*My* baby!" She then spent the rest of the day with her birthmother and sisters.

The Falcos had been invited to Kate's apartment for an "open house." While we were there, the agency social worker met with Tessa and Kyle at the hospital so that they could sign relinquishments of parental rights. At about 5:30, we returned to the hospital for final instructions regarding K.J. and to get Tessa and the baby checked out of the hospital. Tessa helped put the baby in his carseat, and all of us returned to the open house.

Tessa and Kyle wanted to go to the County Fair for hotdogs. John gave them money to bring some for us too. We secretly marveled at their youth and vitality. It was also reassuring to see them so quickly resume the activities that kids do. Emily returned from her time with birth family, and we were a family of four together for the first time.

I marveled at how seamless this was. The responsibility for the baby had transferred from one set of parents to another, but we were all still part of a larger family, sharing living space, meals, and laughter. It was not until the second day of K.J.'s life that I finally held and cuddled him. He had been in so many other arms. And that was okay. In a few days, most of his time would be spent with me. It felt very safe, very *right,* to share him with this larger family for as long as we stayed in Nebraska.

For the next two days, we had a parade of visitors to see and hold the baby. We also took him and Emily to see the pediatrician. She gave both children a clean bill of health and exuded excitement about our adoption.

Most of Thursday had been spent on the phone with Phoebe and the Nebraska agency trying to work out arrangements to get back to

Georgia. The baby could not leave until the requirements of the ICPC had been fulfilled. I had to get back to work. John drove Emily and me to the airport on Friday morning with the understanding that he and K.J. would follow as soon as possible. By the time John returned to Columbus, Phoebe had called to give the go-ahead. The departure on Saturday, July 13th, was tearful for Tessa. She said to John, "Please take care of him." John promised to call when they had safely arrived home.

Our time in Columbus, Nebraska was wonderful. No doubt the contact between our families would ebb and flow over the years. But nothing would change the reality that each of our children had a beautiful birth story. They would always know that their overlapping birth families in Nebraska loved them.

Our announcement to family and friends read: *To Announce the Birth of Kevin John Falco, 5 lbs., 15 oz., 19 inches, on July 9, 1996, in Columbus, Nebraska. Born in Love to His Birth Parents, Tessa [last name] and Kyle [last name]. Given in Love to His Adoptive Family, Rebecca and John Falco and sister Emily*

§ § §

On July 16th, proud daddy John sent an email to his friends regarding K.J.:

> "He's little now but all indications are that he'll be a monster and will have one hell of a fastball. The Braves scouts are already calling to see when they can clock him, but we're keeping him under wraps for now, literally.
>
> "By the way, Emily loves her little brother so much she kisses him incessantly and even slobbers on him a little. She has already helped feed and change him and she'll begin teaching him the alphabet as soon as she learns it herself."

§ § §

K.J. was born at the time of the Summer Olympics in Atlanta. As a tribute to his birth parents, we bought an inscribed brick for Centennial Olympic Park downtown. The brick read: "To Tessa & Kyle for KJ 7/9/96." We also bought a brick honoring Emily's birthmother that read: "Bless Michelle for Emily 7/7/94."

§ § §

Shortly after we left Nebraska with K.J., Kate wrote to tell us that Tessa was doing very well, with occasional sad times. She thought that going back to school would help. In a letter written in October, Tessa thanked us for all the pictures and updates, and the copy of the brick. She and Kyle were getting along. He was working for a lawn service and her grades were good. These communications and others between us were very reassuring.

Three weeks after K.J. was born, our neighbor, Sherry, became his nanny, and I returned to work. I had to. I was the Branch Director of the agency. There were three of us working part-time with barely enough hours between us to complete the minimal tasks. The staff filtered their complaints and requests through me and I made proposals to the Executive Director. My careful notes on phone calls and emails at the time reveal a continuing flow of conflicts and misunderstandings, the details of which are painful to relive even now.

Staff in the other offices mostly supported my positions and proposals, but feared for their jobs as well. There were legal issues, budget issues, marketing issues, employment issues, travel issues, educational issues, compliance issues, issues related to inaccurate statistics, and so forth. One particular statement from the Executive Director in February 1997, seems to capture what I found most distasteful about the approach to adoption that I was being asked to take. He stated: "What is in the adoptive parents interest and our interest is not the same. It's impossible to avoid people suing us. We're never going to be able to meet their reasonable demands." I understood it was a business. But it was more than that. Open adoption, to me, was all about meeting in the middle to solve real human dilemmas. It was about being "reasonably" flexible and compassionate.

In November, Kevin John Falco was baptized at our church, with a brunch at my parents' house following the service. I had put together a program for the brunch, crafted from various religious sources and my feminist spirit. It was, as one might suspect, a program acknowledging, honoring, and praising open adoption. The program included part of a letter written by Tessa one month after her son's birth:

> Dear John & Rebecca,
>
> I wanted to let you know that I really appreciate you adopting K.J. Although it was very hard to watch him go, I know that with a loving family like yours he will be well taken care of and very much loved. I also wanted to thank you for everything you did for Kyle & me while I was pregnant and after K.J. was born. I don't think we could have found a better family.... Emily and K.J. are very lucky.

We chose my brother, Timothy, and his wife, Therra, to be K.J. godparents. We also chose John's best friend, Kevin Elden, for whom K.J. had been named.

John had written a song about the open adoptions of Emily and K.J. entitled, "Given in Love," that he performed at the brunch:

On the day we were married, we prayed for a child
But try as we might, we could not conceive
We questioned the Giver of life to explain
Given in love was the answer received

The child of our dreams surprised and amazed us
Her birth brought us hope like the return of the dove
Chosen as parents, we cried as we held her
Born to another and given in love

Two years later, it happened again
Teenagers in love had created a life
Their love for this child led them to call
Selfless and trusting, their choice felt so right

The child of our dreams surprised and amazed us
His birth brought us hope like the return of the dove
Chosen as parents, we cried as we held him
Born to another and given in love

Twice blessed, we receive these two children with thanks
their presence has filled our lives with such joy
We ask for the wisdom, the humor and faith
Entrusted to us, a girl and a boy

Lord help us raise them honest and proud
Help them learn where they come from and claim all they're due
Help them believe that we love them as their birth parents do
For they were given in love, let them know that is true

Children of our dreams you surprise and amaze us
From the day you were born you have brightened our lives
Chosen as parents, our thanks is unending
Born to these others and given in love

§ § §

In late December through early January, we brought Tessa and Kyle to Atlanta to visit us and see their son with his new family in his new home. They were very appreciative. The visit also seemed to give them more confirmation that they had made the right choice. At one point, John and I took Emily and went on a walk around the block. When we returned, they quickly handed the baby over to us with a sigh of relief. They were kids themselves, after all.

Leaving the Agency, But Not My Calling

January to May 1997

When I was talking to pregnant women who called our adoption agency in crisis or to prospective adoptive parents desperate for a child to call their own, I felt fully alive. I believed in open adoption with all my heart. Moreover, I felt like I was *good* at my job and at being a role model for the end result we were advocating. I appeared in publications and on television programs telling our personal stories and promoting open adoption. A neighbor remarked that she had seen me in my car, driving the children home from daycare, in an animated conversation with them and a smile on my face. She couldn't believe how happy I looked. I was. I had found my vocation. I helped people create their families during the day and loved my own the rest of the time.

As part of my job, I conducted weekend workshops for prospective adoptive parents. There were three-hour information sessions on Saturday mornings that operated as introductions to open adoption and enticed couples or individuals to join our agency. There were also two-day workshops for clients to educate them about all aspects of the process of adopting, including that first phone call or meeting with a birthmother.

As time passed, I accumulated more and more experiences with particular birthmothers and their stories. As a previous client of OAN, I had been told that each birthmother was different. But as an adoption professional, the concept was made real. Our two Falco adoptions had been uneventful by comparison to many of the stories I witnessed and facilitated. Here are a few examples I shared with my clients during their training:

(1) Isabelle is twenty. She and the birth father made the decision about adoption together. They knew they were not ready to parent, though

they planned to marry one day. They are both college students. Isabelle works in a daycare and is opposed to her baby going to daycare.

(2) Karen is a 37-year-old and doesn't believe she needs counseling. She works part-time, has an 11-year-old son, and has been widowed for five years. She had an affair with a 28-year-old and became pregnant. Her mother wants her to keep the baby.

(3) Larry, who is 23, called OAN when his wife, Laura, who is 19, was five months pregnant. He said they wanted to place the baby for adoption for financial reasons. Laura has a 4-year-old from a previous relationship whom Larry is raising as his own. They live in her grandmother's house. Laura's mother later called OAN and said that Larry is not the biological father of the pregnancy.

(4) Chystal is a 23-year-old who lives with her father. She has two years of college and works. She met a man, dated him a couple of times, and then he raped her and stole her money. She did not disclose the rape to her father. Chrystal is very private, shy and independent. She wants her child to have emotional stability and a college education.

(5) Dana is an 18-year-old Asian-Caucasian adoptee who does not get along with her adoptive parents. She ran away with her boyfriend. He was running from the law. They lived together and she got pregnant. The relationship ended and Dana moved back into her father's home.

(6) Frances is in her early twenties and has a 2-year-old daughter with respiratory problems. She is also taking care of her ailing father, going to school, and working. The biological father of the pregnancy is willing to sign papers but does not want to be involved in the adoption because he is married to someone else. Frances has had problems with depression in the past. Her personal goal is to be a lawyer some day.

(7) Gabrielle is 21 and living with a new boyfriend who is the father of her unborn child. She was raped when she was 14 and became pregnant. Her mother is raising that child as her own. Gabrielle has had three other children with a man who lives out-of-state with those children. Each time Gabrielle talks to someone at OAN, something in her story

changes. It appears that Gabrielle is a long-term survivor of abuse, and that her boyfriend is a victimizer.

With respect to each scenario, I asked the clients: (1) Which parts of the description don't fit your assumptions about birth parents? (2) What other information would you need to feel comfortable "matching" with these birth parents? (3) What are your on-going concerns about this situation? (4) Would you take the risk and match with this birthmother?

After the clients and I discussed their answers to the questions about each birth parent situation, I would tell them the rest of the story:

(1) Isabelle and her boyfriend placed their baby with adoptive parents who had written about losing a daughter, and because they lived only 90 minutes away.

(2) Karen placed her baby with adoptive parents who found her through their own networking. They went to doctor's appointments with her and bought her groceries each week.

(3) Laura had to go on bed rest early in her pregnancy. She chose adoptive parents who had experienced a reclaim two months earlier. ("Reclaim" is the term used to describe when a birthmother places her child with adoptive parents but later changes her mind and takes the baby, or child, back within the statutory period for doing so.) The adoptive parents chose to work with a different birthmother who was geographically closer to them. Laura was discouraged, but eventually chose other adoptive parents.

(4) Chrystal chose adoptive parents whose letter reflected that they were equal partners and best friends. She read every letter she received and analyzed it. She prepared a list of reasons why she was placing the baby for adoption and put it in her hospital bag to remind herself when she felt the pain of the loss.

(5) Dana chose adoptive parents who were within driving distance of her home so that she could visit. This turned out to work in the adoptive

parents favor because Dana placed two more children with them in later years.

(6) Frances chose adoptive parents because they appeared to be able to offer the financial and emotion support she wanted for her child. Relatives rushed forward after the baby was born and promised to help Frances raise the child. The baby was reclaimed.

(7) Gabrielle chose adoptive parents who had a picture of a rabbit in their letter. She followed through with her adoption plan.

When I taught my clients how to write their personal marketing piece or Dear Birthmother letter, I provided examples of topics they should include and topics they should avoid based on OAN's experience with real birth parents. In the meantime, my own experiences with birth parents were teaching me that no one could predict the subjective response to one's marketing efforts. For example, no one could have known that Gabrielle would be attracted to a family with a rabbit. No one knew Laura would choose a family that had experienced a reclaim.

In my role as birth parent intake counselor for OAN, I was provided with a list of "red flags." Red flags were behaviors or specifics regarding a birthmother that suggested she was less likely to follow through with her adoption plan. Some examples of red flags were a birth father's or other relative's disagreement with the adoption plan, a very young birthmother who was more likely to have trouble letting go of her idealized infant, or a birthmother who refused counseling. However, I was learning that we often didn't have enough information *up front* to make a good prediction, or that the predictors were just *wrong* with respect to a particular birthmother. Karen's mother was a "red flag," but Karen placed her baby for adoption anyway. Laura's family situation was messy and her first choice adoptive parents broke trust; but Laura followed through with her adoption plan nonetheless. Claire had no support system, but her conviction and organization helped her persevere. Frances seemed to be the perfect birthmother candidate, but no one knew about her relatives or that they would abort the adoption plan. Each case carried unknown risks, but surprising potential as well. I found myself drawn to the human drama in spite of my training in reasoned judgment. I did not know it at the time, but the education I was providing to my clients was preparing *me* for future encounters with prospective Falco children birth parents.

K.J.'s adoption had been finalized on January 22, 1997. As busy as our lives were with work and two young children, I was already thinking about a third adoption as the New Year began. Our two children were wonderful. We might have stopped there. However, before K.J. came along, we had tried on the idea of adopting twins–*two more* children. That had seemed doable. Now, the idea of a third child seemed *preferable.*

Why was I in such a big hurry? There were several factors at work: (1) my age; (2) John's business success; and (3) my knowledge about birthmothers. First, I would be 40 in little more than a year. I had always thought I would complete my family by the time I was 40. If we didn't get started soon, that might not happen. Second, John's business was growing. We could afford another child. We had an extra bedroom. Finally, I had worked with enough birthmothers to know that most were looking for adoptive parents who didn't have any children or had only one other child. I reasoned it would probably take longer to adopt this time. Accordingly, we needed to start searching sooner.

The more I learned about the *typical* birthmother who contacted OAN, the less certain I felt about being successful in finding another birthmother as a client of OAN. This feeling, coupled with the increasing stressfulness of my relationship with OAN's Executive Director, prompted John and me to decide to do a search for a birthmother independent of OAN.

In April 1997, we sent out networking letters with our third Dear Birthmother letter. We would see what happened before deciding whether or not to join an agency or to hire an adoption attorney who might advance our search. The new letter included information about our children:

> Emily - was born on July 7, 1994. She loves books, animals, the outdoors, music, and playing with other children. She gives great hugs, and has the best laugh in the world. Emily met and held her brother in the hospital the day after he was born. She proudly boasts about "my brudder KJ" and tries to help feed and bathe him or instruct him in the use of toys.
>
> KJ (Kevin John) - was born on July 9, 1996. He is a bundle of energy and motion with the biggest smile. He has always loved observing faces and interacting with people. He especially adores Emily, and coos at her whenever she turns in his direction. No doubt he will be equally devoted to a new brother or sister.

§ § §

On May 6, 1997, I submitted my letter of resignation to the Executive Director of OAN. In very detailed letters to the members of the Board of Directors for the agency, I wrote that I was forced to resign because the Executive Director had become far too hostile and distrustful of me. In part, I wrote:

> In the past two years that I have worked for OAN, the Executive Director has demonstrated a lack of sound business judgment. He has demanded that his employees (including me) perform unethical, if not illegal, acts as a condition of their employment. He has managed by threats and intimidation. He has insisted that misleading, and sometimes inaccurate, information be presented to the public and clients as truthful. When I resisted these wrongful practices, I was threatened, harassed, intimidated and ultimately, constructively terminated.

I also requested that the Directors investigate into a number of matters. To the best of my knowledge, this was never done. I was shaken, but not defeated. I had been through more serious traumatic experiences in my life. I could recover from this. But what would I do for work now?

I had managed to squeeze in taking the Georgia Bar Exam earlier in the Spring. I learned in late May that I had passed! I wasn't sure what I would do with my new license, but I had some time to figure that out. I was going to spend the summer being a full-time parent to my children and part-time nanny to another child. Still, I was embarrassed about not having a professional job.

Finding a Match

June to December 1997

On Wednesday, June 18, 1997, I received a call from Phoebe at the OAN. She knew I had spoken with a particular pregnant woman, Christina, in March about open adoption. Phoebe said that Christina had now decided that she definitely wanted to place her baby for adoption, but that she needed some financial assistance with living arrangements. None of the clients of OAN met her specific requests or were willing to work with her. Were the Falcos interested? Yes, we were!

After Phoebe called Christina to tell her about us, I called Christina. She was staying in temporary housing in Lawrenceville, Georgia. She was working as a waitress at Ryan's Restaurant. She was 23 years old and had a son, almost four, who was living with his father's parents. Christina didn't have a car and was taking a cab to work, about 2 miles away.

Christina said that her mother and stepfather lived in North Georgia and didn't know she was pregnant. She wanted to keep the pregnancy a secret from them. Her stepfather had emotionally and physically abused her and her mother, but her mother would not leave him. Christina said she left home when she was sixteen. She said her mother had five other children. Christina was the second oldest.

Christina just recently met her own biological father. For years she had been told that he left her and her mother. Her father claimed just the opposite–that Christina's mother left him. Christina said she was choosing open adoption because she didn't want her unborn child to have to search for her birthmother the way she had had to search for her own father. She also said she wasn't emotionally ready to be a parent.

Christina had been working as an exotic dancer and model in Atlanta before she got pregnant. For liability reasons she could not dance while pregnant, though she hoped to return to that work in the future. Once she lost her dancing job, she moved in with a friend who was living in Lawrenceville. For reasons she did not disclose, he asked her to leave a few days ago.

Her current week-to-week residence was noisy, dirty, and didn't feel safe. She wasn't making enough money at her waitress job at Ryan's to pay the rent *and* take care of her other expenses. She wanted to move into the cleaner, safer Extended Stay America facility that was across the street from Ryan's and close to groceries and her doctor. She hoped the adoptive parents could pay that weekly rent of about $200/ week. She said she could handle all of her other expenses.

Christina was on Medicaid and had been seeing a group of doctors and midwives at the Gwinnett Medical Center since March. An ultrasound in April revealed that she was probably having a girl. Her official due date was August 18, 1997.

Christina and I arranged to meet the next day to get to know each other better. Emily and K.J. were to come along too since John was out-of-town on business. Christina said she liked children. She felt like she had raised her younger siblings.

On June 19th, Emily, K.J., and I picked-up Christina around 3 p.m. and drove to Ryan's to talk and to give Christina an opportunity to eat before her shift started at 5 p.m. If there was ever a birthmother who *looked* like the perfect replacement for my DNA, it was Christina. She was tall, about 5'10 1/2" to 5'11", with a usual weight, she said, of 135-140 lbs. She liked to workout and stay active. She had brown or hazel eyes and reddish blond hair, though it was bleached light blond at the time we met. She was looking for an athletic couple who also valued education to adopt her baby. Christina said she had been a bookworm and good student as a child. She said John and I sounded like just the kind of people she was looking for.

Christina reported that the birth father, whose name was Samuel, had brown hair and blue eyes. Christina thought he was between 5'10" and 6' tall and probably about 27 or 28 years old. They had a short dating relationship. He was a model too. When she contacted him about the pregnancy, he denied he was the father and subsequently changed his phone number. She had had difficulty locating him since then.

I agreed to check out the Extended Stay America facility nearby. I explained that we would like to help her, but that we had to go through a licensed adoption agency, for legal reasons, before we could provide any living expenses. We would be meeting with an agency representative soon to get those arrangements made.

We discussed her doctor's appointments and Christina agreed that I could take her to them. The next one was scheduled for June 25th. I told her that John would be back in town tomorrow and would like to meet her soon. He would be calling her to set up that meeting. In terms of emotional support, Christina confessed that only the people at work knew she was pregnant. She hoped to have the baby, recover quickly, and then go back to dancing, modeling, and maybe eventually work either as a police officer or private investigator.

I was delighted to have met Christina! This was all happening faster than I had envisioned. If it worked out, our two youngest children would be little more than a year apart in age. I couldn't wait for John to meet her. The only thing that concerned me *a little* was the secrecy of Christina's pregnancy. Our other children's mothers had been emotionally supported by their families. Without a counselor or family to support Christina, would she be able to follow through with her plan? Looking long-term, how would the child feel about not having relationships with extended birth family as Emily and K.J. did?

The next day, John and K.J. went to see Christina. The discussion centered on growing up in a small town versus a big town. Christina said that she liked a big town better. She liked the experiences she was having for herself in Atlanta. She said her mom didn't or couldn't understand that. John and Christina acknowledged that they felt very comfortable with each other.

While this new adoption possibility was developing, I was having a spiritual crisis of sorts. At Glenn Memorial United Methodist Church, the church our family attended, the senior pastor had preached on the debate going on between Emory University and Glenn about using the church for same-sex commitment or marriage ceremonies. The university's position was based on equal rights and would permit use of the space for such purposes. The UMC, however, said that marriage included only male-female unions and that practicing homosexuality was against God's will. Accordingly, same-sex commitment ceremonies were not permissible in "sacred spaces" such as the Glenn sanctuary.

I started crying. I couldn't get over how dire it sounded. I had grown-up in the United Methodist Church. But its position was so *wrong!* Weren't we instructed to love one another, to love all people? Weren't we supposed to be making commitments based on love? If Glenn didn't change their position, I couldn't stay. But how long should I wait? How much energy should put into changing something that sounded so permanent? I put my decision-making off to deal with adoption…

On June 23rd, John and I met with Jennifer, Executive Director of the Adoption Agency, to set up an escrow account and to find a counselor who could work with Christina and us. We agreed to put money in the account on an ongoing basis to pay only for Christina's housing and for counseling-related costs. (Subsequently, we modified our arrangement to also include $50/week for groceries.) Medicaid would cover Christina's medical expenses.

Two days later, I took Christina to her doctor's appointment. The midwife calculated that Christina was at 32 weeks and 2 days. She had gained 22 1/2 lbs. so far during her pregnancy. The baby was head down at the present time. Her next appointment would be in two weeks. When she reached 36 weeks, she would have weekly appointments.

I took Christina back to her room to load her things into my car. We moved her to Extended Stay America. The room was very nice, clean, and fresh smelling. Christina said she was glad to be there. She showed me pictures of her son and mother. She also gave me the ultrasound picture of the baby and asked only that I make a photocopy for her. I invited Christina to spend the 4th of July with our family if she was not working that day. She said that she would find out about her schedule and let me know.

I liked Christina. She seemed smart and strong. She was old enough and experienced enough to make this decision about adoption. But I was still anxious to hear what the counselor would say.

I realized that when I was waiting for Emily and K.J. to be born, I had paid employment to distract me. I had no job now and I was postponing making a decision about future employment to *wait.*

In a closed adoption, the adoptive parents are notified when there is a child legally available. In open adoption, there is no guarantee of placement, but anticipation about a particular child begins with the first call from a birthmother. From that point on, every month, week, day, and hour until birth feels significant, weighty, ripe with potential for joy or pain. My journal entries related to Christina are filled with meticulous details about our conversations, activities, and her moods.

On July 3rd, we had a scare when John couldn't reach Christina and then called Ryan's Restaurant only to discover that she didn't work there anymore. Even though everything we had experienced with Christina seemed on track for adoption, her disappearance was concerning. The counselor who had been assigned to us, Dorothy, had also been unable to reach her. Fortunately, after a couple of hours, John spoke to Christina in her room. She said she had taken a cab to do grocery shopping. Yes, she had walked out of Ryan's the day before. The work was too hard. Yes, she would come to our house for July 4th.

On July 4th, I picked-up Christina in late afternoon and brought her to the Falco house where she promptly threw-up, attributing her nausea to the heat. John and Emily gave her a tour of our house, including the new baby's room, which we had scrambled to put together the night before. Then we left for a tailgate picnic and the Decatur Fourth of July Parade and Concert. Christina met most of my family there. My mother drove my sister Joanna and Christina, both pregnant, to the concert, while I pulled Emily, cousin Kylie, and K.J. in a red wagon in the parade. The kids made the evening news.

At the Square in Decatur, my father played his saxophone with the concert band. I took some pictures of Christina. It was so hot, however, that the Falcos and Christina ended the outdoor part of the evening before the fireworks to drive home and visit in an air-conditioned environment.

On July 9th, K.J.'s first birthday, I took Christina to a doctor's appointment again. The midwife was concerned that Christina had not gained weight and that maybe the baby was not growing. Christina was put on a monitor until the baby demonstrated that she was moving well. The clinic also scheduled Christina for an ultrasound. Five days later, the ultrasound confirmed that she was going to have a baby girl. Everything looked fine.

On July 16th, Christina walked to the hospital to find some company and to talk with the hospital social worker. Christina reported to our counselor Dorothy that the hospital social worker had turned cold and disapproving when she mentioned her adoption plan. Christina left the hospital in tears, determined not to give birth there. Dorothy strongly recommended that we move Christina out of Lawrenceville and back to one of the areas where she had lived previously and would be working again after the baby was born. We followed the recommendation and also agreed to assist Christina with housing and food expenses for six weeks after the baby was born.

Paying living expenses: rent, utilities, food, and maternity clothes for a birthmother is legal because it pertains to the health of the mother and child. Payment of the mother's expenses after the birth is also permitted for a limited time to allow the mother to recover and begin work again.

John worked out an arrangement with Sierra Suites in Sandy Springs and Christina loved the place. But it was difficult to find a doctor who would take a 36-week pregnant woman with Medicaid as a new patient. Jennifer finally located one who was in Roswell and delivered babies at North Fulton Regional Hospital.

I told Jennifer that I had recently heard at an adoption law seminar that North Fulton Regional Hospital would not accept a birthmother's Medicaid if she placed her baby for adoption. The adoptive parents would be billed. Jennifer responded that the Adoption Agency had worked with this hospital before and had never encountered that problem.

On July 18th and 19th, Christina came with the Falco family to our community pool. She suntanned in her bikini and received compliments about how good she looked.

On July 25th, I called North Fulton Regional Hospital to get a direct answer about the billing issue when an adoption was involved. The social work department referred me to Kelly in the billing department. I had to leave a message.

Four days later, I had not received a response, so I called Kelly again and left another message. This time she called me back and said that she had delayed responding because she wanted to check with her supervisor. She knew of no reason why Medicaid would not cover the birthmother's and baby's medical care.

On August 1st, Dorothy met with John and me at our house. Dorothy said that Christina loved us and thought of Rebecca as a kind of role model for how she would like her life to be. There was another *potential* biological father, Carl, who Christina was sure was not the *real* birth father, but who would need to sign surrender papers for legal reasons. Carl had been found and was glad to cooperate. Samuel had still not been found. Dorothy outlined the steps that the agency would take to terminate his rights if he could not be found after a diligent search.

Dorothy also told us some bad news about North Fulton Regional Hospital. She had contacted the medical social worker who said that hospital policy did not allow adoptive parents to be in the hospital at all! According to Dorothy, Christina very much wanted me to be in the delivery room with her. We discussed several ways we might address the problem, and agreed to let Christina make the final decision.

Fortunately, Dorothy later had another conversation with the social worker in which she said that they were willing to use the Falcos as a test case: the adoptive parents could come to the hospital and be in the delivery room if that was what the patient wanted.

We used a form, similar to the one that follows on the next four pages here, to help us plan what we intended to have happen at the hospital and after the birth of the baby. For adoptive parents and birthmother, each decision suggests something about their present and future relationship. Any variation at the time of delivery may signal a change in the adoption plan for better or worse. Upon rereading this form from the distance of time, I am struck by how *many* choices there are related to the birth of a baby, and how significant they are to the parties involved. For biological parents who are keeping their child, these decisions may be effortless or not discussed at all.

Tentative Plan for the Birth and Hospital Stay

Birthmother: ______________________________
Age: ____
Adopting Parents: __________________________________
Due Date: ___________
Physician: ____________________
Hospital: ____

At the time of the birth, the birthmother expects to want to:
___ See baby immediately
___ Not see baby immediately
___ See baby later
___ Not see baby at all
___ Hold baby immediately
___ Not hold baby immediately
___ Allow someone else to be the first to hold the baby:

____

The birthmother wants the following people to be with her:

1. ______________________________ during labor ___ during birth ___

2. ______________________________ during labor ___ during birth ___

3. ______________________________ during labor ___ during birth ___

4. ______________________________ during labor ___ during birth ___

For the birth, the birthmother wants the adopting mother to:
___ Be at the hospital in the waiting area
___ Not be at the hospital
___ Be present during labor
___ Not be present during labor
___ Be present during the birth
___ Not be present during the birth

For the birth, the birthmother wants the adopting father to:
___ Be at the hospital in the waiting area
___ Not be at the hospital
___ Be present during labor
___ Not be present during labor
___ Be present during the birth
___ Not be present during the birth

Photography - The birthmother requests that:
___ Hospital Baby Photos be taken
___ No hospital Baby Photos be taken
___ Still and video photography be taken during labor and delivery
___ No photos allowed during labor or delivery
___ The following persons be allowed to photograph the birthmother:

____

____

___ Still and video photography of the newborn infant be allowed
___ No photos be allowed of the newborn infant
___ The following persons be allowed to photograph the newborn infant:

____

____

Post-Partum, the birthmother expects to want to:
___ Room on the Obstetrics Unit
___ Room on non-maternity unit
___ Have baby "room in"
___ Not have baby "room in"
___ Have baby brought to her room on request
___ Not have baby in her room at all
___ Visit baby in the nursery
___ Not go to the nursery

In caring for the infant, the birthmother plans to:
___ Give the first feeding
___ Not give the first feeding
___ Give some/all subsequent feedings
___ Not give subsequent feedings
___ Have the baby brought to her for all feedings
___ Have the baby brought to her only upon request
___ Breastfeed the baby
___ Not breastfeed the baby
___ Share feedings with adopting parents
___ Not share feedings with adopting parents
___ Share all care-giving with adopting parents
___ Not share care-giving with adopting parents
___ Share some care-giving with adopting parents
___ Delegate most/all feeding and care-giving to adopting parents
___ Allow the adopting parents to spend time with the baby in her room
___ Authorize the adopting parents to have access to the baby privately (e.g., in the nursery)
Comments: ____

Confidentiality - The birthmother's request regarding publicity and release of information are:

___ No restrictions on information given out by the hospital. Treat as any other maternity patient.
___ No special measures within the hospital, but please do not release birth information to the press.
___ Restrict access to information, with the exceptions listed below.
___ Absolute confidentiality - Please deny the birthmother's presence at the hospital. Birthmother will notify those she wants to know about the hospitalization, and they will ask for her using the room number.
___ The birthmother does authorize release of information to the parties indicated below:
___ Staff of adoption agency (Partners in Adoption)

___ Adopting Parents: ______________________________

___ Other: ______________________________

___ Other: ______________________________

Naming the baby - The birthmother plans to:

___ Choose the name used on the original birth certificate, but the adopting parents may call the child by another name which will be on the final adoption decree and revised birth certificate
___ Allow adopting parents to choose the name on the original birth certificate

Medical Care and Consents - The birthmother plans to:

___ Meet with the pediatrician
___ Not meet with the pediatrician
___ Allow the adopting parents to meet privately with the pediatrician
___ Authorize adopting parents to give consent for medical care*
___ Sign consents for medical care
___ Refuse circumcision
___ Sign consent for circumcision
___ Authorize adopting parents to consent to circumcision*
**If allowed by the hospital*

At the time of discharge, the birthmother plans to:

___ Sign the state or hospital form authorizing the hospital to release the baby to the adopting parents
___ Leave the hospital together with the adopting parents & infant
___ Discharge infant to herself
___ Leave hospital before baby does
___ Leave hospital after baby does

Comments: ______________________________

Length of stay desired:
___ Early discharge (12 hours or less)
___ "Normal" or maximum allowed by insurance or Medicaid
___ Extended stay if possible based on medical or psychosocial justification

In the event of a Cesarean birth or medically necessary extended stay for the birthmother, she would prefer that:
___ The baby remain in the hospital until she herself is ready for discharge
___ Early discharge of the infant be considered, with the final decision to be made by the birthmother following the birth
___ The baby be discharged to the adopting parents as soon as she or he is medically eligible

Accommodations - Private/Semi-Private, etc.: * *[see note below]*
___ Whatever is available and covered by the third-party payer
___ Private room or no roommate is very important to birthmother
___ Private room if hospital can arrange it at no extra cost

Financial arrangements - Payments for prenatal, delivery, & hospital expenses:

Birthmother	*Baby*	
___	___	Adopting parents to guarantee payment
___	___	Birthmother's medical insurance or HMO
___	___	Birthmother's Medicaid, Case #: _______

Comments: ____

* *NOTE: At the present time, private rooms are the norm because of HIPAA regulations and other concerns, but at the time of the birth, semi-private rooms were available.*

§ § §

On August 3rd, we invited Christina over for dinner. My brother Timothy and his wife, Therra, also stopped by to meet Christina and to discuss professional wrestling, baseball, and dancing.

On August 4th, I took Christina to her first appointment with her new doctor. Christina was 38 weeks pregnant. He said everything looked good and that if she was dilating at all next week, he would admit her to the hospital.

On August 10th, John took Christina to the Braves game. He told her we were going to name her baby "Skye." She said that was a cool name. John and I had also decided to give the baby the middle name "Joelen" for my sister, Joanna, and mother, Helen.

On August 11th, when Christina was 39 weeks pregnant, she and I went to her scheduled doctor's appointment. The doctor said, "Nothing is happening yet." He sent us away for another week.

On Friday, August 15, 1997, Christina called me about 3:30 p.m. and said that she was having labor pains and discharge. The doctor's office had told her to get to the hospital. I said I would be there as soon as I arranged childcare for Emily and K.J. I then called John. While I waited for my dad to arrive, John called Christina. She told him to come right away - her contractions were four to five minutes apart now!

John got to Christina just a couple of minutes before I could get there, so I followed John's car. We arrived at the hospital about 5:00 p.m. I rushed Christina to the labor and delivery area by wheelchair and Christina was soon in bed with monitors attached. The nurses monitored contractions and heartbeat for 30 minutes and then did a pelvic exam. The nurse came out of the exam to tell us that the baby was breech, that is, feet first instead of headfirst. The baby would be delivered by C-section. Christina told the nurses that I was supposed to go with her.

The doctor on call arrived to do the procedure. In record time, Christina was medicated and wheeled into the OR while I changed into scrubs and doctors and nurses set up the equipment. Christina was scared and crying when I was permitted in the OR to be with her. I put my hands on her shoulders and head–the only parts in front of the drape–and reassured her that everything would be okay. One of the doctors told me that I could stand and watch if I wanted to. I reported what I saw to Christina, leaving out some of the bloodier details. I watched the doctors pull Christina's baby girl by head and neck from her body.

Beautiful Skye Joelen was born at 6:32 p.m. Her APGAR scores were 8 and 9. She was measured at 20 inches long and 7 lbs. 11 oz. Christina began to fall asleep as the doctors cleaned and stitched her. She was moved to the recovery room for about two hours.

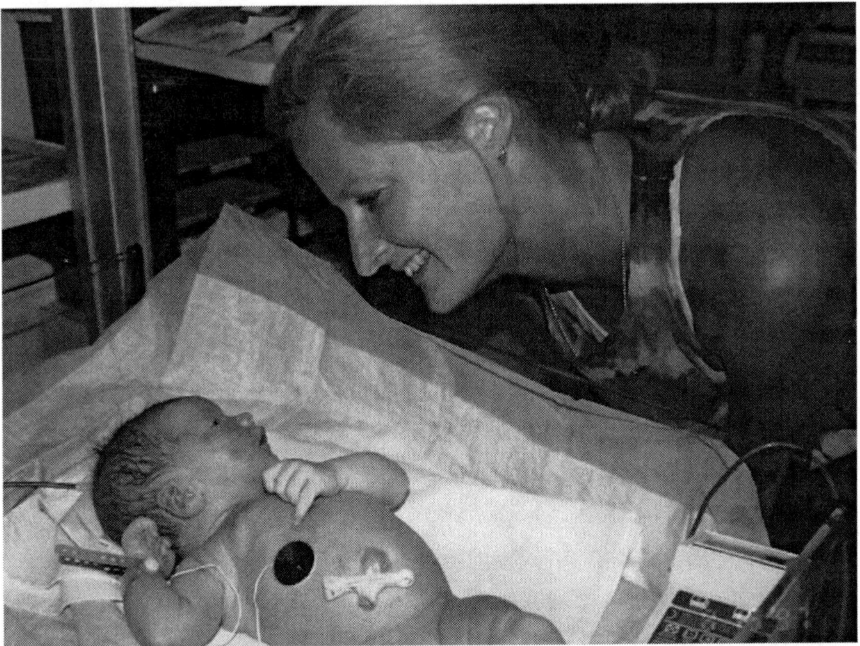

After Christina had fallen asleep and the baby had been taken to the nursery, I left to find John in the Family Waiting Room to report on the birth of his newest daughter. We called our families in Atlanta, New York, and Chicago to tell them about Skye's birth while we waited to be permitted into the nursery. A nurse took us to the baby and bathed her before we did the first feeding. Skye loudly protested the bath, and the nurse commented, "This one will be a handful."

Because Christina was still in recovery, we took a dinner break at a restaurant across the street. When we returned to the hospital, Christina was in the post-partum area, but she was very groggy. We visited briefly and agreed to see her again in the morning. As we left, the nurses warned us that only the adoptive parents–not other adoptive family members–would be allowed in the nursery.

On Saturday, August 16th, we returned in the morning to the hospital with Emily and K.J. Christina was still sleepy. A different nurse allowed me to bring Emily in to meet her baby sister. Later John and K.J. came into the nursery too.

We took a break for lunch and to play in a park. Then I came back to the hospital to stay with Christina while John took Emily and K.J. home for naps. About 4 p.m., Christina came out of her fog and began to act more like her old self. She also got hungry enough to eat a real meal when dinner was served. Joanna arrived about 5 p.m. and she, too, was allowed in the nursery to see the baby. Contrary to what we had been told the night before, all the nurses were helpful and welcoming.

On Sunday, August 17th, Emily, my mother, and I went to the hospital. Mom brought flowers for Christina. Christina was preparing to take a shower and get ready to sign surrender papers when Dorothy and witnesses arrived at 3 p.m. Carl would also come to the hospital to sign papers around 4 p.m. Mom, Emily, and I fed Skye.

John went to the hospital in the afternoon to see Skye and to be available to take Christina home. However, Dorothy volunteered to transport Christina because she wanted to continue their conversation. The plan was to discharge the baby the next morning. After signing surrender papers, Christina and Dorothy sat and talked with John while he held Skye in the nursery. Christina said everything felt right and that she was very happy with her decision.

That evening, Dorothy called to say that she had spoken with the medical social worker again. The social worker said the adoptive parents could *not* be in the hospital at discharge. Only the agency representative could be on the unit. We had to wait in the parking lot! In fact, we were not supposed to have been in the nursery all weekend, much less our other family members.

On August 18th, Emily went to school and Mom came to the house to wait with K.J. while John and I went to the hospital to get Skye and bring her home. Jennifer did not arrive at the hospital until 11:30 and told us to "hide" outside while she paged the social worker. After what seemed like an eternity, Jennifer appeared again and told us to meet her in the ER parking lot. It was there that we received Skye, some supplies, the baby's medical report and discharge instructions, and a signed placement agreement.

In an agency adoption, the baby is relinquished or surrendered to the agency by the birthmother or both legal parents; and the agency places the baby with adoptive parents. Although the adoptive parents are given the right to make medical and other decisions related to the care of the child, the agency is ultimately responsible for the child until the adoption is finalized and the child receives new legal parents.

Jennifer then told us that the social worker had informed her at discharge that the hospital would not bill Medicaid for Christina's and the baby's expenses, but would charge the agency. This was alarming after receiving different information when I talked to the billing department. We told Jennifer that we were not authorizing her to pay hospital bills from our escrow account.

Nanna had prepared lunch, which K.J. was wearing, when we arrived home. Our neighbor Sherry had put welcoming baby balloons on the mailbox. She also prepared an evening meal and presents for all three Falco children, which her family brought over later in the afternoon. Papa, Aunt Joanna, and cousins Nathan and Kylie were also on hand to welcome Skye home.

The next day, Jennifer called me to report on the status of the Medicaid issue. She had been calling the billing office but no one was returning her calls. She had also called the hospital administrator and spoken with his assistant. Jennifer told the assistant that if the Adoption Agency received Christina's bills, she would put them in the trash. She stated that if bills were sent to Christina, it would be hard to keep her from going to the newspapers. Jennifer explained that the Adoption Agency had provided only counseling for the birthmother and assistance at discharge. Neither the Adoption Agency nor the adoptive parents guaranteed payment of the hospital bills. She was now waiting for a call back from the hospital administrator.

Later in the day, Jennifer spoke with John about a conversation she had just had with an adoption attorney. He warned that it was North Fulton Regional Hospital's policy not to bill Medicaid when an adoption was involved. John reiterated to Jennifer that the Falcos were not authorizing her to pay medical expenses from our escrow account. There was a silence. Then Jennifer stated, " If this matter is not cleared up, the adoption can not be finalized." I felt betrayed and outraged, but shared these emotions only with John. The Adoption Agency had the fate of our child, our family, in its hands. Sadly, I was not surprised to hear an adoption agency administrator turn sour when money was involved. My experience at OAN taught me that adoption agencies were sometimes more interested in staying in business than in making every client happy.

Dorothy called to check on our family and report about birth father termination. The attorney for the Adoption Agency would be handling the petition to terminate birth fathers' rights. The petition would ask to terminate the rights of Samuel and to confirm the terminations, after the 10-day-period, of Christina and Carl. A private investigator would be creating his report of the steps taken to locate Samuel by September 2, 1997. On the Medicaid issue, Dorothy thought the hospital's policy was discrimination against birthmothers.

The next day, Jennifer called John to report that no one from the hospital had called her back. Upon reconsideration, she had decided to tell the hospital that the adoptive parents never agreed to pay medical bills and there were no funds in their account to pay the bills.

A day later, Jennifer called John to report that she had spoken to a supervisor in the billing department at the hospital, who said that the reason they bill the agency/adoptive parents is because of the way the hospital's licensing agreement with Medicaid reads. If they billed Medicaid, it would amount to Medicaid fraud. Other hospitals got around this by discharging the baby directly to the birthmother.

The billing supervisor also said that she was aware that Kelly told me the wrong thing. Dorothy had had several conversations with the hospital social worker who knew the birthmother was on Medicaid and never mentioned the policy until the baby was being discharged.

Jennifer learned that Christina's bill was $7000 and the baby's bill was $900. Jennifer told her that Christina was ready to go to the newspapers with this story. Jennifer also told the billing supervisor that the adoptive parents had not paid a big agency fee. It was an "identified adoption." In an identified adoption, the adoptive parents come to the agency with a specific birthmother, and pay for services related to that situation only. We had only authorized payment of $50/hour for counseling. The billing supervisor seemed surprised. Finally, Jennifer said she needed a decision about how the hospital would handle billing by tomorrow. John and Jennifer also discussed that the "unplayed card" was to tear up the surrenders and tell the hospital that the birthmother was keeping the baby.

All of this drama related to the medical bills was unexpected and stressful, but we hardly had time to focus on the worst-case scenario as we were so busy incorporating a new baby into our young family. Fortunately, the hospital finally came to its senses and billed Medicaid.

Nine days after Skye's birth, John picked-up Christina to come to our house to take pictures of the adoptive and birth parents, Emily, K.J., and Skye Joelen. In that week and a half, Christina had dropped to her pre-pregnancy weight. She looked great with her hair done and her make-up on. From our perspective, she seemed content with her adoption decision.

Our birth announcement read: *To Announce the Birth of Skye Joelen Falco, 7 lbs., 11 oz., 20 inches, on August 15,1997 in Roswell, Georgia. Born in Love to Her Birthmother Christina [last name]. Given in Love to Her Adoptive Family Rebecca and John Falco, sister Emily and brother K.J.*

Skye, like her older brother and sister, had a special lullaby that her daddy or I sang to her every night. She also received godparents who had been special people in our lives: Ruth and Gary Musicante, and Bobbi Patterson.

Adoption is a complicated legal proceeding, governed by statute, which must be completed precisely to be airtight. I was going to be filing the Petition for Adoption of Skye, but I was depending on the Adoption Agency to complete its responsibilities in the process first. After Wednesday, August 27, 1997, the tenth day after Christina and Carl signed surrenders, the attorney for the Adoption Agency would petition the Superior Court of DeKalb County (our county of residence) to confirm the terminations of rights of Christina and Carl, and ask the Court to terminate the rights of Samuel, the alleged biological father of Skye. Assuming the private investigator had been unable to locate Samuel, the judge was likely to order notice to Samuel of the pending adoption by publication. The Adoption Agency would place the appropriate notice once a week for three weeks in the "official organ" of DeKalb County and in the county of Samuel's last known address. Service was deemed received on the date of the last publication. Following that date, Samuel had 30 days to file a petition to legitimate the child, if he so chose.

Assuming Samuel did nothing during the 30-day notice period, the agency's attorney would again petition the court to terminate Samuel's rights; and the judge would enter an order so doing. Once the termination order was entered, I would file a Petition For Adoption on behalf or John and myself, and the Court would set a date to hear the petition not less than 60 days from the date of filing.

I would need a number of documents from the Adoption Agency to complete our Petition for Adoption. These included:

(1) Surrender of Rights signed by Christina;

(2) An Acknowledgement of Surrender signed by Christina;

(3) An Affidavit of Agency Representative re: Christina's Surrender;

(4) A Mother's Affidavit signed by Christina;

(5) A Surrender of Rights of Biological Father signed by Carl;

(6) An Acknowledgement of Surrender signed by Carl;

(7) An Affidavit of Agency Representative re: Carl's Surrender;

(8) The Petition to terminate the rights of Samuel (and exhibits);

(9) The Order terminating rights of the alleged biological father, Samuel;

(10) An affidavit from the Adoption Agency stating that all of the requirements of certain sections of the Georgia Code had been complied with;

(11) The written consent of the Adoption Agency to the adoption;

(12) Completed forms containing background information regarding Skye; and

(13) The report of the investigation done by the Adoption Agency on the adoptive parents following the filing of the Petition For Adoption.

In September, John's mother, Barbara, came to visit us. Later in the month, Michael J Patton Breazeale was born to my sister Joanna and her husband.

In October, we took a trip to Nebraska to spend time with Emily's and K.J.'s birth families and to introduce Skye to them. Unlike the two older children, Skye was without an extended birth family. In the midst of all these loving relatives, it hit me how sad this would someday feel to Skye. I expressed this feeling at dinner one night, to which Emily and K.J.'s mutual great-grandfather said, "If she's one of yours, she's one of ours." John and I were very touched.

Later that month, we also took a trip to Chicago to visit the LaRusso family. While we were away, my beloved 14-year-old dog, Adagio, died. She had been my best friend through many of the ups and downs in my life.

Although John and I took pride in having equitably divided household chores, we had now fallen into traditional roles when it came to who brought home a paycheck and who had primary responsibility for childrearing. I was torn between wanting to be a professional, working mother and the kind of role model I long envisioned I would be for my children, and recognizing the very real financial and emotional barriers to pursuing paid work at this point in time. Could I find a job I liked that paid enough to cover the cost of three children in daycare/school? If the job paid *enough*, would I ever be at home with these wonderful, beautiful children we had worked so hard to add to our family? If I stayed at home for a few years, would I really be able to begin a new career in my 40's?

By the end of 1997, Emily was attending the Montessori School at Emory during the week, enjoying both the work and her friends. She enjoyed playing with K.J., and cousin, Kylie, and helping to take care of Skye. She refused to wear dresses or things in her hair, except on special occasions. She loved animals–especially our dog, Meeko, who had come along to fill some of the absence left by Adagio.

K.J. was an affectionate 17 month old, who clung to his parents, but, in a safe environment, was happy and curious about everything. He loved to read his books, to wrestle with his dad and Emily, to kiss his sister Skye, and to feed himself with *no* assistance, creating a giant mess. He was working on naming the parts of the face, the sounds animals make, and the types of food he most enjoyed eating.

Skye was long, lean, and in constant motion when she was awake. She had learned to rollover and was beginning to sleep through the night. The name Skye was Dutch for "scholar." It seemed fitting since her birthmother claimed to have been a good student. "Skye Falco" also sounded like a great name for a basketball player; and since Christina was 5'11" and an athlete, we could dream that Skye would love sports as much as we did.

Falco

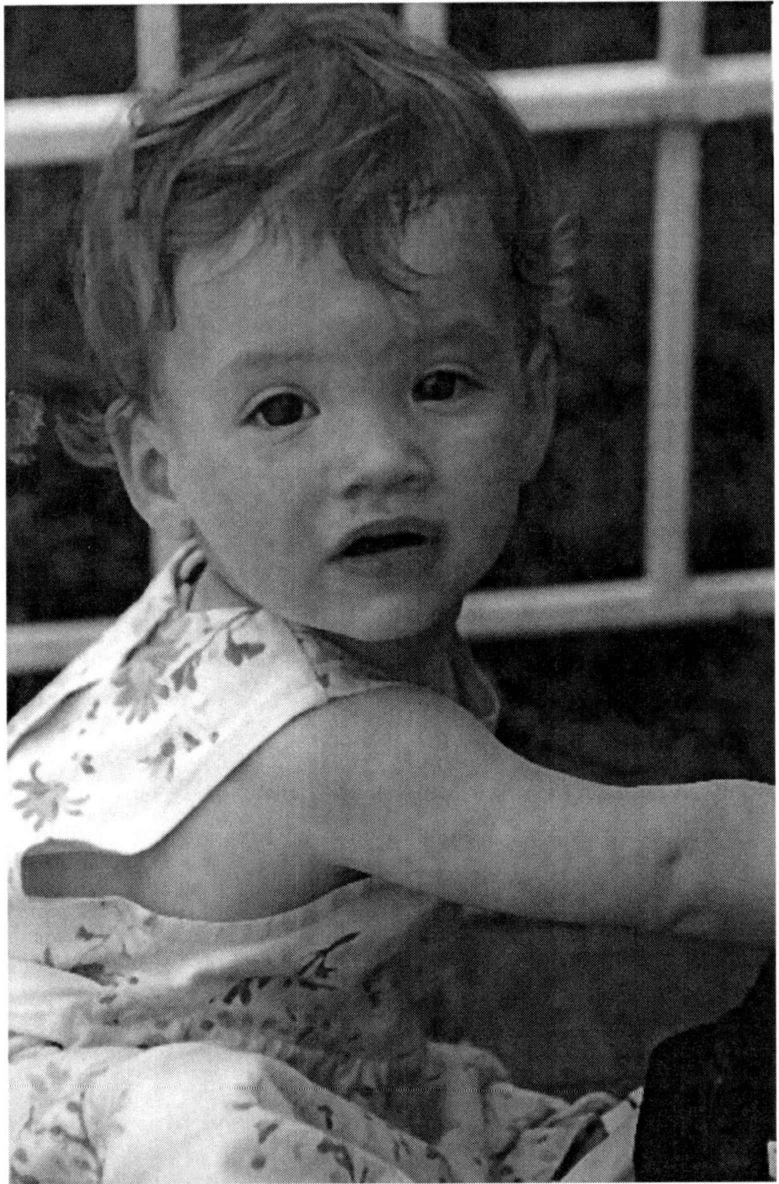

A New Church Home for a Non-Traditional Family

January to December 1998

John could not have been a better partner to me or father to our children. He had not given up on us when infertility broke me. He had been an equal partner in the work of the adoption process each time. He was gracious to and appreciative of our children's birth relatives while, at the same time, never doubting his identity as "Daddy."

John shared parenting responsibilities with me. We took turns getting up at night to respond to a child's cry. He transported children to school and I picked them up. He shared in the bedtime rituals of bathing, reading, and singing. If I was preparing a meal and he had just walked in the door from a day at paid work, he would drop his briefcase to receive the embraces and outbursts of Emily and K.J. and then lead them off to play with him away from my work. When it was time to eat, we sat down at the table as a family and John patiently shared in the overseeing of the supper chaos in our joint quest to create nurturing and stabilizing routines for our young family that, we hoped, would endure as they matured.

John also gave me time to myself to pursue my other-than-mothering interests. He didn't assume that I would stay home with the children indefinitely. He understood that how we configured our paid and parenting work was something that we would always stay in conversation about and that would require sacrifices from us both.

My primary work was stay-at-home parent. I also taught classes on abuse of others (sexual and domestic violence) and on family issues (infertility technologies and adoption) as part of my father's pastoral care classes at Columbia Seminary. I began some volunteer work with The Giving Tree, an adoption agency that focused on finding permanent homes for the thousands of children in Georgia and throughout the U.S. who were free for adoption but waiting in foster care. I was also a volunteer attorney for the Grandparent Project with Atlanta Legal Aid. I was helping a grandmother adopt her five grandchildren, ages seven to sixteen, who had been living with her for several years. Once she became their *legal parent*, she would be entitled to an additional $1000/month in adoption assistance money.

John was traveling more, but he loved his job as a real estate consultant. Business was good; and his company had opened an office in London.

I put my extra energy into organizing parties and events. 1998 was the year of my 40th birthday. To commemorate this milestone, I created the "40th Birthday Challenge." It involved twelve 40-minute exercise periods, alternating running, cycling, and walking, which began at 6 a.m. and ended at 6 p.m., with a party to celebrate that evening. I mapped out a 60-mile course through metro-Atlanta, which passed by places I had lived, worked, or studied. Several friends and family members participated in parts of the "challenge" with me. John drove the support van and provided food, drink, and encouragement throughout the day. It was so much fun that I had decided to come up with yearly birthday "challenges." My other big fitness venture in 1998 was participating, for the first time, in the Bike Ride Across Georgia (BRAG), a weeklong cycling event covering in excess of 400 miles.

As Easter approached, I thought it would be fun to host an Easter Tea and Egg Hunt. Roughly two and a half days before the party, Skye began to cry when I lifted her right leg to change her diaper. For the next two days, she had a runny nose, fever cooled with Tylenol®, and more complaints that seemed related to her leg.

On the day of the event, at 2:30 p.m., Skye woke from her nap with a fever of 101.5 and went rigid with pain when I lifted her. I knew I had to take her to a doctor. After hurried instructions to John, my mother, and friend Jodi about the food, crafts, activities, and schedule I had planned, I left them in charge. When thirty women and their children arrived, John made "straw-bunny milkshakes" and served other Easter treats. My stand-in hosts directed the group in making Easter baskets out of diaper wipes boxes and then led them on two Easter egg hunts–one for infants and another for older children.

Meanwhile, I took Skye to the nearest Urgent Care Center. Between 3 and 7 p.m., Skye was examined, had x-rays made of her legs and hip and had blood taken and analyzed. Her doctor thought she might have a serious condition that could destroy her hip if untreated, so he sent us to an orthopedic specialist at Egleston Children's Hospital. The specialist examined Skye and agreed: she needed surgery right away for a condition called "septic hip." Skye would receive general anesthesia. Then the doctor would stick a needle in her hip to remove fluid causing inflammation and test it to find out what bacteria was causing the infection. He would make a small incision and go between her muscles to create a hole for a tube to drain the pus. The tube would remain in her hip for two to three days. The doctor thought we had discovered her problem early and that it was unlikely Skye had sustained much, if any, damage to her hip yet.

After the surgery, Skye would be in the hospital for several days to a week on strong IV-antibiotics to make sure the infection was killed, followed by four weeks of oral antibiotics. The doctor explained the risks of surgery and I signed the consent while I waited for John to arrive at the hospital.

Somewhere around 9 or 10 p.m., the surgical team had assembled and the operation was done. It seemed successful. They removed a teaspoonful of pus and inserted the drainage tube. When we saw her after recovery, Skye was dazed, but awake, and took some apple juice from me while I rocked her. I stayed the night in her room while John went home to be with Emily and K.J.

Skye slept fitfully, but managed the night pretty well. As I looked at her, I thought: "She is so beautiful and so strong. And aren't we lucky she came with such a good alarm?"

One of the most significant changes in our lives in 1998 was our transfer of church membership from Glenn Memorial UMC to St. Mark UMC. I had been looking for a United Methodist church with a more enlightened view regarding homosexual unions, and a greater emphasis on mission and outreach. St. Mark was a congregation of mostly gay and lesbian persons who had come from many religious (and non-religious) backgrounds, who were committed to serving others, and who had found a home that was accepting of all persons regardless of their sexual orientation. I was particularly delighted with the out-pouring of love and the nurturing our children received, and their exposure to diverse forms of family. As a family constructed through open adoption, we were out-of-the-norm as well. John and I were asked to chair the Family Council. We were also going to be teaching a parenting course. I would be a member of the Council on Women's Ministry.

At St. Mark UMC, I collaborated with others to write a play about the diversity of families. I also created a handout to assist persons who were beginning to explore adoption as a way of enlarging their families. *[The handout can be found in Appendix A.]* I did a presentation at church about open adoption. Emily participated by telling her version of her adoption story and sharing her storybook.

In May, I took Emily and K.J. to Nebraska for Tessa's graduation from high school. Kyle was still in and out of employment, but he and Tessa remained a couple and shared an apartment. Tessa hoped to get an office job soon and eventually go to junior college.

On the same trip, Emily met her birthfather, Jason, for the first time. At this point in her life, however, it made a *bigger* impression on her that she rode her grandmother Vera's horse, Cody, and that she played with her half-sisters, Michelle's other daughters.

It was also during the Spring of 1998 that we received a letter from Eve, a woman who identified herself as Christina's mother and Skye's maternal grandmother. Some months after Skye's birth, Christina told her brother about the baby and he reported this to Eve. Since Christina had intentionally hidden Skye's existence from her mother, I wasn't sure what to do about this new avenue of contact with Skye's extended birth family. I called Christina and she suggested that we arrange a visit at her home so that she could see Skye at the same time her mother met Skye. Later I tried to call Christina again to set a date for this visit, but her number was disconnected. We had also invited Christina to come to Skye's baptism. She had said she would come. But when the day arrived, she did not show-up. I tried sending a letter to her apartment, but got no response. She had "vanished."

On July 1st, I wrote to Eve and explained my efforts to contact Christina. I told her that I didn't want us to get together without Christina knowing about it and approving the contact. I hoped she would understand. In the meantime, I was glad to send her pictures and updates about Skye. I reported:

> Skye is in constant motion. She is standing alone now, so I expect she will be walking any day. She eats anything and everything, and gets completely covered in food. She also drops food off the side of her highchair for our dog, Meeko. As you can

imagine, Meeko is never far from her side. Skye especially loves pasta of all kinds. She is very comfortable in the middle of the chaos that her brother, K.J., and sister, Emily, provide. She loves playing with them. She is not very fearful of strangers, though she looks to see where I am. Skye is a good sleeper and nap taker. She climbs up stairs great, but she scares me because she won't turn around to go down the stairs. She is a very happy and easy-going child. I feel very blessed.

Emily continued at the Montessori School through August 1998. On the day she was to begin Pre-K at Laurel Ridge Elementary, our local public school, Meeko, was struck and killed by a car. The placard over Meeko's grave carried Emily's sentiment: "I love you, Meeko, in the whole wide world. And that's a long way." Two weeks later, we adopted a new puppy from the Atlanta Humane Society and named her Mikayla. Emily enjoyed school and was one of the resident experts on tying shoes. She liked her teachers and made lots of friends.

In September, I submitted an article to the United Methodist newspaper, the "Wesleyan Christian Advocate," which was published on October 2, 1998. It was an opportunity for me to summarize and restate what I had learned and experienced about open adoption and to celebrate it publicly with my extended faith community. In concluding the article, I wrote:

> I believe fully open adoption makes me a more compassionate person. It teaches me that while adoptive parents give children the reality of parenting and nurturing, birth parents give them the reality of birth and heritage. One cannot take the other's place. Each parent is real in a unique way, not better or worse; and we should each be proud of the role we play in our children's lives.
>
> Children are God's miracles. They belong to God. Whether we give birth to our children or adopt them, they are not our possessions. Love for our children ought to include a commitment not to cut them off from the people who partly

> represent their past and future. Our children need to have whole identities. Living open adoption reminds me every day of our connection to and responsibility for other people...
>
> One of my greatest desires for my children is that all of their families, both adoptive and biological, will continue to nurture and support them with our different kinds of love as they mature into the unique and special individuals they are and are becoming.

The termination of Skye's biological father's potential rights had not occurred as originally planned. Instead, in late June, a private investigator finally located Samuel. He signed the appropriate papers and wanted no further contact with us. On October 8, 1998, Skye's adoption was *finally* finalized. To recognize this momentous occasion, our immediate family and a few others participated in an Adoption Finalization Ceremony. At that time, we presented Skye with a *Wisdom Book*, a collection of "words of wisdom" gathered from friends and family in the form of poems, sayings, philosophy, song lyrics, and personal letters.

The more time I spent with my new church family at St. Mark, the more excited I got about the possibility of starting an adoption agency whose clients would be gay and lesbian individuals, as well as single adults and adults over 40 years of age, who had more difficulty adopting because of adoption agency restrictions, legal restrictions, sexual orientation, and/or societal prejudice. What I didn't have was the money to get started. However, I was pretty sure I could get the financing if I found support in the community for my ideas.

I made an appointment with a couple of attorneys who I knew, by reputation, to be advocates for same sex couples. At our meeting, I was shocked to discover that they were *not* supportive of my plan. According to them, such an adoption agency would bring the issue of gay parenting into the public light and potentially instigate conservative legislators to close loopholes in existing adoption laws that these attorneys were using to help create legal two-of-the-same-sex-parent families. I left the meeting with my tail between my legs. If I couldn't or shouldn't do this, what could or should I do to help create a more tolerant world?

I continued to receive calls and emails from friends, old and new, for advice about adoption. Most of the information I shared was practical and straightforward. Occasionally, I shared more personal feelings about being an adoptive parent. To a childhood friend who knew my family of origin I wrote:

> I remembered that when I was growing up, I often heard the story of my birth–my mother's pioneer effort to give birth 'naturally,' without medication, without complaint about pain, while my 1950's father remained in the waiting room. And I remembered what my father said about seeing me for the first time: 'I knew you were mine because you looked like me.' They were words of claiming, of belonging, of love.
>
> When my husband John and I began to consider the possibility that we would not conceive a child and might have to look at alternatives to becoming parents biologically, I struggled and struggled with the memory of my father's words. Would or could a child be my child if s/he did not look like me? Would or could I love him or her as much as my parents loved me?
>
> I have known since the beginning of our journey to and through open adoption that my children's birth stories would be important to them. It is only now that I am discovering how important they are to me also. In those stories are my connections to my children's other set of parents. They are like umbilical cords my body could not create on its own. The stories help my children define their identities by helping them understand where they came from, but they also give me a replacement for my father's words, "I knew you were mine because you looked like me."

"I knew you–Emily, Kevin John, Skye–were mine because I loved your mother.
We connected in deep places inside both of us. A grace-filled transformation occurred and you began to grow inside me too."

By the end of 1998, K.J., at two and a half years old, was still attending the Montessori School. He loved his books, cars and trucks. He loved to wrestle and be tickled. His most distinctive characteristic–other than his blond curly hair–was his habit of twirling the tags on his stuffed animals while he sucked his thumb.

Skye, at almost one and a half, had completely recovered from her septic hip earlier in the year and showed no signs that the hip or joint had been damaged. She was attending a two-morning-a-week church school program. Skye was energetic and adventurous. She ate more than her brother and sister combined and remained thin. She loved babies, blankets, her kitchen, her dollhouse, markers, and her siblings. She was especially fond of me. If I left the room, Skye called out: "Mama, wh' are you-u-u?" She had one disturbing habit: She could hold her breath long enough to pass out! Her doctor said this was an attention-getting mechanism that would pass if we ignored it. That was easier said than done.

In December, I made contact with Christina again who gave me her approval to take Skye to meet her relatives. Two days after Christmas, we traveled to northwest Georgia to meet Skye's grandmother, step-grandfather, two aunts and an uncle–Christina's half-siblings. They were gracious and loving, but it was clear they did not understand why Christina had done this. I wondered how Skye would feel about these relatives and their ambiguity about her adoption in the years to come.

Thinking About a Fourth Adoption

January to November 1999

Back in November 1998, I had seen Skye's birthmother, Christina. She looked pregnant to me, but I didn't say anything then. Christina called me just before Christmas to say she had new jobs at two French restaurants. She also hinted that she wanted to see Skye. It wasn't convenient then, but I called her in early January and we agreed to come by one of the restaurants. She was clearly pregnant now, so I commented on her condition, asking what her plans were. She said she was going to keep this one. She said she had gotten pregnant "sort of on purpose to fill the void left by Skye."

I had been to Christina's apartment. She had pictures of Skye everywhere. Suddenly, I was seeing the pictures like a shrine. I felt guilty for "taking her baby" even though I believed it was better for Skye this way. I felt angry and sad at the same time.

Christina acted surprised when I asked her about being pregnant. She said the Falcos were the only ones who knew. Her boyfriend didn't know yet. Her family didn't know. I found it very hard to believe that a boyfriend who was intimate with her could not tell she was pregnant. A month ago she told me she was depressed and couldn't pay her bills. Now she presented a different story: she was happy and ready to be a parent.

Christina said that her French boyfriend was the father of the child and that he was buying a house and had asked her to move in. I could do simple math. It was not possible for this new boyfriend to be the father of a baby that was due to arrive in April. What did she think she was doing?

I had reason to doubt her mental state. When I showed her pictures I had taken of her family in northwest Georgia with Skye a few weeks prior, she commented how much she loved her baby sister April, while pointing to a picture of her sister June. She didn't recognize her own sisters? Christina's mother had told me that Christina left her first child with his father when the baby was five weeks old. Christina couldn't recall that detail either. Of course, I'd known birthmothers who got pregnant again quickly after placing a child for adoption. But I couldn't understand why *Christina*, who had seemed so at peace with Skye's placement, would do this now.

I had to admit to myself that I also felt jealous in two different, but related, ways. First, I would probably always feel jealous of women who could become pregnant when they decided to do so. I was jealous of my own sister! I was less comfortable admitting the second form of jealousy. It was jealousy that extended to this particular child. Seeing Christina this way, I realized that I wanted one more child; and that *this one* would be the perfect one for our family. Emily and Kevin John were blood-related. Skye and the unborn baby would be blood-related. I knew I had no right or claim to this baby. But the feeling was there. I wondered if there was any way *both* to let Christina know that we supported her *and* to let her know that if things didn't work out as she planned, we would be happy to adopt the baby. Of course, I had not yet discussed this with John.

I wrote an email to Dorothy, the counselor who had worked with Christina on our adoption of Skye, and shared my story and questions. Dorothy cautioned me not to let myself get excited about possibly adopting this baby. I tried to keep my emotions in check, but they poured out in my journal entries that winter: anger, sadness, jealousy, powerlessness, and more.

At church, when I mentioned to our associate minister that Christina was pregnant again, her first reaction was, "Does this mean there may be a baby for *[name of couple at our church who wanted to adopt an infant]*?" Privately, I was angry about that response. Didn't she understand we were talking about *Skye's* sibling? This baby was related to *us* and to Skye. If Christina didn't want to parent the new baby, *I* did. I wrote for myself:

> It isn't like children are pieces of candy and everybody is entitled to have some. Children, unlike candy, are not interchangeable. They are more related to some people than others. Those relationships have to be honored.

In my emotional state, I was unaware of my hypocrisy–prioritizing biological connection over other reasons for a child's placement with particular parents. I would not have made this argument a few months earlier, but now it seemed to work in my favor. I kept my mouth shut around Christina, but I doubt she misunderstood that I was "waiting in the wings" if she changed her mind.

On January 25, 1999, Emily and I called her birthmother to wish her a Happy Birthday. Michelle had had a tough go of things lately. She divorced her husband in 1998. She had recently put all her trust in a new beau who then stole from her, forged checks, and forced her to drop out of school to deal with a huge financial mess. I was impressed by Michelle's resilience. Though she had seen good times and bad since placing Emily for adoption, I could always count on her support. We trusted and respected each other. We always managed to remind one another how valuable each of us was as mother, friend, and family member. Because of Michelle's diligent efforts, Emily now knew her birthfather too. And, according to Michelle, he hung her pictures on his wall along with pictures of his other children.

I also spoke to Emily and K.J.'s Great-Grandpa that day. I told him about our lives, John's travel, and John's invitation to me to go with him to a conference in France. I laughed, saying, "But what would we do with the children?" Grandpa immediately offered their extended family in Nebraska to take care of all three kids. I thought to myself: I really would trust our Nebraska family to take the Falco children for a week. This is the way it should be. Why don't I feel this way about Christina?

I told Michelle about Christina and my dilemma. I asked for her perspective: Was there any way I could tell her I wanted to adopt her baby, *if* she changed her mind about parenting, without damaging my relationship with her? Michelle said she had always valued my honesty. She thought I should be honest and tell Christina how I felt as long as I emphasized that I would support her no matter what her decision about parenting.

In late January, we also received some presents for our kids from Tessa and Kyle, as well as a lengthy report on how each person in the extended family was doing. I reported back to them on how each child spent his or her Wal-mart gift card:

> K.J. picked out a Space Explorer. It's a rocket ship with two smaller rocket ships and Sesame Street characters in space suits. Emily selected a Champion Horse that comes with a stable and the various pieces for feeding and cleaning the horse. Skye picked out a roller-skating, talking Big Bird. They all thank you very much for their gifts.

By early February, Christina's boyfriend had left her. We talked regularly on the phone. Christina needed a friend. She also needed someone to drive her to the grocery store and other locations because she didn't have a car. Christina had not yet told her mother she was pregnant. She commented, "I bet I'll see her a lot more once I have a son. She is much more interested in grandchildren than in me." I was sad for her, but also curious. Was positive attention from her mother part of the reason Christina had gotten pregnant?

By mid-February, Christina had lost her job. Her employer said she was sick too often and that working must not be good for the baby. Christina had run out of money. She used WIC vouchers for food, supplemented by trips to the food bank. Christina finally told her mother about the baby. Reportedly, the first thing Eve said was, "You better not give this one away!" Eve wanted Christina to move back home and work a night shift in a factory so that Eve could look after the baby. Christina said she had no intention of doing that.

I remained calm, logical, and a good listener with Christina. Emotionally, I was distraught. Close friends cautioned me not to bail Christina out, not to get too involved or she might become angry and resent me for abandoning her in her time of need. It all made sense, but I just couldn't imagine walking away. Christina was, and would always be, my daughter's birthmother. A voice inside me kept saying: "You are her only friend. Love her."

There was also the message from my friend, Lee who wrote:

> Hang in there. This painful experience may be your 'labor.' Our time is not God's time. I don't know why this is happening to you and to Christina, but don't take yourself out of a situation where you may be supposed to make the difference… Follow your heart. I believe in the wisdom inside of you and the wisdom God will send you.

For whatever reason, this bit of advice made more sense to me than all the cautionary messages I received from others.

In March, Christina moved to her aunt's house; but the next day she called and asked me to pick her up. She couldn't stand the clutter and the foul language. Somebody told her she needed to have her legs sewn together. Christina came home with me to spend the night and make other plans. She convinced someone at an anti-abortion organization to give her two months rent so she could get back in her old apartment. We gave her our space heater and $25 to get her heat back on. I knew she wanted more money. She kept talking about 'all the rich people' who could help her, and how she was going to start a home for pregnant women herself.

With each encounter, I learned something new about Christina or confirmed something I already suspected. She really believed she was *entitled* to material possessions that others gave her. She barely batted an eye when I offered to pay the turn-on fee for her heat. When her cousin suggested yard sales for clothes, Christina's comment was, "I don't like to wear clothes that other people have had on."

There was more drama. But, ultimately, baby Isaac was born at Grady Hospital on April 18, 1999. Some of Christina's relatives were there for the birth. I came the next day to take pictures of mother and child. She kept him. It wasn't as hard for me as I thought it would be. By then, I had no illusions about her suddenly deciding to make an adoption plan. We did not hear from Christina for a while.

The Falco children were growing and defining their own unique personalities as I reported to our Nebraska relatives in April:

> Emily is playing soccer now. She is sometimes more interested in socializing than playing the game, but she is picking up the skills and she is proud to wear the uniform. She scored her first goal two weeks ago. Emily is still practicing her letters and likes for me to spell things to her so she can write actual words.
>
> K.J. is enjoying his Elmo computer game a lot. He seems to be pretty smart and he enjoys school and helping the other children obey the rules. He is a creature of habit. Things must be done just so and the same way each time….
>
> Skye has just joined K.J.'s Montessori class. I think she likes having big brother there, but she is pretty darn independent. Skye talks constantly and tries out every new word she hears. She can say K.J. pretty well. It sounds like 'Tay-Jay'. Emily is harder. She calls her big sister, 'E-e-e.'
>
> It's interesting to me to observe their personalities–Emily and Skye are both more social than K.J. who clings to me (or his dad) around new people. In fact, if asked to say 'hello' or 'thank you' to someone new, he hangs his head and turns away. He is also cautious about doing new things. Yesterday, I showed him a kid-size jeep he could actually ride and steer. He is crazy about cars and trucks, but he was very hesitant at first. But by the end of our visit with these friends, he was ready to ride. By

then he had observed Emily driving the jeep.

Another example: K.J. and I have been going to a music class for parents and their children ages 18 months to 3 years. One of the things the teacher does is sing notes or rhythms into a pretend microphone and have the kids copy her. K.J. clung to me for three weeks, but on week four he sang, in perfect pitch, back into the microphone exactly what the teacher had sung. My mom says K.J. is like me in that he wants to be sure he can do it right before he is willing to try something new. Skye, on the other hand, walks into new and dangerous situations all the time. She is the one I have to watch. Emily is cautious, but she tends to trust my judgment and try new things with encouragement. The thing that gets her in trouble is her sensitivity. She gets her feelings hurt easily and then has to pout about it.

§ § §

All those months of thinking "what if…" regarding Christina's baby left me with the conviction that we needed a fourth child in our family. It wouldn't be Skye's brother; but that was okay. John thought we had our hands full with three little ones, but he was willing to follow my lead. We began our search for Number Four with a networking letter to friends and family. In this letter we made it clear that the child need not be full Caucasian. We had tried on some of the feelings associated with adopting a child outside our race when we contemplated adopting Mary's biracial twins. We thought we were comfortable with the idea of raising a child who was not like us–racially. We decided we would see what situations presented themselves and make our decisions then.

In June, we took a 10-day driving vacation with stops to visit friends in North Carolina, Washington D.C., and Maryland, on our way to New York for a wedding and visits with family. Midway through the trip, we got a call from Dorothy about a birthmother who had selected us to adopt her baby. There were some health issues; and the counselor was having a hard time making contact with her to set up a meeting. Still, it was hard not to get excited.

That particular pregnant woman disappeared. However, the experience with her let us know that adopting a fourth child was really possible. It was time to get serious and prepare. I contacted an adoption agency to get started on another home study and wrote, with John's help, an updated Dear Birthmother letter.

In August, we took another trip to Nebraska where Emily and K.J. visited relatives, including their great-grandfather who would die two months later. K.J.'s birth parents announced that they were getting married in October and expecting twin boys in March!

On August 23rd, I suddenly heard from Christina again. She said she was in Marietta, just north of Atlanta, living in a Sierra Suites with a new boyfriend. She had a waitress job. She reported being "boiling mad" that her old landlord had thrown all of her stuff away because she had not been living in her apartment since May. All of the pictures of Skye, letters, birthday party invitations, and birth pictures of Isaac that I had sent to Christina were gone. Every memento of Skye since her birth was in a trash heap somewhere. I felt angry about Christina's irresponsibility!

I asked about Isaac. She said she had found a babysitter to watch him while she was at work. She spoke of him lovingly.

§ § §

With each passing month, the computer was becoming a more accessible tool for research and marketing. I had never been much of a phone-talker, but I could write all day long–children permitting. Email was a dream come true for me. I contacted everyone I could think of who might have some connections to birthmothers or have ideas about how to find birthmothers.

In the course of doing some research online about adoptions, I discovered that there was a company that posted prospective adoptive parents' letters to potential birthmothers on their site. I knew it wasn't legal to advertise for birthmothers in Georgia unless you were a licensed adoption agency. But this company was in Maryland. Our information could be available to anyone anywhere who went to the site.

On August 31, 1999, I sent to Adoption Online Connection: (1) our "Dear Birth Parent" letter; (2) a photo of John and me to be used with the letter; (3) nine additional photographs and their captions; (4) a list of 10 search terms and descriptive text to be used with each term; (5) and payment for a three-month listing. If a woman looking for adoptive parents for her baby/child came to this site and found our letter, she could click on underlined words in our letter and go to pictures. The last line in all of our descriptions emphasized our openness. This was our calling card. This was the characteristic, I believed, that set us apart from so many other prospective parents.

In early September, I heard about a potential adoption situation through an adoption facilitator located in northern California. In conversations about the birth parents and with them, I learned that Denise and Scott, from Idaho, were married at 17 and 16 years of age and had been married 2 ½ years. They wanted to join the Job Corps after Scott finished an anger management program in six months. They had a son, Mitchell, who was two, and a daughter, Paula, who was one. They admitted to having no patience with the children and to being very poor. But they were not asking for financial aid. Paula's leg was broken and "one story" was that Scott had jerked it while changing her diaper. The parents both denied this. They stated that both children were healthy and promised medical records to the parents who adopted the children.

The placement had to be done quickly. The family was going to lose their home in a few days and become homeless. The couple did not want the children to be homeless too. The birth parents wanted an open adoption. We spoke with Denise on the phone several times. She sounded great. We felt compatible. She wanted us to adopt the children. She said we were the kind of family she was looking for.

Our plan was to fly the family of four from Boise to San Francisco, near the offices of the adoption facilitator. John and I would also fly to California for the weekend, visit and meet with the family and facilitator, and possibly bring Mitchell and Paula home with us. There were lots of details to take care of: agency contacts, attorney contacts, travel arrangements, and childcare.

I had lots of questions about the emotional well-being and the life experiences of the children, but John and I were ready to act. It was of paramount importance to get approval to spend any money related to the children, including the plane tickets for the family, from the Georgia agency that did our home study. Jennifer at the Adoption Agency got straight to the point. She didn't think we should go forward. We didn't have medical reports in hand on the children or psychological assessments. She had seen "tragedies" when non-genetically related same-age children were adopted into families. In this case, Skye and Mitchell would be the same age. She didn't think we had thought about this enough or that we had enough education about toddler adoption. In any event, our home study would have to be amended first because it stated that we were approved to adopt one child or twins, but not siblings of different ages. We would have to be interviewed and reevaluated for this type of adoption.

We reluctantly told the Idaho couple that we could not move forward with adoption. I was discouraged, but still hopeful. There was a lot about adoption that was mysterious and magical to me. It seemed spiritually significant the way people found each other–like in marriage–and connected to create "whole" families out of disparate or broken pieces. I was sad about the lost possibility, but I trusted another opportunity would come. I continued to network, and to investigate agencies and facilitators around the country.

In October 1999, we received another adoption lead from a friend at church who was a social worker. She was currently working with a foster mother whose adopted 21-year-old daughter was pregnant.. There was some concern that the pregnant woman, Nancy, might have an "attachment disorder." She had lived in 14 homes before coming to her adoptive parents home. Nancy was white. They thought the biological father was African-American. Then the story got murkier. It was thought that the presumed father was a pimp who had taken Nancy in. But there were questions about who else might be a possible father, about drug use, about Nancy's health and the baby's health. Nancy was eight months pregnant and in some sort of homeless shelter, but her mother wanted to bring her home for the birth. Nancy didn't get prenatal care until she was 6-7 months pregnant. However, the doctor reported that everything "looked good."

I called Nancy's mother, Jane, the next day to try and arrange a meeting with Nancy. Jane was very excited about the possibility of our adopting the baby, based on what the social worker had said about us. She told me more about Nancy's early life and the recent year. She had talked to Nancy about adoption and about us. Reportedly, Nancy started to cry. She said, "I have been praying and I know I can't raise this baby. I just wanted to know I could have some contact in the future."

I got a call from Jane a few days later. She reported on her recent visit to see Nancy. The people who ran the homeless shelter seemed to have taken on the project of convincing Nancy that she could keep the baby with their support. Jane said that when she and her husband arrived to talk to Nancy, they were treated like "the enemies." With the shelter manager standing by, Nancy claimed she was keeping the baby. Jane said that Nancy calls every few days and tells her how much she hates the place. Jane and her husband were convinced that Nancy would eventually walk out of there, at which point Jane would like to call us. In the meantime, the adoption plan was off.

John and I were learning more about what other adoptive parents had gone through to find their child. This was very hard. I was beginning to wonder if there really was another baby for us out there somewhere.

A few days later, we got a response to our online adoption letter from Diana. She claimed to be a thirty-six year old white, American, educated housewife, happily married for ten years, with a seven-year-old daughter. She never expected to get pregnant again and did not consider it good news. She was miserable and couldn't wait to be done with the pregnancy. Her husband and daughter were in agreement that they were an "only-child family." Diana then went on to describe the extensive legal, medical and living expenses she would need, and cautioned that anyone not willing to pay these should look elsewhere for a baby. We declined Diana's offer, but it added another *type* of birthmother to our growing list.

The contacts we made through the Adoption Online Connection were sometimes strange. There was no agency or attorney to mediate or filter what got through to us. Some were easy to dismiss. But the mail in my inbox always made my stomach lurch.

John said he sometimes wondered: 'What's wrong with us?' Leads to possible adoptions were great except that then so much of our energy got focused on adoption. We were suspended in time. We didn't know whether to make renovations to the house for our existing family or a family of six. Did I look for part-time work? Not if we were expecting a baby. How long did we wait? Was the expiration of a home study at the end of a year the signal to stop looking? Should we do more networking? Should we put money into hiring an agency to find a birthmother? It was confusing and emotionally draining. Of course, if there *was*, eventually, another adoption, another child for us, it would be worth it. Maybe it was worth it anyway. As John said, "The worst thing that can happen is that we raise three great kids."

A Texas Birthmother

December 1999 to March 2000

The adoption search continued. We added another source of potential birthmothers in mid-December. We signed on as clients with Families Forever, Inc. It seemed like a good agency for us because our initial investment was very low until we were matched with a birthmother. We were still concerned that a birthmother would not choose us because we already had three children. This way we didn't take a huge financial hit until we'd actually been chosen. Meanwhile, if we found a birthmother independent of the agency, we didn't have to pay the lump sum agency fee. John and I told ourselves that if we were not successful in the next few months to a year, we'd stop pursuing a fourth adoption.

Less than a week later, everything changed again. The next part of our story is told mostly by emails written at the time of these events:

Email to family members and friends on December 19, 1999

> While I went to bed early Friday night to prepare to get up early to run a practice marathon (26.2 miles), John received a call from a birthmother in Texas who found us through an attorney friend of hers in southern California. We still don't quite understand how this corporate attorney found our letter online and recommended us to her, but he did. Stacy told us that she is 23 years old and is 5'9" tall. She spent four years in the Marines. She is the 6th of 7 children in her family and a professional horseback rider with a B.A. from Pepperdine University,. Stacy sent us pictures of herself by email. We think she looks like the actress Minnie Driver.
>
> She said she knew from the beginning she wasn't going to raise

this child. She was in southern California and contacted an adoption agency in Texas. Relying on the promise of help from the agency, she bought a Greyhound ticket and moved to Texas. Stacy says her work moves from place to place, so she really didn't mind moving and doesn't intend to stay in Texas.

The agency she was initially working with did some things she didn't like, and now Stacy doesn't want to have anything to do with them. For instance, they told her to lie and say she didn't know who the birthfather was. She does. His name is Jamie and he is the only possible birth father. He's 6'4" tall. He is athletic and is planning to try out as a pitcher for the Diamondbacks. Stacy has his last known address in Colorado. But he has nothing to do with Stacy these days.

Stacy says she has had prenatal care from the beginning. She is very healthy. No drugs or alcohol. She had medical insurance, but now she's on Medicaid. Her original due date was Feb. 28th, but her recent ultrasound showed the baby was big–already 4 pounds and 19 inches long, so they may induce around Feb. 10th. At 20 weeks, she had an ultrasound that suggested the baby was a boy.

That's what we know so far. We've talked with the director of our agency in Atlanta and the plan is to have a Texas attorney interview and check out Stacy. If everything seems legitimate, we will be able to help Stacy with some living expenses. Then, if her doctor agrees, we will fly her to Atlanta for a couple of days the week between Christmas and New Year's Day so that she can meet our family and some friends and see where and how we live. She said she'd like to do that....

John was so excited about Stacy that he woke me Friday night to share the good news. Of course, I couldn't sleep very well after that. But, I swear, it was the excitement of maybe having found the right birthmother that kept me going for 26 miles on Saturday.

§ § §

I didn't write to my friends about the expenses or calls to attorneys and agencies involved, but my notes reveal a different story. At the recommendation of our Atlanta attorney, I called Janice Longhorn, a Texas adoption attorney, to discuss the adoption and legal ramifications for paying living expenses to Stacy. We sent a retainer for the attorney to do an assessment of Stacy. Janice recommended Children's Hope, a Texas adoption agency, to provide counseling and to terminate parental rights. We were told we could pay up to $150/week in living expenses from the time of the assessment moving forward. Children's Hope's fee was $2500. We had to pay $750 up front, non-refundable. The rest would be due when the baby came home to us. Legal work would be billed separately, by the hour. We were to escrow money with Children's Hope for estimated living expenses.

Janice Longhorn called after she met with Stacy. She said Stacy was delightful and very bright. She thought Stacy was "legitimate." She also said that expenses could be substantial. Although we could not pay for debts Stacy had incurred before we met her, we could help her by paying full rent for December, January, and February, at $750/month. Stacy also needed $100/week for food and toiletries for two weeks in December, four weeks in both January and February, and four to six weeks post-delivery. The minimum total would be $3250. Legal fees were estimated at $3750, but could go up because of the missing birth father. Texas required the adoptive parents to pay for an attorney for the birthmother and a guardian ad litem for the baby.

Email to family members and friends on December 24, 1999

> Stacy is flying to Atlanta next week. She will be here from December 28-30. We are very excited; and Stacy says she is really looking forward to the trip. We seem to have retained a competent attorney and agency in Texas. Things are moving along.

My parents are hosting a gathering at their house on the evening of the 29th so that Stacy can meet our family and vice versa. Stacy told me she is open to meeting anyone and everyone who will be part of our child's life. If you are going to be around and want to meet Stacy, give me a call and we'll work something out. To me, this is one of the great things about open adoption: you are confronted with the fact that (in most cases) a baby doesn't just appear one day parentless. He or she has a parent or parents or family of origin that determine his/her physical characteristics and some of his/her aptitudes and abilities. As adoptive parents in an open adoption, we get to meet and know one or more of those original parents and members of the families of origin.

John and I are not in agreement about names. As you may know, "Kevin"' is the only boy's name that John likes, and K.J. has it. He also thinks he'd like a one syllable first name. Got any suggestions? If you do, be prepared for rejection. John is a tough cookie when it comes to boys' names. But, you may have an idea we haven't thought of, and we need ideas.

Merry Christmas! Happy Holidays! – Love, Rebecca

Email to family members and friends, December 30, 1999

Stacy just left a few hours ago, headed back to Dallas. We really enjoyed getting to know her. She is direct, not afraid to voice her opinions, worldly, bright, and articulate. It was very easy for us to talk to one another and she knew how to give John a hard time in a light-hearted way. She wasn't very interested in our children. For most of my children stories, Stacy could give a horse analogy. She was much more interested in our dogs. She is clear that she wants to place her baby for adoption.

On Tuesday, after getting Stacy settled into our house, we decided to go shopping. She loved Lenox Mall. I get the impression that Stacy has lived very comfortably in her life. Her childhood was spent mostly in Sonoma County, California, on a vineyard where her family raised the grapes for Cardinal wine–which Stacy says sells for $120 a bottle. Her father owns a number of businesses. Stacy, herself, owns some horses, though she is currently cash poor. She has traveled quite a bit, both as a Marine (electrical engineer) and for her horse-related work. She seems very motivated to get back to work as soon as possible.

It was mid-afternoon on Tuesday and the kids had not eaten, so we stopped in the food court at Lenox. Stacy was truly grossed-out by the amount of food Skye got on her body and the table, and the general messiness of feeding my crew. Of course, Skye and K.J. were also more irritable because they had not yet napped. While I cleared the table, Stacy chased Skye who was being chased by Emily as they ran for the doors to the parking garage.

We had one more stop after lunch to return some items to Richs Department Store. While I stood in line, Stacy watched the kids run around some area rugs. Skye fell on her face and passed out. Stacy said her friend had warned her she wouldn't last three days in a house with three young children. I was afraid we'd scare her into choosing another family for her baby!

Stacy said she had not been able to sleep the night before her flight. She had gone shopping at midnight. At 2:00 a.m., she was taking a shower when someone broke into her apartment and bathroom. She screamed so loud, he ran away. She dealt with the police before catching a cab to the airport. So, by Tuesday night, she was ready to crash. Unfortunately, from that point on, she was sick. She couldn't keep anything down. We had plans to do sightseeing on Wednesday that never happened because Stacy needed to be near a bathroom or needed to sleep. On Wednesday night, she rallied to go to my parents' house for a gathering of family and friends. Every 15 minutes, she bolted to the bathroom. What a good sport she was.

About 2:15 a.m. this morning, Stacy appeared in our bedroom and asked to be taken to the emergency room. She had been awake for two hours with terrible abdominal pain. I quickly dressed and drove us to DeKalb Medical Center. It turned out that she was having contractions every five minutes! She was given a shot to stop the contractions, which, though it made her very jittery, worked. Stacy came home, ate, and then slept until the afternoon. My main job for 36 hours was keeping the children entertained and quiet while confined to our house. With two hours to go in the visit, Stacy and I were finally able to talk about plans at the hospital and other aspects of the adoption.

Other bits of information we learned: Stacy is meeting with a group of birthmothers on a regular basis. She meets with a young adult minister at the United Methodist church she attends in Dallas. Though she professes not to need counseling from an adoption agency, we are glad she is getting her emotional needs met elsewhere. The birth father is still trying to keep his whereabouts hidden from her, though she thinks he'll be in spring training with the Colorado Rockies or Arizona Diamondbacks in February. He is a pitcher and has 103 mph fastball!

We have made no progress in finding a name that we can agree on. Stacy has strong opinions about names as well. We'll see....

We will wait to hear how her doctor's appointment goes tomorrow. Stacy is convinced she won't last until Feb. 10th before delivery. We may have to rethink the Disney Marathon and Magic Kingdom plans. Again, we'll see.

Email to family members and friends on January 1, 2000

I talked to Stacy tonight. Since she returned to Dallas, she started having contractions again. This time it took two shots of Brethene to stop them. She is dilated 2-3 cm. According to Stacy, her doctor says that they won't let her deliver until 4 shots in 2 hours don't stop the contractions. He told her that she could go on this way for two hours, two days, a month, etc. She has a lot of back pain and she's not keeping much food down, but she is drinking lots of fluids. Stacy is making a book for the baby, which is keeping her busy.

To those of you who have labor and delivery experience and/or knowledge: what do you know about premature contractions or how long it is likely to be before she delivers? I'm scheduled to run the Walt Disney Marathon next Sunday, Jan. 9. I'm supposed to fly to Orlando on Friday. John, my parents, and the kids are driving to Florida on Saturday and Sunday. We had planned to stay through Wednesday to take the kids to Disney World. We are trying to figure out our emergency plan or alternatives.

§ § §

Advice from friends was *not* to cancel our trip, but to be prepared to leave our vacation abruptly. We adjusted our plans so that it would be only John and Emily to follow me to Disney World. We felt that she would get the most out of the trip anyway. This "adjustment" turned into a "tradition" of the two Falco parents taking one child on a special trip to Disney World when he or she reached the magical age of five years old.

Email to family members and friends on January 5, 2000

I just got a call from Stacy. She has a cold, but has not been back to the hospital. Her chief complaints are that her back hurts and that she is stuffed-up. She says she is gaining weight and is hungry all the time. She told me she had 3 oranges, a banana, and some kind of avocado sandwich today. I told her that sounded awfully healthy to me. I'd be eating bags of chocolate chip cookies.

Stacy said her sister (and main support person) is on a ski trip until Jan. 16, so she can't have the baby until after that date. That's fine with me. Stacy says she sleeps most of the day, but needs to get out some and has been able to do grocery shopping and trips to the bookstore. She is reading a lot, and working on her book for the baby. I can tell she is really proud of it. She has pictures, poems–her whole life in it.

Her landlord filed eviction papers against her. The court date was yesterday. He didn't show up and Stacy was able to tell her side of the story to the judge. She just has to show a copy of her lease to the judge and then she can get back all the stuff her landlord took from her apartment.

Stacy is feeling down. She said it's been hitting her hard now that the pregnancy is almost over. Her doctor said he was concerned about her being depressed. She said, "There would be something wrong with me if I wasn't sad about this. That doesn't mean I need to keep the baby." It sounds to me like she understands the distinction between feeling sad because this is sad, and feeling sad because of a bad decision that would be cured by keeping the baby.

Stacy has had two more job offers that she can respond to as soon as she has recovered from the delivery. One friend told her that, after a relatively easy labor and delivery, she was back on a horse in 3 weeks. Stacy is hoping for that scenario.

As to the name of the baby–the name on our list that received the most votes from those of you who gave us your opinion also happens to be our mutual favorite. If the baby is indeed a boy, his name will be Luke.

§ § §

I ran my first marathon and raised $5000 for the Leukemia Society. John, Emily, and I spent three wonderful days at Walt Disney World. We came home to continue waiting for Luke to be born.

Email to family members and friends on January 14, 2000

We talked to Stacy a couple of days ago. She is having irregular contractions, her cervix is starting to efface, and she is about 3 cm. dilated now. She was told she would probably have the baby within 2 weeks.

We received copies of Stacy's medical records and there doesn't appear to be anything of significance that would affect the baby's health.

Our home study has been updated for Texas purposes.

There are some questions about insurance and Medicaid payments, but we have been led to believe that all of this will work out and we won't be paying Stacy's medical bills.

§ § §

We were confident about this adoption; and our friends supported this view. One friend wrote:

While nothing is ever guaranteed in life, this looks like a good bet. Stacy seems, from what you have written, to have a good head on her shoulders. She really does know that she does not want to keep this child. I think things are going to go smoothly with her, and Luke will be home with his new mom and dad, and brother and sisters very soon. I haven't felt this confident with all of the potential birthmothers you have contacted, but Stacy seems to know that you and John are in this child's best interests. I feel quite sure that everything will be just fine.

On January 17th, Stacy emailed to tell us she was meeting with the social worker that day and to suggest a name for the baby: Lucas Alexander Falco. She preferred to put the same name on the original birth certificate that would appear on his amended birth certificate after the adoption became final. I wrote back with a compromise suggestion: Luke Haynes (my mother's maiden name) Alexander Falco.

I had learned that naming a baby could become a pivotal issue between the birth and adoptive parents. In one case I worked on, birthmother and adoptive parents had agreed the baby would be Noah Seth. The problem was that the birthmother thought he was going to be *called* Noah. After the baby was born, the adoptive parents called him Seth. The birthmother revoked her consent during the statutory period and took the baby back. Eventually, she realized that she still did not want to parent and had chosen good people for the job. The baby went back to the adoptive parents. But the whole thing taught me to pay more attention to the naming process.

§ § §

Stacy sent us an ultrasound picture of the baby. I wrote to thank her and to tell her that I was packed and ready to go when she called.

Email to family members and friends on January 18, 2000

Stacy went to Ft. Worth where there is a big rodeo going on for several weeks. Stacy would ordinarily be working at this rodeo. She met a beautiful horse and couldn't resist riding him. She said she felt her hips move. This led to another trip to the emergency room. Imagine pregnant Stacy and six cowboys in the emergency room. The doctor told her she had dilated to 4 cm. Although she could have been admitted to the hospital under these circumstances, the doctors feel that her body is taking the process of having this baby very slowly. They told her to call the adoption agency and us, but didn't see any reason we should rush out to Dallas. Stacy is ready to have the baby, but, today, she was mostly feeling happy to have her cowboy friends around, knowing they'd keep her spirits up once she placed the baby for adoption.

§ § §

We heard from Janice, the Texas attorney, on January 27th. She wanted us to know that they had not received papers back from Jamie, the alleged biological father, after making several attempts to contact him. She planned to file a petition for termination and have him officially served the next day. She wanted to know if the petition should state only Jamie's name or include all "unnamed and unidentified fathers" of the child. She recommended the latter, but said that it took longer and would cost more because it required two hearings. We also needed an attorney to represent the "unknown fathers."

Stacy seemed offended that I would ask about other possible fathers. I explained that it was for the safety of her adoption plan and for Luke's security. But I emailed, "John and I really do trust you, and we wouldn't want to do anything to jeopardize our relationship." I told Janice that we didn't see the need to terminate the rights of "unknown fathers" unless Stacy had indicated to her that their might be someone else. She had been very clear with us.

We continued to talk and email daily. Stacy asked if we wanted to cut the umbilical cord, to which we responded, "Yes!" She wanted Jamie to see the baby. She wanted us to videotape the birth and send a copy to her mother. The social worker continued to visit with Stacy.

I had no problem complying with Stacy's list of requirements, but I was uncomfortable with the negotiations. I resigned myself to the fact that having a baby was never going to feel exactly the way I wanted it to feel. It was just too complicated when there were two moms. I didn't have any right to claim exclusive maternal role at the hospital. Stacy was the one who had done all the work. She was the one who had paid a price with her life and livelihood. I was just a lucky observer.

Email to family members and friends on February 3, 2000

At her last doctor visit, Stacy was told she could have the baby in 3 days or 3 weeks. Ever since she was put on bed rest, she hasn't had pain. She is ready for the pregnancy to be over, but her body is still moving very slowly. All this "hurry up and wait" has made me feel like I've been pregnant for many months.

Other than the "no news yet," there are a few other noteworthy things to mention. Stacy and I are planning an adoption ritual of some sort to occur at her United Methodist church when she and the baby are discharged from the hospital. Her minister (and possibly my dad, if he can make it) would officiate. It would be a brief ceremony acknowledging the gift of the baby from birthmother to adoptive parents. I have heard about these before, but never personally participated in one. Stacy would bring the baby to the ceremony and the Falcos would leave with him.

The agency's attorney located Jamie. He said on the phone that he would sign papers. He has had them for weeks now and has not signed. An anonymous female keeps calling Stacy and harassing her, saying things like: "Leave my man alone." At this point, the agency has re-sent the papers to the sheriff's office in the Colorado town where Jamie is located and they are supposed to be personally serving him. Once that is accomplished, the clock will start ticking to terminate his rights involuntarily.

Stacy is more thorough than any birthmother I've worked with before. She is really thinking through all the anticipated details at the hospital. We talk daily and there's always something new on her list. She asked about her sister and brother-in-law having access to the baby. She told us about a room at the hospital for adoptive couples to spend time with the baby. She has bought a stuffed bear for the baby.

Email to family members and friends on February 8, 2000

Good news! The Texas agency received signed "termination of parental rights" papers from Jamie yesterday. It was big surprise to them and a big relief to Stacy.

Stacy went to the hospital last Friday night to be re-hydrated. She had been throwing up everything, including water, for two days. She took three bags of fluid intravenously and went home.

At 1:30 a.m. on Monday, we received a call from Stacy. She was at the hospital again, having contractions every 8 minutes. The hospital staff wanted to monitor her longer before deciding if this was it. Stacy said she would call back in two hours and John thought we could catch a 6 a.m. flight to Dallas. About 5 a.m., Stacy called again. She was being released. They called it non-productive contractions, probably produced by the dehydration.

Stacy sees a new doctor today and may discuss setting a time to induce labor. Do we understand all these changes in doctors? No, except that it has to do with insurance and Medicaid. Also, Stacy told John that she might be having the baby at a different hospital too. Meanwhile, we wait.

Email to family members and friends on February 9, 2000

Stacy called in tears. She had received a call from one of her friends in England. He told her that he had waited two and a half weeks, but finally had to call and tell her what a cold-hearted bitch he thought she was. A man she had known for half her life had been killed and she had not even had the decency to send a card. Stacy had no idea what her friend was talking about. In short, it soon became clear that an old friend and occasional lover, Bert, had been killed three weeks ago. Bert's family had wanted to fly Stacy to England for the funeral.

Stacy's friend, thinking Stacy was still working with the adoption agency she left last Fall before contacting the Falcos, talked with a counselor there and told the counselor to tell Stacy that her friend, Bert, had been killed. Instead, the counselor called Children's Hope, the agency that Stacy is now working with, and told them that there was another alleged birthfather–Bert. This led to a series of phone calls and emails to and between the agency, Stacy, and the Falcos trying to determine whether other legal steps should be taken to terminate the rights of "all possible" birth fathers. We, ultimately, decided to believe Stacy's adamant position that Jamie was the only possible birth father. Our agency also received a letter from the old agency asking the Falcos to pay the expenses incurred by them while working with Stacy. This request was for several thousand dollars. But, at no point in time did that agency tell Children's Hope or Stacy that Bert had been killed!

§ § §

On February 10, 2000, I contacted Adoption Online Connection to tell them that we no longer needed their services as we were awaiting the arrival of our baby any day now.

Email to family members and friends on February 13, 2000

Disturbing news comes from this week's visit to the clinic/doctor. They ran tests for four hours. In the end, it was decided that the baby is already 10 pounds. Stacy has stress fractures on her pelvis. Because of the baby's size, Stacy will have to have a C-section. But there will be no scheduled C-section any time soon. If she goes into labor on her own, they will do an immediate C-section. If she does not go into labor before the end of February, a C-section will be scheduled for March 1st.

I don't understand this and neither does Stacy. Apparently, she has decided not to try to understand, as long as someone gives her sedatives and painkillers so she can sleep–which has been a big problem. I realize that, under ideal circumstances, it is best for a baby to go full term. But with all of Stacy's illnesses and the stress fractures, I just don't get this decision. Is it Medicaid driven?

Email to family members and friends on February 22, 2000

The last time I wrote we had just learned from Stacy that her baby was estimated to be 10 lbs. and that she needed a C-section. Well, it doesn't take long for information to change with this pregnancy. On Stacy's next visit to the doctor, a different doctor at the clinic told her the baby was 8 lbs. and they expected her to try to deliver vaginally. No mention of pelvic stress fractures. Who knows what is really going on!?

John went to Dallas on business last week and had dinner with Stacy while he was there. She showed him her apartment, the book she has made for the baby, and pictures of her horses. They had a great time together.

Stacy later called me about the hospital situation. She had been to tour Parkland Hospital. According to Stacy, there is only one other hospital in the country that delivers more babies per year than Parkland. Even so, their arrangements for special situations seem archaic. Stacy says her only choices are to room with one or more other mothers and to have the baby "room in" or to be in a private room and have no contact with the baby whatsoever. Stacy is not willing to give up all contact with the baby, but she doesn't want to have the baby with her at all times either. She is sure it would be upsetting to have us visiting with the baby in her room, which seems to be the only option at this hospital. On the other hand, the adoption agency social worker says there is a "waiver procedure" that we/Stacy can pursue. However, it must be initiated with the social worker on the floor where the patient resides, and we won't know what floor Stacy will be on until she is admitted.

On Friday, Stacy called me with her latest plan. Apparently, there is a doctor who delivers at Presbyterian Hospital who has seen Stacy a few times and who is willing to take her as a patient when she has her actual Medicaid card. Stacy has had the Medicaid number for a while. But, in Texas, the actual card makes a difference. The provider can swipe the card like a credit card and guarantee payment. Stacy is hoping to hold out until the actual card arrives in the mail. At that point, she can reconnect with the doctor at Presbyterian and deliver the baby there. Presbyterian Hospital has special rooms for adoptive parents to visit with the baby.

Friday night, Stacy went to the hospital emergency room because she had been having pains every 20 minutes. According to the on-call doctor, she was in early labor. They would not admit her because she had not dilated to 4 cm., but she was told to expect to deliver within 3 days at most. Stacy had a doctor's appointment scheduled for Monday. John was going to be in Dallas on business, so Stacy said she would call him with any news.

Here it is, Tuesday morning, John is back from Texas, and we haven't heard from Stacy. I'm packed. John is packed. My 5-page list of the children's daily schedule and calendar of events with permission slips and other necessary documents is ready and waiting for my parents when they arrive to take over my duties here. I am at a point where I don't know if I believe this is really going to happen or if it is real at all. I feel slightly crazy. I will be back in touch when there is more to report.

Email to family members and friends on February 24, 2000

The social worker called today. She had been in touch with Stacy. Stacy told her that she is sick and tired of being pregnant, that she doesn't want any of us to call her anymore, and that she'll be in touch when she goes into labor.

Email to family members and friends on February 26, 2000

I just got off the phone with Stacy. She is spending the weekend with friends, but forgot her iron pills, so she came home to get them and decided to call us. She apologized for cutting us off, but said it was getting so hard to talk to us. She went on to say that she has been reevaluating the whole adoption plan. She remembers how scared she was when she found out she was pregnant. She knew she couldn't terminate the pregnancy, but she knew she couldn't parent either. Lately, she has been wondering if she is being selfish or if it's the best thing for the baby. I told her that, although I could not really know how she felt, I thought that everything she had done to prepare, including being honest with herself about how much this does and is likely to hurt, is incredibly admirable. I also told her I understood that we weren't necessarily the right people for her to talk to about her doubts and that we respected her decision to call only when she wanted to.

Stacy went on to talk about some bad experiences with hospital staff at Parkland. For example, the nurses have been questioning her adoption plan: "How could you give away your baby?" It's very hard for her. Also she has been receiving calls from friends in the D.C. and Virginia, the area where Jamie's parents live, saying he isn't the father. But, Stacy also said that she was so glad she found us, and that she knew her baby would be better off with us as his parents. She's even wondering if she can stand to see him when he's born. She thought maybe she needed to wait a few weeks. I told her I thought it would be good to leave her options open.

Stacy says that everywhere she looks she sees babies, and she is already feeling the loss. I told her I did know how it felt to not have a baby and see everyone else with babies. And I talked a little about the feelings associated with infertility–something I've never been able to share with a birthmother before. Stacy seemed to think we did have some feelings in common.

It was so hard for me to hear how fragile she feels and to know she's also having to deal with so many people who don't understand what she is doing and why. It's so clear to me that she is a remarkable, brave woman.

The bottom line on the delivery is that she must go two weeks past her due date of Feb. 28th before they will induce her. Can you believe this baby we expected in late December may not arrive until mid-March?

§ § §

I stopped emailing my family and friends. We waited to have good news to report.

Email to family members and friends on March 7, 2000, a.m.

I hesitate to write this, but since I've brought you along this far, it seems to make sense to let you know about these latest developments.

Last week, after Stacy went to her doctor's appointment on Tuesday, she called to say that she'd been told: if she didn't have the baby by Monday (3/6), they would induce on Tuesday or Wednesday. As Stacy predicted, nothing happened. John talked to Stacy on Saturday night and reported a good conversation. The agency social worker, Anne, talked to Stacy on Sunday night and reported a positive conversation. John told Stacy on Saturday that, unless she had the baby sooner, I would fly in on Monday night for an anticipated delivery on Tuesday or Wednesday. She was fine with that. John would already be in Dallas because he had business there on Monday. Stacy told John and Anne that her appointment at the clinic was on Monday morning. She would call Anne and us when she learned when the inducement would occur.

Monday morning came and went. We did not hear from Stacy. Recalling that Stacy sometimes had to wait at the clinic for several hours to see a doctor, we continued to wait patiently until late Monday afternoon. I called John. He had not heard anything from Stacy. I called Anne. She had not heard anything from Stacy. I called the adoption agency. They had not heard anything from Stacy. I called Stacy. Her answering machine had the disturbing message: "It's Sunday night. I am going out of town for an emergency." None of us knew what that meant – whether it was a true emergency or a code of some kind. And why had Stacy not called any of us about this "emergency"?

The hours dragged by. John decided to stay in Dallas for the night. I stayed in Atlanta. Anne, John, and I left messages for Stacy to call. It is now 11 a.m. on Tuesday. Stacy has not called. John is coming home on an 11:30 a.m. flight.

When I talked to John last he said, "I go from feeling angry to feeling depressed to being worried about Stacy to feeling like a fool." I too share those feelings as well as feelings of fear and sadness.

This is where we are. I hope there will be good news to share in the not-too-distant future. But, right now....

Email to family members and friends on March 7, 2000, p.m.

You are not going to believe this. Anne just called. Stacy had just called her. On Sunday night, after Anne talked with Stacy, three of Stacy's friends were killed in an automobile accident in San Antonio. Horses in a trailer were also badly injured in this accident. Stacy left Dallas for San Antonio. She just called Anne a few minutes ago to tell her that she was now on her way to Oklahoma for the funerals. She said she knew it probably wasn't advisable, but she had to go. Stacy has been crying since she heard the news Sunday night. Stacy said she'd call from Oklahoma if she has the baby there.

Thanks to those of you who sent love and prayers my/our way after my last message. Please pray for the families of Stacy's friends and for Stacy now. She has had one hell of a pregnancy. She needs all our support. I don't know that there is anything else we can do from here but wait and pray.

Email to Rebecca from Stacy on March 8, 2000

Hi,

I am sorry that I have not been in touch with you guys lately. I am just trying to cope with everything that is going on in my life and it is becoming more difficult by the minute. I hope that you both understand why I have to attend the funerals. I can't lose any more without being able to have some closure.

Rebecca. Thank you so much for your offer to come and help me. I really appreciate it and cannot tell you what it means to me that you are willing to come support me. Unfortunately it is really hard to talk to you guys right now. I know what is best for me to do, and I know what I have to do. I just can't help but feel resentment that you are able to provide for Luke what I cannot. I wish I could, but I know in my heart what will be best for him and that is you, John, two sisters and a brother.

I also want to thank you again for allowing me to meet you at your home. When I can't sleep at night it gives me a lot of comfort to be able to visualize the environment that he will be growing up in.

Well I need to get some rest, so I will close for now. I hope you understand why I can't talk to you. I don't want to stop communication. It's just that I will start crying all over again if I hear your voices. I know that you guys are happy about him, and I really want to be happy for you and share in your joy. I just can't right now. I hope you understand.

Love, Stacy

Email to Stacy from Rebecca on March 8, 2000

Dear Stacy,

Thank you for your email. I couldn't believe it when I heard from Anne about the accident. You have suffered so much in the past few months–physically and emotionally. This seems incredibly unfair. Please know that you and the families of your friends are in our hearts and prayers. And, yes, we understand your need to have some closure.

We also want you to know that we continue to want to respect your needs regarding communication. I'm still impressed with your ability to share your feelings about the baby with us. He'll know how much you love him and have sacrificed to bring him into the world and to plan for his future well being. We love you too.

If you feel like it would not be a violation of your privacy, we'd like to know where you are in case you suddenly go into labor and want us to be where you give birth.

Love, Rebecca

Email to family members and friends on March 13, 2000

Today, Stacy is officially two weeks past her due date of February 28. We have not heard from her since the middle of last week. We don't know where she is or how she is feeling. We don't know her state of mind regarding the adoption plan. We are trying to "keep the faith," but it is harder with each passing day.

In church yesterday, it was announced that one of our associate pastors, Mary Lou, would be leaving in June to be appointed to her own church. I've known Mary Lou a long time and I adore her. She is smart and funny and one of those people you feel blessed to have as a friend. And I am really, really happy for Mary Lou that she is moving in the direction that she believes God has called her.

But, yesterday, the announcement set me off on a crying jag for an hour. I was not crying only over the loss of Mary Lou. I was also crying about losing Luke, Stacy's baby boy. This may sound crazy, but I had the feeling that my crying was not just a biological function of releasing too much stored tension or stress. I had the feeling I was being given some insight that might help me.

One of the things I've learned from my father, the pastoral counselor and professor, is a way to understand forgiveness: Forgiveness happens when you stand in the other person's shoes. It happens in the moment when you experience what it must have felt like to the other person at the time s/he did the troubling act(s). As I was crying, I wondered if Stacy felt like I did–if Stacy felt hollowed out and empty from all her losses, and so out-of-control of what was happening to her. I began to think that leaving Texas to drive to Oklahoma for the funerals of friends might be the only thing I could do, too.

I hope that Stacy will resurface very soon. I hope that she got what she needed from her travels. I hope the baby has not suffered in the process. I selfishly hope that we will still be chosen to adopt Stacy's baby. In the meantime, I will try to remain open to receive whatever it is I need to receive.

P.S. While I was typing this message, I was interrupted by a phone call from K.J.'s birthfather, Kyle. He called to let us know that on March 6th, Tessa gave birth to twin boys: Adam, 5 lbs., 12 oz., 18 ½ in. long, and Chad, 6 lbs, 19 ½ in. long. They are all doing well. K.J. now has full biological brothers in Nebraska!

Email to Stacy from Rebecca on March 14, 2000

Dear Stacy,

We are going out of our minds with fear. Are you all right? Please, please let us know.

Rebecca & John

Email to Rebecca from Stacy, received on March 15, 2000

My cousin has disappeared in China and my mother's family is quite freaked out. I have been having contractions for two days now and will have the baby at a military hospital or VA hospital, Balboa or Pendleton are most likely. I have been seeing the doctor and taking care of the baby. I am very confused right now and don't know what to say. I am worried about my family, and am scared to say goodbye to Luke. Today is the 10th and I am not sure when they will get this out to you. I will try to call when I know more and have some privacy. My mother is getting increasingly unhappy with the adoption and is letting everyone know how she feels, but I need to be here. Anyway I need to go so I will talk to you later.

Email to Stacy from Rebecca on March 15, 2000

I know this is a very stressful, crazy, emotional time for you. Are you in California with your mother now? We just received the email you wrote on the 10th. Has the baby been born? Actually, the answers to those questions are not as important as your decision regarding parents for your baby. It sounds from your email like the adoption plan is up in the air. You know John and I can't be completely objective about this. We have ordered our lives and jobs and finances and opened our hearts to take the baby, you and your family into our lives. But I don't know that it's fair to lay our pain on you at this time.

What I keep thinking about is that all of your words and actions and our observations of you indicated that you did not consider yourself ready to be the day-to-day parent to a child. I think about how we planned that all of us could fulfill our dreams through this adoption plan. You would be able to pursue your career and the things you love the most. Your baby would get the love and resources of two parents, siblings, and extended family. You, your mother, and as much of your family as you choose, would be part of our lives and add more love to your child's life. In fact, I envisioned you seeing him several times a year with all the traveling you do around the country.

John and I have always felt that we "clicked" with you. The fact that we chose each other to pursue this adoption plan seems right and good and almost preordained. I hope you know us well enough to trust that our openness is not some kind of trick to get you to give us your baby. I don't know what else I can say, Stacy. Ultimately, this is your decision. We have to keep trusting you.

Email to family members and friends on March 16, 2000

I received a call from our attorney in Texas last night. Stacy has resurfaced in Dallas. She had the baby a few days ago. She has decided to keep him even though she tells the attorney she's not bonding with him and her situation hasn't changed. She says she can't place him for adoption because of all the other losses she has experienced.

When I started this adoption story in December, I believed it would have a happy ending. I am sorry now that I dragged you into something that turned out to be a tragedy.

Thank you for being there – Rebecca

§ § §

The outpouring of love and support from friends and family was enormous. I saved many of the email messages for a scrapbook entitled, simply, “Luke.” But I wasn’t ready to let this dream go entirely. I thought and thought about what to say to Stacy. In my grieving state, I wrote to her on March 17, 2000. I wrote about infertility. I wrote about being raped in my twenties and learning to be a survivor. I wrote about almost adopting the twins. I wrote about K.J.:

> I’ve been unpacking the suitcase that was packed for two months and putting away the little baby things. That’s hard. But what is harder is seeing the children struggle with the loss of ‘Luke.’ Last night I was helping K.J. undress and get ready for bed. His shirt was a little snug so I suggested it might be time to give it to someone smaller. K.J. said, “How about Luke?” I said, “K.J., do you remember that I told you Stacy has decided to keep her baby? He won’t be coming to live with us.” K.J. hung his head and said, “Then I won’t have a little brother.” That was tough to hear.
>
> I can’t judge your willingness or ability to be a parent, Stacy. Maybe something has changed that we don’t know about. If it has, we certainly do not want to stand in your way. I imagine that you are one of those people who can do almost anything you put your mind to. But do know this: If, after some time passes, you begin to think you’ve made the wrong decision–we are still here. The Falcos will not pursue another adoption. This is the end of the line for us. For financial and emotional reasons we can’t start over again. But we are here for your child. Remember that if you ever need us.

§ § §

To my surprise, I heard from Stacy the next day.

Email to Rebecca from Stacy on March 18, 2000

Dear Rebecca and John,

I got both of your letters and have been trying to figure out what to say. I am so very sorry for hurting your family. That was never my intention. I don't know how to explain what is going on with me so if I start to ramble please understand.

I still want the world for this baby. I know that I can't offer him as much as you can. I can't even provide him with a father who loves him. But I am so damn scared to say goodbye. I don't think I can right now. I keep reading over the papers that I am supposed to sign and they make my stomach turn. I am not sure if my original reasons are good enough anymore. What if he hates me? Is my career more important? There are other jobs in my field that require no travel, and yes they pay a lot less, but don't they say that money can't buy happiness? I have had so many horrible things happen in the last year, and I feel like I just keep losing.

I don't know how you have gone through having an infant 3 times, and still want to do it again. I don't know if I am doing everything right or not. But I do know that I love him. And I want what is best for him. CC told me that she thought you would both be open to still taking him. I wish that I had signed in the hospital but it all happened so fast, and there were so many people there that I never picked up the phone. Then for 2 days I kept telling myself that I needed to call someone, and I couldn't do it. I couldn't stand the thought of having to say goodbye in such a cold, sterile environment. I didn't want placing him to be a part of my month from hell. I can't blame my family, though I know where they stand. Ray came from Virginia to stay with me. He is so helpful. I know that I am not being fair to you and I am so sorry, but I didn't want to have any doubts within myself.

Ray is taking me to talk to a counselor tomorrow, and that is all that I can say for now.

Email from Rebecca to Stacy on March 18, 2000

Of course we would "still be open to taking him." We hoped for it, planned for it, dreamed of it, and counted on it. But we can't make this decision for you. It's yours to make alone. I hope you do get to talk with a counselor who is familiar with adoption. And I hope you can make your decision soon so that you can get on with planning the rest of your life–either with your son as a daily part of it, or without him on a daily basis, but still part of your life. As I think you knew, but may have forgotten, either choice can be a decision motivated by love.

§ § §

I was torn-up. While I said to Stacy all the understanding things a good adoption professional might say, I silenced the wannabe adoptive parent in me who was screaming, "Don't take my baby!"

Late that afternoon, I was in our basement doing some cleaning when the phone rang. The message was from a pregnant woman in North Carolina named Grace who said she had seen our adoption letter on the Internet. This seemed strange to me because our letter had not been posted since early February, but I took down her number.

The next day, I called Grace. She told me she was 32 years old, and that she was having a baby due on May 12th. She said she was from Grove, Oklahoma, but wasn't close to her family. She now lived in Sunset Beach and had been getting prenatal care in Wilmington, North Carolina. She was on Medicaid.

Grace found out she was pregnant five months ago. She had been afraid of adoption because she thought the homes were unsafe until she read our letter. She loved our letter and had been carrying it around in her car for a couple of months. She had friends who supported her plan to place the baby for adoption, and they had encouraged her to call us.

Grace said that she was just now starting to get grounded in her life. She had a positive group of friends. It had been a "bad situation" with the birthfather. He was gone by the time she found out she was pregnant, and she didn't know how to find him. When I delicately asked about his race and ethnicity, Grace said she didn't know. "He was 'tan,' but not African-American."

John and I talked. To my surprise, John said we should go and meet Grace right away. We made plans to travel to her. But, then, calls came from Texas again, and we cancelled our plans with Grace, calling it a "family emergency."

Email to family members and friends on April 3, 2000

> I've had enough inquiries about Stacy that I've decided to send another group email. We did hear from Stacy about two weeks after her baby was born. She called the attorney to say that she had changed her mind and did want to place him with us. Everyone scrambled to prepare. In Texas, you have to hire separate attorneys for the birthmother, the baby, and the agency.
>
> I talked to Stacy the night before she was scheduled to go in and sign termination papers. She told me not to bring a car seat or clothes because she wanted to give me the ones she had. She went through a long explanation about the time that had passed. She went to Oklahoma to attend a funeral of a friend who had been killed in a car wreck. While she was there, she was contacted by family in California who wanted her home because a cousin (exchange student) was missing in China. She flew to southern California and began having contractions. She delivered in a military hospital there on March 10th. Her mother and sister changed their minds about the adoption and wanted her to keep the baby. Her mom couldn't take time off from work, so Stacy flew back to Dallas with the baby and solicited help from various friends for a few days while she tried

to figure out what to do. She called Jamie, the birthfather, to tell him she had his son. He basically told her that he might get married some day and didn't want the little bastard in his life. Stacy said she still wanted her baby to have two parents and she knew we'd be good ones.

The attorney and social worker thought Stacy sounded "for real," but advised us not to come to Texas until they called and said Stacy had signed the papers. I packed and waited at the Atlanta airport. John was in Chicago waiting at the airport. Stacy never showed up. No one has heard from her since. Thanks again for your supportive thoughts and prayers.

§ § §

How was I feeling? How could I consider making a new adoption plan with another birthmother so soon after Luke was gone? I didn't really want a new birthmother to make me feel better before I was done feeling bad or just *feeling* about losing Luke and Stacy.

I had a complicated set of emotions. On the one hand, I had professional and personal experience with adoption that enabled me to realize: even the best-laid plans sometimes fail. Our commitment to Stacy was one we took very seriously. There were human lives involved. But then she broke the commitment.

On the other hand, I was also an experienced survivor of sexual assault. I had learned both to bury painful emotions and to carry on in the face of them. It was too soon to know what might happen with Grace. We didn't have the money to start over. Moreover, I was embarrassed about how this would look to others if we seemed to move on from Stacy so effortlessly.

But there was Grace. Innocent. Unknowing. Telling me the Falcos were the family she wanted. Telling me things Stacy could never have said about my parenting style and other details that demonstrated how much attention she paid to our relationships to each of our children.

I went to Cannon Chapel, where John and I were married, thinking it would help somehow. I really wanted to fall apart to make room for a new spirit to enter. It didn't happen exactly as I'd hoped, but I did hear two things that stayed with me: *To love God, we have to love our brothers and sisters... God does not leave broken what God has made.*

I wrote:

> I'm trying to be loving and rational and open-minded. I'm trying to listen, to relax, and to enjoy the life and family I have. I'm trying to just be in these moments and learn whatever it is I am able to learn.

§ § §

The Stacy baby adoption was over; but there was still the issue of the money we had spent and promises made to us. I wrote to Stacy on April 5, 2000, to request repayment of living expenses as she had promised if the adoption did not go through. Stacy left a phone message a few days later, stating that she intended to pay back the living expenses *and* the legal and agency fees. We never saw the money or heard from her again.

Many months later, after I published a story in *Adoption Today* magazine about this failed adoption, I received an email from an adoption agency professional. She wrote:

> I would be most interested in talking to either of you about a young women who told and acted out, almost verbatim, the story about a birthmother you called "Donna." Her real name we believe is Stacy *[last name withheld]*, aka Stacy *[different last name]*.
>
> I am the co-director of an adoption agency in Plano, Texas and worked with Stacy for over six months, and have learned this woman scammed at least four other persons. I have documentation gathered by an irate neighbor when Stacy left suddenly one day that proves clearly she defrauded us, and at

least three other agencies not to mention several families like you. This young lady belongs in jail for the hurt and pain she has caused you and many others. The district attorney's office here in Dallas is aware of her as well. Please call me....

§ § §

This was shocking and devastating news of a different kind. There were conversations and letters with this agency and others that followed and pieced together a tale of deception and, perhaps, mental illness. But, to the best of my knowledge, charges were never filed against Stacy. At least, we never heard about her again.

Grace Appears

March to December 2000

Stacy had called to say she was ready to place her baby for adoption on March 21st. On March 22nd, she failed to show up to sign papers. On March 23rd, we called Grace and arranged to take the family to meet her. After that first visit, I returned alone to North Carolina to go with Grace to the doctor on April 14th. I was afraid to make a new birthmother commitment, but Grace was so sweet. It wasn't her fault that we were fragile. By the end of April, we were ready to let others in on our secret.

Email to family members and friends on April 29, 2000

We have decided to break the silence...

I was hesitant to write about a new possible adoption because I had written so much and so intensely about Stacy–and you know how that ended. Miraculously, we were contacted by a birthmother in North Carolina not long after Stacy changed her mind about placing her baby with us the second time. This birthmother, Grace, received a copy of our letter through a network of friends back in January and, for some reason, kept the letter. If she had called in January, we would have told her that we had an adoption pending with Stacy, and Grace would have disappeared. Instead, she called when we were feeling emotionally raw and financially depleted. Surprising me, John said, "Let's meet her right away." Of course, his response was very practical. If we met her and didn't like her, we could get out before we got too involved.

We decided to make a family vacation out of it. Grace lives on the North Carolina coast, and our children had never been to the beach (except for Emily as an infant). We figured the time together would be well spent whatever the outcome with Grace. And it was. The children loved the shells and sand. They met a crab and played with waves.

To make a longer story shorter, let me summarize what we learned about Grace that weekend in March and since that time: Grace is a very attractive, 32-year-old, single mother of a 7-year-old daughter, Hope. Grace grew up with an abusive father and her continuing focus in life seems to be recovery from that abuse and concern for the safety of all children. She was drawn to us because she believes we will provide a safe and nurturing environment for her child. (Unlike Stacy, she pays close attention to our relationships with each of our children.)

Grace was a devoted member of the Church of Latter Day Saints and was married when she gave birth to Hope. She was a certified massage therapist and very interested in holistic and alternative healing methods. About the time Hope was born, Grace realized her marriage was also an abusive relationship. She divorced her husband and attempted to raise Hope on her own. Unfortunately, Grace was also dealing with depression and anxiety that impaired her ability to make ends meet. Ultimately, after five years, she allowed her mother (now divorced from her father) to take Hope. Grace then began a journey in pursuit of emotional and financial wellbeing that will eventually lead her back to Hope.

Grace refers to herself as right-brained. She was/is a dancer and singer, not a rational thinker. She discovered that she had an aptitude for exotic dance. However, Grace drifted from club to club and roommate to roommate. It was during a one to two week period when she roomed with a man she met at a club that she conceived the baby she is now carrying. She had taken a birth control shot and been told that she might not have menstrual periods.

She was 4 to 5 months pregnant before she discovered that she was pregnant. Grace was quite upset about it because she knew that she had been drinking and smoking during these early months. We are confident that Grace is not an illegal drug user.

Because of her concern about the baby's health, Grace was sent to a genetic testing center where she had a level two ultrasound. It is my understanding, after listening to Grace and talking with her doctor directly, that this type of ultrasound allows the doctor to take an up-close look at the baby's brain and other organs, as well as facial features, which might indicate fetal alcohol syndrome. No abnormalities were found. Having researched this issue and discussed the specifics of Grace's case with our pediatrician and others, John and I are fairly confident that the risk of serious special needs is minimal.

Grace is now living with a New Jersey-born and bred guy named Vito who runs an Italian restaurant in Calabash, NC. As you can imagine, he and John hit it off immediately. Vito and Grace's other close friends are all supportive of adoption. Grace knows what is takes to raise a child. Her goal is reunification with Hope. She knows that would not be possible with another mouth to feed, particularly when she is still trying to get on her feet.

Grace is a very sweet person from a small town who seems genuinely committed to placing her baby with us. I have been to Wilmington with Grace to talk with her doctor and arrange for the hospital experience. Grace was at our home for several days to meet family members and get a visual picture of where her child will be living. She tolerated our chaos very well. In fact, she was the desired playmate of the children while she was here.

Grace is due May 12. Yes, in two weeks. She is having a baby girl. There are no guarantees in life. This seems like a risk worth taking. We wanted you to know.

§ § §

This was an independent or private adoption driven by attorneys instead of an adoption agency (or two). Because the *connection* between Grace and us had happened independently of an agency, and because there were no living expenses involved in this placement, an adoption agency was not necessary. The fact that there were no agency costs or living expenses also meant that we could afford the adoption despite our losses with Stacy. That alone felt miraculous, an answer to prayer.

However, because there was no agency involved, there was also no counselor to mediate, to listen, to advise, or to collect information. I took it upon myself to collect information from Grace and to listen as intensely as I could to her concerns and fears. It was a difficult role to play–and not one that I would recommend to other prospective adoptive parents, but it didn't seem like we had an alternative. In the first place, because of Stacy, our financial resources were limited. Moreover, Grace had been betrayed by strangers and loved ones alike. However, she trusted *us*. To try to interject another person into the equation didn't make sense in this case. Either we would work this out between us, or it was not meant to be.

I created my own "background information form" and proceeded to fill it out from conversations with Grace. *[This form can be found in Appendix B.]* This information was passed on to the attorneys involved in the case. Grace defined her ethnic background as Dutch and German on her mother's side and Spanish and Cherokee Indian on her father's side. Grace said that her father was a "small percentage" Indian. This fact might have created an obstacle to the adoption because of the Indian Child Welfare Act, a federal law that requires notice to Native American tribes when the adoption of an "Indian child" is contemplated. Each tribe has its own rules regarding what percentage of Indian blood creates an Indian child. If the child meets their definition, the tribe can object to an adoption outside the tribe. In our case, notice was given, but the percentage was inconsequential to the Cherokee nation. Our adoption could proceed.

In response to my question about the reasons for placing her child for adoption, Grace wrote: "So that my baby can have the most healthy, balanced, and unconditional loving home possible. So he/she has the chance to know how to make it in this world. Every child deserves and has the right to be safe and feel safe and have unconditional love."

Grace wanted us to be in the room when she delivered the baby, if possible. As to contact after the birth, she gave the Falcos complete discretion to decide what was best for the child. She could not have been more accommodating.

Grace's pregnancy was a secret from her parents. She wrote: "I do not have a relationship with my parents any longer. This has been necessary to my emotional health. I am on my own and have finally found my own healthy family of friends that are very supportive of helping me believe in myself and finally make my life work."

When asked what she wanted her child to know about her, she wrote: "I love this child with all my heart and have prayed for his/her well being and perfect health in body, mind, & spirit every day since December/January. I am thankful to know the Falcos love you with all their hearts, Rebecca, John, Emily, Kevin John, & Skye. They both know how to and have the desire and ability to be there for you all your life with love, guidance, and understanding."

How different it felt to be in relationship with Grace versus Stacy. Grace listened and paid attention to our family. She was reassuring and comforting. Stacy had seemed smart and worldly. She was exciting and unpredictable. Upon reflection, I saw an analogy to dating. Exciting, unpredictable men were very intriguing to me. But the reassuring, comforting men, like my husband, were the ones I had learned I could trust.

I hired an attorney in North Carolina and prepared all the documents he needed from us. We hired a Georgia attorney to handle the interstate compact process on this end. I contacted the hospital where Grace planned to deliver and provided the staff with information about our adoption. I planned to pursue termination of the alleged birth father's rights and filing of the petition for adoption when it was time.

Email to family members and friends on May 12, 2000

We have some good news on the birth father front. The private investigator we hired was able to get an address, phone number, date of birth, and social security number for Charles *[last name]*. After trying unsuccessfully for a day to get in touch with our attorney and to get her opinion about how to proceed, we decided to forge ahead and contact Charles ourselves. After all, we are the open adoption "gurus," aren't we? John was elected as our spokesperson.

Turns out that the phone number we had was for Charles's grandparents' home. John was very careful not to reveal the reason for his call–only that it was "personal." He left toll free home and work numbers with the grandfather and asked that Charles call him ASAP. Charles had moved to a town outside Charlotte, NC, and was living with his younger brother, mother and father.

Last night, about 12:30 a.m., Charles called. I couldn't understand John's sleepy mumbles for the first five minutes of their conversation, but apparently that didn't bother Charles. John was able to tell him about the pregnancy and impending birth and his alleged role in all of this. Charles was shocked, but not antagonistic. He asked questions about Grace and us. John was careful in his responses. The only troubling thing was that Charles thought he might come to the hospital to see the baby. We know that Grace thinks of Charles as an abusive individual and that she would be very upset by this news; but we could not very well tell him he couldn't come. I was muffling my laughter as John told Charles that he wasn't sure of the name of the hospital or where Grace would deliver. In the end, Charles agreed that adoption seemed like the best plan. He didn't have the money to parent. He wasn't even convinced he was the father. They ended the conversation with the plan that an attorney would be calling him the following evening to set up the specifics of what he needed to do.

I spent the day talking with our NC and GA attorneys about the logistics. It was decided that the NC attorney should call Charles and that Charles would be told to meet with another attorney in Rock Hill to sign papers next week. He can deny paternity or not–as long as he agrees to terminate any potential parental rights he may have. The NC attorney called Charles, but he was not home. He left instructions with John to give to Charles if he called us.

An hour or so ago, Charles called and John filled him in. Charles had decided to tell his parents what was going on. The family all agreed that adoption was the right thing to do. He had decided he didn't have the money for a paternity test, and never mentioned to John about going to see the baby. Charles agreed to go to the Rock Hill attorney's office to sign papers next week.

We are feeling pretty good about these developments. There are certainly other things that can go wrong, but this helps.

John just made reservations for us to fly to Wilmington on Sunday evening. We'll take an earlier flight if Grace calls before then. Assuming she doesn't, the plan is still that she will go to the hospital in Wilmington to have her water broken on Monday.

We will keep you informed as it goes...

– Rebecca

§ § §

On the evening of May 14th, John and I took a plane to Wilmington, leaving the children with my mom and dad. We were to meet Grace and Vito at the doctor's office at 1 p.m. We were there on time, but Grace wasn't. The minutes dragged between 1 and 1:40 p.m. Finally, Grace and Vito appeared with his father and girlfriend too. There had been a series of delays, but they were fine.

Eventually, the doctor checked Grace and decided that "conditions were not favorable" for inducing labor. There was too much space between the baby's head and her cervix. He could force it, but the labor would be long and hard. The doctor broke some membranes around the cervix and sent Grace home. The plan was now for her to come back to the hospital on Thursday at 7 a.m. if she did not have the baby sooner. We were all a little disappointed, but recognized that it would be better to let her body get there on its own, if possible.

We decided to go to the river for lunch at Elijah's. The food was great and the conversation was entertaining. Carol (the girlfriend) knew all the real life people who are the basis for the characters in "The Sopranos." At 4:45 p.m., John and I left to take him to the airport so that he could get prepared for a big work presentation the following morning. I suggested we turn in the rental car to save money because Vito said he would pick me up on the way to the hospital when Grace went into labor. After getting John to the airport, I walked the 5 miles back to the room. I picked up a few groceries, watched a movie in the room, and went to sleep.

As I waited for Grace's baby to be born, I kept a detailed journal of my activities:

May 16, 2000

> From 7 to 10 a.m. I completed a handwritten version of one of the home studies that I brought with me. (At this time, I had a part-time job as a caseworker for an adoption agency, doing home studies for families interested in domestic or international adoptions.) I ran 4.5 miles and showered. I then walked to a

strip mall and bought a big sister gift for Emily–her first real watch–some snacks and some lunch. I watched a TV movie, ate, and took a nap. Dad called. John called. A local Presbyterian minister and friend of Dad's called. I bought more drinks and food. I am now going to start the second home study. Maybe tomorrow I can find a way to borrow a computer. I might walk to the big mall we saw on our first day's run. I should do more reading, but I am fidgety.

May 17, 2000

Finished the second home study by hand. I then ran for 62 minutes. It was muggy and warm. I called Grace and left a message as it started to pour rain outside. I napped off and on for two hours. What a luxury! Than I walked to the "mall." It turned out to be another larger strip mall; but there was a Wal-mart, so I walked around inside. Then I started the walk back, stopped at Appleby's to buy a chicken Caesar salad for later. It's so strange to have nothing to do! I read part of a marathon book, ate, and watched TV. John, Grace, Joanna, and Emily called at different points. John says Charles hasn't made his appointment to sign papers on Friday yet. I hope he will follow through. I watched the final episode of "90210," gave John a packing list for the kids, watched "Law & Order," and went to sleep.

May 18, 2000

Thursday. Got up at 5:50 a.m. to prepare for the day. Grace and Catherine *[the friend who helped Grace find our letter on the Internet]* arrived about 6:30 a.m. to pick me up for the ride to the hospital. We got to the hospital before 7 and began the registration process.

The rooms are nice; and the baby will stay in the room with Grace (assuming she is healthy). The doctor on call checked

Grace. She is only 1 ½ cm. dilated. He decided to give her Pitocin by IV to get contractions started. The contractions could break her water. If not, the doctor will break it later. Vito arrived. I'm now in the cafeteria getting coffee and writing. I'll go back now.

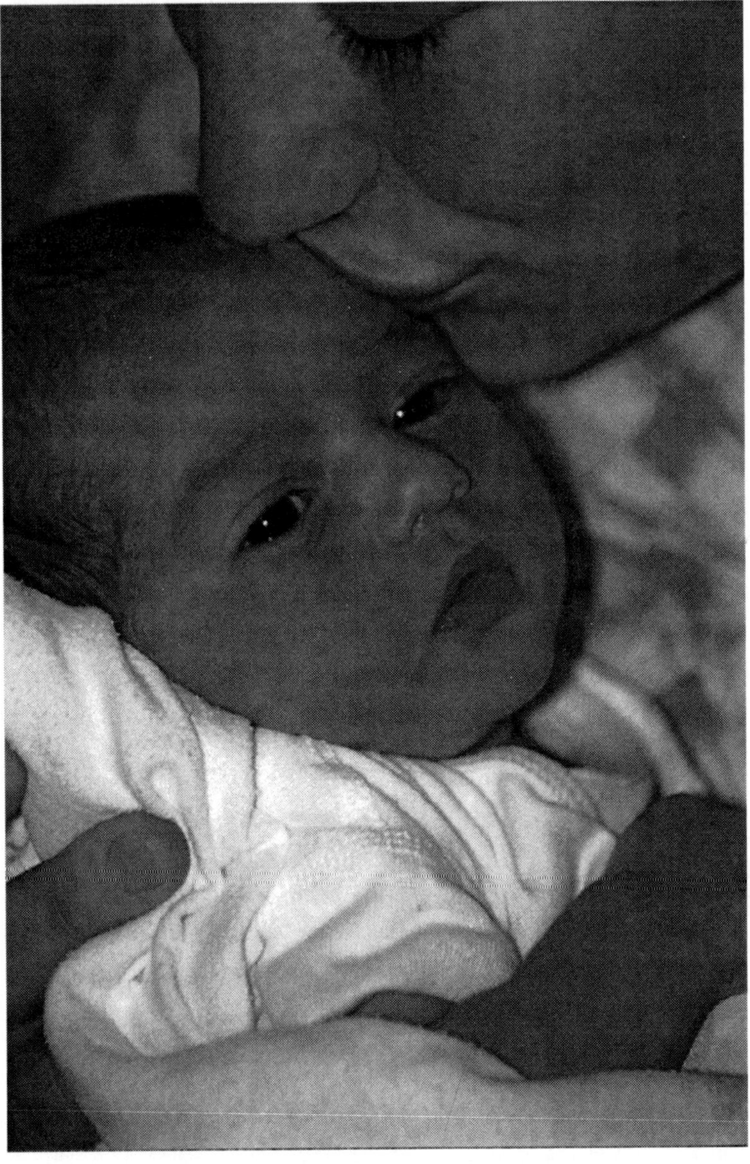

Grace's water broke around 5:30 p.m. The nurses have steadily been increasing Pitocin all day. Grace got her first pain medication around 6:30. Nurses checked her at 7. Grace was 3 cm. dilated and 80% effaced. Grace received an epidural around 8:30 p.m. Then the nurse put her on oxygen for the baby.

Baby Journey Leigh was born at 11:32 p.m. She was 7 lbs., 6 oz. and 20 inches long. APGAR scores were 9 and 9. Beautiful baby and she looks like Grace.

Grace's friends arrived at 11:30, but came in after the birth. Vito drove me back to the room after 2 a.m. I couldn't sleep until 3 a.m.

I love this hospital. They put a hospital bracelet on me (as well as Grace and Journey) because, "You're the baby's mother, aren't you?"

May 19, 2000

Woke around 7:30, ate, dressed, and walked to hospital. It took an hour and a half. Vito had spent the night with Grace. John called. I spent the afternoon with Grace and Journey. I walked back to my room around 6:15/6:30. I bought dinner and ate it. Then I walked to Target for diapers, wipes, and baby clothes. By the time I returned to the room, John and the kids were in town. We camped out with sleeping bags in the room, while John went to the hospital to meet his daughter.

May 20, 2000

Up early with the children. We ate a continental breakfast. John swam with the kids while I packed. Before we left, Grace called to say they were discharging her and the baby that day. We arrived at the hospital about Noon. The attorney was there with papers for Grace and us to sign. Grace could not find her picture ID, which delayed things a bit.

The children were very excited about seeing their new sister. On the walk down a hospital hall, K.J. turns to me, slaps his forehead with his hand, and exclaims, "What am I going to do with three sisters?!" Emily, K.J., and Skye loved Journey and couldn't wait to hold her. While we waited, the kids bounced off walls in an empty patient room. Vito had to work, so we were going to drive Grace to Sunset Beach.

Mid-afternoon, we went to check-in at an extended stay hotel. No luck. Everything in Wilmington was booked for the weekend. We also had a hard time finding a rental car for Journey and me to use for the week.

We picked-up Grace, dealt with the discharge process, and drove to Sunset Beach. A friend of Grace's arranged for us to stay at a resort apartment for $110 a night. Then Catherine offered her condo to Journey and me for the week after the rest of the family left. Grace didn't have her key. She had forgotten she gave it to the landlord so he could fix her flooded carpet. We went back to Calabash and the restaurant to get Vito's key. I gave Grace a photo album with pictures as we parted company. The "resort apartment" had no air conditioning! But we did the best we could. Journey ate at 12:30 a.m. and slept until 5 a.m.

May 21, 2000

The kids were up early, but John fed them. At 9 a.m. we went swimming. Skye found a frog and wanted to keep it as a pet. Emily has the magic touch with Journey. She wants to feed and hold her all the time. Catherine came by and took Skye and me to see her place and get the information on what to do. I made lunch while the others cleaned-up. The family left after 1 p.m. Emily and I were super-sad. Journey had a fussy two hours in the late evening, then ate and slept 5 hours, ate and slept more.

May 22, 2000

We checked out at 10 a.m. and drove to a K-Mart in North Myrtle Beach to buy baby clothes, blankets, and formula, and to develop pictures. We moved in to Catherine's condo. Later we walked to the Food Lion and bought groceries. The baby carrier works great. Journey had another two hours of fussiness late in the evening and then a 5-hour sleep, followed by more sleep.

May 23, 2000

I typed one of the home studies. We walked, did laundry, and just hung-out. Spoke with Grace who says she is doing fine and resting to be prepared to work this weekend.

May 24, 2000

Another great sleep night. Journey was fussy until 12, but slept until 5:45, ate, and went back to sleep. Sleepy day for Journey. She barely budged while I shopped for bottles and diapers at Wal-Mart, and then walked around Calabash taking pictures. I also did my exercise routine. Journey became alert around 5:30 p.m. and then was fussy until about 11 p.m. Made a plan to see Grace tomorrow.

May 25, 2000

Journey slept until 4 a.m., ate, and slept again until 10:15. Did exercise routine again. Started laundry. Made a to-do list. Rainstorm and no lights. Out to dinner in Little River with Vito and Grace. Journey awake. Catherine came home.

May 26, 2000

Catherine watched Journey while I ran 3.3 miles and walked to the grocery store. Took Journey to Larry's Seafood and saw Grace and friends.

ICPC screw-up. North Carolina administration leaves early. We are stuck through Memorial Day.

§ § §

Back in Atlanta, John sent an email to family and friends:

This is John again writing to update you on Rebecca and Journey. They are still stuck in North Carolina!!!

Unfortunately for all of us who miss Rebecca terribly and are dying to spend more time with Journey, we have not yet received the approval from the individual responsible in NC that would allow our two loved ones to return to their home state. We hope that will occur Tuesday. In the meantime, Rebecca asked me to send this email so you would know why you haven't heard from her or why she hasn't responded to a call or an email.

As for Journey, she is doing very well. And why wouldn't she be: she's getting what every Falco child wants, Mama's undivided attention. They are bonding quite nicely, and Journey is even letting Rebecca get upwards of 5 hours continuous sleep at night. I'm sure that habit will change right about the time they get home. I have been assured that I have not yet missed out on any walking, talking, nor even teething. In fact, they tell me it's only been two weeks that Rebecca hasn't been here. I would have sworn it's been months. Hang in there. Rebecca will return to this computer someday soon. In the meantime, thanks for all your thoughts and prayers. They mean a lot to us. –John

§ § §

From May 27th to 30th, I continued to chronicle when Journey slept and ate, where we went, and how much exercise I got. I took Journey to the beach. I tried to figure out my future with four children. Catherine was a great conversationalist. Journey and I met with Grace again.

Email to family members and friends on June 1, 2000

Journey and I returned Tuesday night. When the word finally came on May 30th that Journey and I could leave, Grace and Catherine (her honorary birth-grandmother) were with us. We said our "good-byes" and "see you soon(s)." I drove the 50 miles back to Wilmington and got a stand-by flight home.

It was great to get home, though I knew the real adjustment was only beginning. Emily, K.J., and Skye almost gobbled Journey up. They wanted to hold her and feed her and smother her with kisses. They were pretty glad to see me, too. I really missed them all. The only sad thing was that John missed the homecoming. He has been gone Tuesday, Wednesday, and Thursday (today). My mother, who can only be described as an angel, has taken care of the three older children when John and I were away. Now she is helping me get adjusted to being the mother of four.

I still have most of my emails to read. If you've written, I will respond soon–I hope. Be patient. Thank you for all your prayers and warm thoughts/wishes. This is a miracle. I hope you will get to meet Journey soon. I will be sending a birth announcement and picture in the next few days so you can see just how beautiful (and strong and smart and kind…) she really is.

§ § §

Catherine wrote the next day to say:

I have looked at the entire experience as truly a spiritual thing that happened to us 4 females: Journey, Rebecca, Grace, and Catherine. Take care and hug our baby for me.

I could not have said it better myself.

Email to Catherine from Rebecca on June 7, 2000

I talked with Grace yesterday and she sounded good. I should be getting a birth announcement out soon. Journey is doing well. The first 24 hours were a little hairy as she made the adjustment to the noise and siblings who wanted to hold, feed, carry, and touch her all the time. Emily is actually very helpful and nurturing. K.J. is gentle and helpful at times too. Skye wants to be helpful, but so far she mostly distresses Journey because Skye is in her face, stroking and touching her. John got home from a business trip and is learning the routine.

We've got a double birthday pool party for Emily and K.J. tomorrow and we are trying to get the bedrooms ready for our new family. This requires moving K.J. to Skye's room and moving Skye and Journey to K.J.'s room (which is the bigger room). It means painting both rooms and building a loft for K.J. It means sorting through everybody's stuff and figuring out which furniture, shelves, boxes, etc. go in each room. In other words, we are busy.

Journey went to the doctor yesterday. She is up to 8 lbs. 2 oz. She seems healthy and perfect. Several of the staff members came in to see her and hear the story.

§ § §

While I was stuck in North Carolina waiting for approval to come home, I had contacted my friend, Lee Highsmith, asking her and her husband, Bucky, to be Journey Leigh's godparents. We chose John's younger sister, Julie Falco, as Journey's other godparent.

Journey's birth announcement read: *To Announce the Birth of Journey Leigh Falco, 7 lbs., 6 oz., 20 inches, on May 18, 2000, in Wilmington, North Carolina. Born in Love to Her Birthmother Grace [Last Name]. Given in Love to Her Adoptive Family Rebecca and John Falco, Emily, Kevin John, and Skye*

On the back of the announcement, we included an explanation of Journey's name: "Naming a child is an awesome responsibility. Our older children, Emily and Kevin, are named for two people we love and admire (Emily Saliers and Kevin Elden). With the third child, Skye (meaning "scholar"), we looked for a name with a meaning that would honor her birthmother. Our fourth child's name also pays tribute to her birthmother. Grace has been on a "journey" to emotional and financial stability. In the course of her journey, Grace found us on our own journey to find the child who would complete our family. For Grace and for us, our journeys have sometimes been very difficult, complete with moments of despair, and experiences that gave us reasons not to trust in the way that trust is necessary for an open adoption. But, miraculously, like two puzzle pieces meant only for each other, we met. And together we create a picture of Journey who begins her life's journey supported by the love of her parents, our Creator, and all of you who, in different ways, made our meeting possible."

§ § §

I resumed my journal writing when I could. No longer did I write about pursuing adoption. I was consumed with day-to-day parenting. I wrote of potty training, gas management, Journey's milestones, sleep habits, behavioral problems, and learning issues.

As a feminist who had worked in religious and academic communities, and in the fields of adoption and sexual violence recovery, I knew that language was important. Persons could feel alienated by words. For example, "God the Father" might not comfort a survivor of incest. Her father or stepfather may have been her abuser. God the Nurturer, the Mother, the Creator might be better choices. In adoption, there were also language issues.

In September 2000, I wrote to the director of Skye's school to point out one such issue:

> I would like to suggest that you change a word in your 'Authorization to Consent to Medical Treatment for a Minor

Child' form. The word is natural, as in 'natural parent.' I am the mother of four children by adoption. My husband and I are their legal parents, not their guardians. Using the word 'natural' alienates me. If I am not the 'natural parent,' am I an unnatural parent? And what does 'natural' mean anyway? Does it mean biological parent? As I am sure you know, most parents who have become parents by means of adoption have been through years of emotional, physical, and financial agony to become mother or father. I hope you can adjust the wording of the form to respect the position of all parents, whether biological or not.

§ § §

One final story from a memorable 2000:

Email to family members and friends on December 27, 2000

Our church had a 6 p.m. "child-friendly" service this year. Several of the children dressed-up to be characters in the Christmas story. Journey was asked to be Baby Jesus. Skye was an angel. K.J. was a shepherd. Emily was a lamb.

Unfortunately, Skye had not been feeling well for several days and was actually running a fever off and on. But, she wanted desperately to be an angel. We spent a day going from store to store looking for the right costume. Finally, we found a white leotard with a large gold star on the front and small stars on the puffy sleeves. There was also a white tutu with a large gold star to match. She wore white tights and shoes. The church provided a halo and angel wings.

I should also mention that I called my mother at 8:30 a.m. on Christmas Eve and said, "I don't have anything to make a shepherd's costume. Can you help?" It won't surprise many of you that K.J. was the best-dressed shepherd in his newly sewn garment that night.

At the time we arrived at church to dress the children, about 5:20, Skye was feeling good. However, once the service began, the children were required to sit with their parents for an hour, waiting their time to perform. Imagine 3 and 4 year olds "patiently" waiting for an hour. Indeed, the minister's son, a 6-year-old, had undressed from his cow costume and was rolling around in front of the pews by the time the children were called into action. Our seven-month-old baby Jesus was bopping up and down. She had lost her "swaddling clothes" and was practicing deep knee bends in my lap, dressed only in a diaper.

By 7 p.m., Skye's fever had returned and she had almost fallen asleep in my mother's lap. At the appropriate time, Emily the lamb, K.J. the shepherd, and Journey the baby, took their places at the front of the church. Groggy Skye never made it past the front pew. Everything proceeded smoothly for a while, but then Journey became agitated. Mother Mary, a young teenager, popped a pacifier in Baby Jesus' mouth. That worked for about 30 seconds. Meanwhile, a soloist stood above at the lectern, beautifully singing "O Holy Night" as the baby wailed. I leaned across to Skye and whispered, "Do you think you could take this bottle to Journey?" The next thing we see is a lovely angel walking to the front of the church, handing a baby bottle to the lamb, who hands it to Mary, who feeds the baby. The crying stops. The angel turns and returns to the pews.

A few minutes later, when the lights are dimmed and the candles lit, the little angel donned her halo and returned to the front of the church to stand with the host of angels while we sang "Silent Night."

Living with Inequalities In Open Adoption

January 2001 to April 2002

Not all open adoptions are created equal. I worried about those inequalities. Emily and K.J. had relationships with and/or knowledge about both of their birth parents. Skye and Journey were in a different position. Neither of the younger girls knew their biological father. It was too soon to explore Journey's paternal heritage. But enough time had passed since Skye's birth that I thought I could look for Skye's biological father without ruffling any feathers. If he was not a safe person with whom she could have a relationship, I would find that out and deal with it. Skye was young enough that she didn't even need to know that I was looking.

I did an Internet "White Pages" search for all the Samuel or Sam *[last name]* in the metro Atlanta area. Then I sent a letter to each possible candidate, telling him who we were, describing what we understood about his relationship with Christina, and enclosing a recent picture of Skye. I defined open adoption and asked that he be willing to have some contact with us too. I did not receive any responses....

We stayed very busy in 2001. In our annual letter at the end of the year, I would summarize the activities of our everyday life:

Winter 2001

> Emily was in First Grade and K.J. was in Pre-K at Laurel Ridge Elementary School. Skye was in a 3-year-old class at Decatur 1st UMC. Journey went to Children's Morning Out, one day a week. Emily played basketball and Skye took a dance class at the YMCA. Emily and K.J. took karate in Midtown. Emily began working with a reading tutor. Rebecca and John continued as

co-chairs of the Family Council at St. Mark UMC, organizing events such as Happy Adoption Day, the Blessing of the Animals, and "That's A Family."

John continued work at Kingsley Associates. Rebecca continued very part-time contract work with The Giving Tree, doing home studies, and with the DeKalb County courts, doing adoption investigations. Rebecca's 43rd Birthday Challenge included a 10-mile run, 28-mile bike ride, 5-mile walk, 43 tennis ball returns, and 43 baskets made. K.J., Skye, and Rebecca took the Amtrak train to Washington, D.C., for a long weekend to visit with our friends, the Musicantes.

Spring 2001

In March, Rebecca and John took a marvelous 10th anniversary trip to Miami, leaving Rebecca's parents in charge of the children. (Helen was limping when we returned.) Rebecca had Lasik surgery to correct severe near-sightedness. The whole family took a trip to Chicago to visit the LaRussos, and to Nebraska to visit Emily's and K.J.'s birth families. K.J. met his twin brothers, Adam and Chad, for the first time. Renovations on our home began. These included remodeling the kitchen, redoing and adding hardwood floors, and replacing windows.

K.J. started spring soccer season. We co-hosted an Easter Tea and Egg Hunt with another family. Our family attended Rebecca's 10 Year Law School Reunion and John's 15 Year College Reunion at Duke University. Journey celebrated her first birthday on May 18th. Rebecca's article, "The Journey to Journey," was published in *Adoption Today* magazine.

Summer 2001

Emily and K.J. chose to have birthday parties at our community pool. Emily started her 2nd season on the Pangborn Swim Team and K.J. started T-Ball. Emily went to swim practices in the mornings, followed by "summer school" with Teacher Rebecca. Skye and K.J. attended several fun-filled weeks of morning camps. Rebecca participated in the weeklong Bike Ride Across Georgia. This year, it started in Hartwell and ended at St. Simons Island–387 miles. John brought the children down for the final three days, and the family spent an additional day enjoying the beach together. John then had "minor surgery"–which felt like major surgery–on his left shoulder.

In July, nephews Joshua *[my brother Marcus's son]* and John David *[my sister Joanna's son]* were born. Emily went through educational and behavioral testing. We learned that she has auditory and visual processing problems. When school began, she took some supplementary tests. The result, by November, was that Emily spends part of her school day with resource teachers to help with language arts and math. She seems to be responding well to this program.

The girls traveled to Myrtle Beach, SC, to visit Journey's birthmother, Grace. The entire family then took an end-of-the-summer trip to Chattanooga, TN. Skye celebrated her 4th birthday with a party that included hunting for eggs filled with plastic bugs, several "messy" arts and crafts, dress-up, and swimming. Skye started Pre-K at Laurel Ridge. Emily started Second Grade and K.J. entered Kindergarten. Three children at one school!

Fall 2001

Emily and K.J. played fall soccer. Journey attended the Preschool at the Heights, four mornings a week. Rebecca and Journey took a 10-week Music Class. K.J. and Skye took gymnastics. Emily discovered that one of her gifts is working with the severely handicapped children at her school. The family attended a wonderful retreat at Camp Glisson with other church members.

On September 11th, John was in New York City–Midtown, not Downtown. The day before, I had run past a home for sale, less than a mile from our house. We were about to start a new remodeling project, but I wasn't sure we were doing the right thing. I arranged to see the home-for-sale right away. On September 11th, I called John to say, "Are you all right? This is crazy, but you need to get home and see a house that I've fallen in love with. You will too." He did. On September 13th, we signed a contract to buy our new home. Then, in a sluggish market, we miraculously sold our first house in 22 days. On Thanksgiving Day, Rebecca ran the Atlanta Marathon, slowly and with a lot of pain–but successfully! The next day, the movers came for our furniture.

Winter again

As Christmas approached, we, along with some relatives and friends, adopted two families from DFCS and the Women's Resource Center to make Christmas possible for them. We also purchased a goat for a needy family in a third world country and participated in other service projects. The end of November and December has been spent unpacking and organizing our new home. Our goal was to make the house presentable in time for our annual Caroling and Potluck Party last weekend. We hope to have a more restful end of December now.

§ § §

I reported on our trip to visit Journey's birthmother in August. We did not know it would be the last time we would see or hear from her for years to come.

Email to family members and friends on August 7, 2001

Emily, Skye, Journey and I have just returned from a trip to Myrtle Beach, SC to visit with Journey's birthmother, Grace.

Grace had not seen Journey since we left to return to Georgia after Journey was born in May 2000. We had been invited to stay with Grace, who doesn't have extra beds or kid stuff, so we had lots of bags to manage on our trip: a port-a-crib (which Journey refused to sleep in), a duffel bag with sleeping bags, 3 suitcases, a car seat, and a stroller, plus the backpack stuff the girls wanted on the plane. (By the way, John and K.J. stayed home for their last tee-ball game and two birthday parties. They said they would otherwise be sitting around in their underwear watching baseball on TV.)

Vito (Grace's boyfriend of more than a year and a half) works at a restaurant many hours–usually 10 a.m. to 1 a.m., 6 days a week. Grace was working as a hostess at the restaurant until recently. Now she is dancing 3 or 4 nights a week, which is less exhausting to her. When we arrived after midnight, they were blowing up an air mattress for us. Other than their mattress and box springs, a sofa and a TV, the townhouse was completely unfurnished. That worked out fine because it gave the kids more room to run and roll around. Grace looked great. Every time I look at her, I think how beautiful she is.

Although we got to bed no sooner than 2 a.m., the girls were up by 7. Grace and Vito continued to sleep while we ate some of the snacks we brought with us and dressed for a trip to the beach. The beach was just minutes away. The girls collected shells, but were afraid of the waves. After playing there for a while, we headed back, stopping by the grocery store to accumulate enough food to last for our three-day trip. Back home, we ate and I forced us all to take naps. Once refreshed, we walked over to the pool. Grace joined us and enjoyed the way Journey leaps to me fearlessly in the pool, kicking and moving her arms to "swim."

After swimming, Emily found a Christmas video in Grace's house and wanted to watch it several times. Grace went outside to smoke and the girls followed her. Emily began saying to Grace, for the first of 100 times, "Smoking is so disgusting. I can't stand the smell." Grace was very patient with her and conceded that it was not a good habit. Skye asked, "Why do you smoke?" Grace responded, "I don't know." Emily told her she should stop. Grace said, "I don't know how." Skye interjected, "Why don't you do the Noodle Dance?" For those of you who are not big followers of cartoons, there is one called P, B, & J Otter. Whenever the otters can't figure out a problem, they do a Noodle Dance and the answer occurs to them.

For dinner, I went out to find pizza, leaving Grace to watch the girls. That gave her some time to bond with Journey.

On Sunday, Vito did not have to be at work until 2 p.m., so we all went to the beach. Vito brought his boogie board and tried to teach Emily how to ride waves. Grace seemed particularly pleased that Vito was doing something fun and relaxing. This was the first time they had been to the beach all summer! Skye finally got comfortable with me holding her in the waves. Journey dug and piled wet sand.

After the beach and some sandwiches, we went back to the pool. Skye went from holding on to the edge to paddling around in her padded suit to jumping off the side to taking off the suit and swimming to me under her own power! It was amazing.

Catherine, the friend of Grace's who had allowed Journey and me to stay with her in North Carolina after the baby was released from the hospital, came by to see us in the afternoon. It was great to see her. She has been my email contact with Grace since Journey's birth.

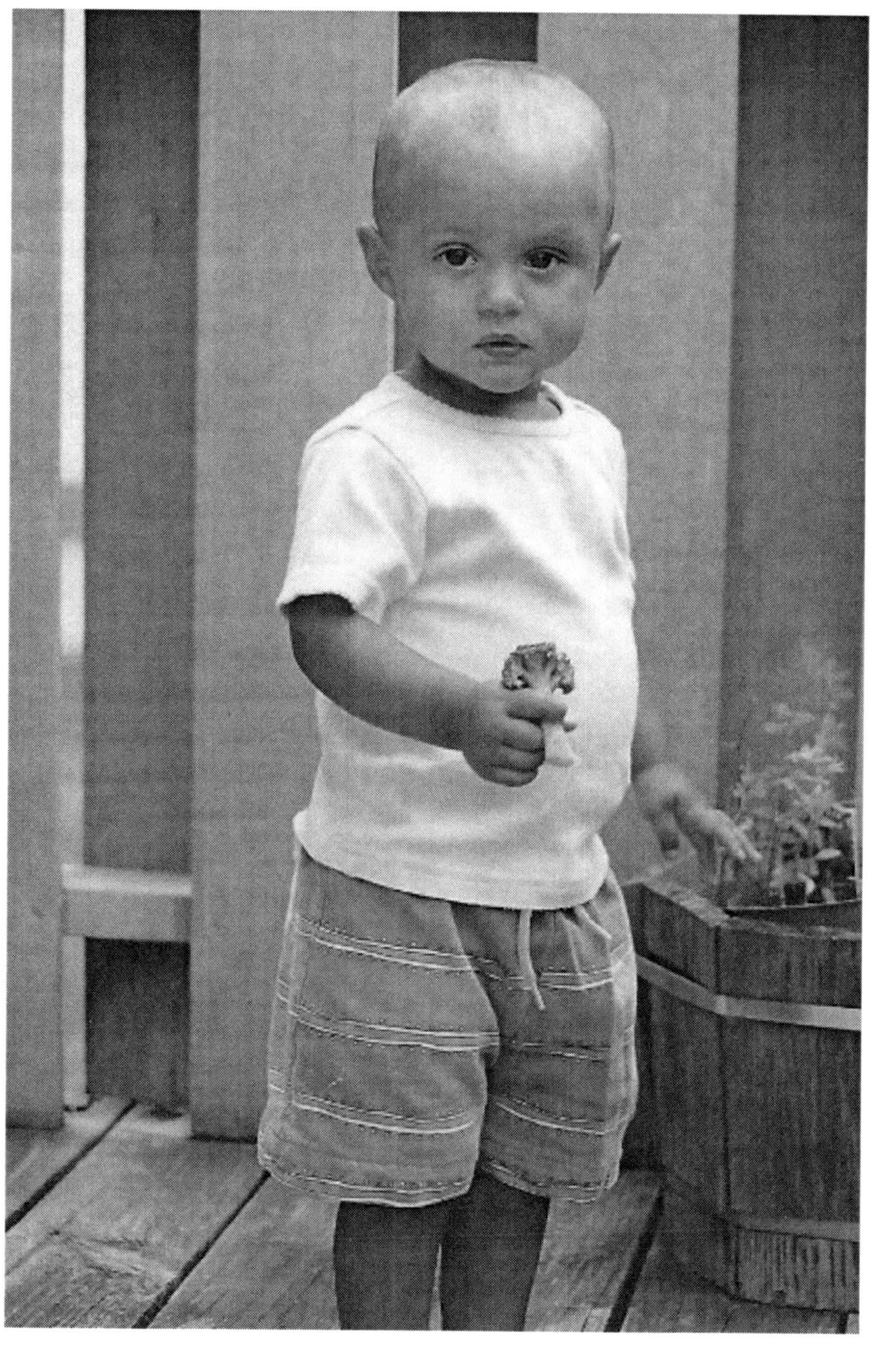

That evening, we went to the Aquarium at Broadway on the Beach. The kids had a GREAT time, and Grace had never been to the Aquarium either. They saw stingrays and sharks swimming overhead, all kinds of crabs and beautiful fish, etc. In one area, you could pick up a horseshoe crab. Once I got brave enough to do it and showed Skye how, she must have picked up all 20-30 floating around in the trough, demonstrating the technique to child and adult alike. After the Aquarium, we walked, ate ice cream, and played at the playground before heading home to bed.

On Monday, we hung close to home. We swam at the pool and packed. I could tell that Grace was getting sad, but holding back the tears. When it was time to leave for the airport, we did a pretty good job of appreciating each other, I think.

That brings me to one thing I want to share, but don't know if I can express it very well. I have this great sadness about taking away another mother's child. Don't get me wrong: I know each of my children's mothers made sane and loving decisions. And, I have never heard or suspected that any of them later or now feel the decision was wrong. Still, there is this sadness in addition to an overwhelming gratefulness and joy about being the mother of Emily, K.J., Skye, and Journey.

§ § §

In late August, I learned about some developments in Christina's life from a conversation with her mother, Eve. Christina had given birth to two more children after Skye. Isaac had been born in April 1999. A second boy, Jacob, was born in August 2000. We didn't see Christina often. That was her decision. The last time we had seen her had been in the Spring when she came by to get our double stroller for her boys. Accordingly to Eve, Christina had been arrested in July and the children went into temporary custody of DeKalb County Department of Family and Children Services (DFCS). They were in separate foster care homes. I would later read the Guardian Ad Litem report (dated July 7, 2002) stating that Christina "was escorted to the DeKalb Crisis Unit and admitted after the police found her in her apartment with the door open, furniture in disarray, holes in the wall of the apartment, and a strong odor of alcohol coming from her person. She was in a distraught and aggravated state. There was very little food in the home and the children were dirty and in need of a diaper changing." Eve told me that Christina was not doing what she needed to do to get them back.

I couldn't help myself–my first thought was: "If Christina can't get the boys back, I want to adopt them because they are Skye's brothers." We were not looking to adopt again as a general matter. But these are Skye's half-biological siblings! However, when I told John the story and my reaction, his eyes bugged-out and he asked for a hammer to begin smashing in his head. I couldn't believe it! How could we see or feel things so differently? Surely, if I pushed him… but did I want to "win" by bullying, and live with that the rest of our lives?

I reasoned that chances were very good that Christina could pull it together and get her kids back. If she couldn't, chances were also good that one or more or her relatives would want to raise the boys. So, I really didn't know if it was worth making an issue of this with John. Nevertheless, I knew that I would continue to think about this mini-drama being played-out in the DFCS-world until it was resolved….

In September, Michelle called to tell me that she and her boyfriend Mike are getting married on October 27th. I had always loved Michelle, but she often seemed unhappy to me. She seemed different now. She acknowledged that moving away from Columbus was a positive step for her. When we last saw her in the Spring, Mike was injured from a work-related accident and Michelle was unemployed. I was worried about that. Now, Mike was back to truck driving. Michelle had steady work with disabled adults until a couple of months ago when she learned that her excessive weight gain, no menstrual periods in 3 years, wild mood swings, etc. were due to a benign pituitary gland tumor.

Now that she was on medication, she felt much better. For Emily's sake, she also wanted me to know that the condition was not hereditary.

Michelle said something about Mike being supportive of her adoption plan with Emily. We talked a little about that and my experiences with other birthmothers, and she helped me realize (again) how important that support is. One of the things I really love about Michelle is how seriously she took/takes her commitment to us and Emily and how much she loves Emily.

By November, I was ready to share what I'd learned about the ongoing Christina-situation with select family and friends. After giving some background, I reported:

> The last time Christina saw Isaac and Jacob was around August 8th for Jacob's first birthday party at DFCS. She has not complied with the requirements to get her children back. These include attending a parenting class and alcohol treatment. She has not kept a steady job. She told the DFCS caseworker that Isaac and Jacob have the same father. She didn't tell them about her first child, now 8 or 9 years old, who is being raised by his paternal grandparents. As of last Sunday, she was in jail in Cobb County related to a debt she failed to pay back.
>
> The Falco kids and I recently met the foster parents with Isaac and Jacob at DFCS so that Skye could spend some time with them. Skye, Journey and I have just been to visit with Skye's birth-grandmother, aunts and uncle who live there. They always express gratitude for our contact. This time, Skye's grandmother spent most of her time worrying aloud about Christina and her inability to get the boys back. She and the rest of the family are scared about losing contact with Isaac and Jacob.
>
> I am torn. There is a part of me that is certain John and I should declare ourselves available to adopt Isaac and Jacob should Christina not get them back. In the interim, we should foster parent them so that they can live together. They are Skye's

brothers. Further, with us, they could continue to have contact with their birth relatives because of our commitment to open adoption.

On the other hand, the 'cons' stack up: John is overwhelmed with work and the move to a new house, and can't even think about adding more responsibilities to his plate. What would adding two more children do to our four? Is it fair to them? The current foster parents seem fine. Are Isaac and Jacob better off in homes where they are one of two instead of one of six children? Does the biological relationship mean that much, really? Yes, they would want to know each other, but do they necessarily need to live in the same family? Christina is likely to pull herself together again, at least temporarily. If the children were in and out of our home, would that be more harmful than good for them? Could I be a good enough mother to SIX children? Others do it, but could I? And if I could, if John could, what would we sacrifice? What would we gain?

I will confess that if I had to decide today about whether or not to foster parent and, possibly, adopt Isaac and Jacob, I would say 'yes.'

§ § §

I received some advice from a counselor who cautioned me not to place too much emphasis on biological ties. What these boys needed was the love and stability of a permanent home, and the Falcos might have a role to play in finding that home–even if it wasn't ours. She also cautioned that becoming certified foster parents would not guarantee the boys' adoption by us or any other parents. DFCS's goal was reunification with the biological parent(s). Christina would likely get her children back.

I heard every logical, well-reasoned thing she said. And then I followed my heart anyway. In spite of a promise I had made to John not to discuss the foster care situation until the new year, I contacted DFCS in early December to get an application for the Model Approach to Partnerships in Parenting ("MAPP") course that was the first step toward becoming certified foster parents.

On January 5, 2002, we went to Christina's mother's house. I had promised that we'd make one more visit before the holidays were over. We learned that Christina had been in jail for seven weeks. She would be getting out in four days. "Christina is saying all the right things now about working to get her boys back," said Eve. We were startled to learn that Christina was *pregnant* again. According to Eve, this father wanted her to run off to Texas with him and leave Isaac and Jacob. He also didn't want her to have a relationship with Doug, the friend who found her an apartment and bought her a car. Doug had a steady job at a local television station. I couldn't imagine that Christina was ready to give up Doug's support.

My gut reaction to this information was to want to take care of the boys. I was worried and sorry for them. It wasn't fair what Christina was doing to her babies. Why did I have to care? Why couldn't I just be grateful for my lovely, demanding, delightful daughter Skye, and *not feel* for Christina's boys?

I shared the stories of Christina with select friends by email:

Email to close friends and family on February 6, 2002

Today, Skye and I went to DFCS in DeKalb County to visit her half-brother, Isaac, and birthmother, Christina. (Jacob, the younger brother, was supposed to be there too, but his foster family did not show up.)

By January, John and I had both come to the conclusion that we should go through the MAPP 30-hour training program for foster parents, to be in a position to take both boys into our home if Christina had not gotten the boys back by the time we were certified as foster parents. We both thought it would be better for them to be together, if possible.

Today, Christina showed-up! She was charming, convincing, and motherly toward Isaac. And, clearly, he knew her and missed her. I watched as two social workers bought every word of her enthusiasm about single parenting and doing what she needed to do to reclaim her children. I silently thought about all the times she had not followed through. I thought about the years trying to keep tabs on her as she changed addresses, changed phones, changed jobs, and changed men. I thought about her history of opportunistic behavior. And, now, her mother and stepfather were going to buy her a car with their tax refund. This is a family who lives in a very small, rented house, heated by a kerosene stove, with three teenagers, and supported by the paycheck of a mother with health problems who works in a factory. Doug, the friend who loves her, is getting her a phone and provides other support. Christina doesn't have a job.

And yet, she could make it. She could pull it together if she really wanted to, if she really tried. It wouldn't be the life I'd choose, but so what? Who am I to judge? And so, I find myself more comfortable than I ever would have imagined… waiting. John and I will take the MAPP course; and we'll be ready in the event those children need us. But maybe they won't. And we will applaud Christina for doing what needed to be done to give her children a happy, healthy, safe, and loving home.

§ § §

In mid-February, I wrote to Grace to ask if we could visit her during our Spring Break trip in April, on our way to New York. We had not heard from her in a few months. I got no response to my letter.

Email to family and friends dated February 22, 2002

We are bogged-down in paperwork related to the MAPP class

that John and I are taking. We also have to complete a new home study that includes special requirements and forms that are not part of the usual private/agency adoption home study. I'm irritated about the time and money it takes to get new physicals, statements from pediatricians and vets, drug screens and fingerprints, etc., but I still feel like we are doing the right thing. The more I think about it, the more I'm convinced that fostering Christina's boys is a natural extension of our "openness." Aren't you supposed to help out family, if and when you can? I mean, it wouldn't be helpful to bail her out financially. Given her track record, that would not really help her over the long term. But, making sure her boys are growing up together, instead of in separate foster homes, is a good thing, a helpful thing, I think.

Last night, at the session of the MAPP course, I was talking to the instructor about our situation. I told her that Isaac and Jacob were in two separate foster homes, and I wondered if it would be a priority with their caseworker to move them to a home where they could be together–especially if the children are thriving in their separate homes. The instructor said that the move would, more than likely, be made because Skye is their sister. Did you hear that? For years now, I've been teaching and preaching that love makes a family, not blood. But in the world of our government, it is blood, not love, that counts first.

§ § §

Email to select family and friends dated March 5, 2002

Last week, Christina's social worker, Sandy, agreed that it would make the boys' transition back to their mother easier if they were in a foster home together. (She also brought up the fact that they would be with their sister–a confusing point to me, but it seemed to be working in my favor.) Moreover, Sandy said that when Christina showed-up unexpectedly at the county office demanding to see Jacob, she had exclaimed, "If only Rebecca had them!"

Christina told Sandy that she was diagnosed with bipolar disorder when she was in jail last Fall. Sandy wanted to get her records, but Christina protested that it was her private business. My guess is that Christina doesn't want Sandy to know she is pregnant. Sandy said there was to be a staffing on the case at the end of the week and encouraged me to call her afterwards to find out how the group felt about the plan to move the boys to our house.

Today I called Sandy. She snapped, "I have no control over placement. Someone else makes that decision. The boys are fine in their separate homes. Unless someone makes a complaint or they are not doing well, they probably won't be moved." Then she softened a little. She said they need to go back to court and set new goals for Christina based on the information about her mental illness. Is she mentally competent to be a parent, or can she be?

Before I called, I had a brainstorm. I thought how great it would be if the boys moved in with us right after we returned from our driving trip to New York in mid-April. Isaac will be three on April 18th. I imagined loading the boys, our family, and Christina in our new 12-passenger van, and taking a trip to Eve's house to have a birthday party with the grandparents, aunts and uncle. But, after I got off the phone with Sandy, I felt defeated and sad.

John and I had a conversation recently in which he shared his fears: that the boys would come to live with us, that we would enable Christina to see them, but that Christina would continue to live a lifestyle that prevented her from getting the boys back, and that this would go on forever. John has been worried that I am too anxious to adopt the boys and that I can't see the negative side of doing that. It's not true. Where we differ, at the present time, is that I see adoption as a possibility if Christina fails and if her family decides not to parent them. John can't contemplate adopting any other children.

As I sat with my sadness this afternoon, I realized that it is not about losing out on fostering or adopting. This is a time-consuming and rather expensive process we are going through. No. This has to do with my relationship to Christina. With our other children's birthmothers, I have never doubted their decisions to place their children with John and me. Certainly, they wished their circumstances had been different. And they each loved their babies enough to bring them into the world and to find good parents for them.

But, with Christina it has always felt a little different to me. She didn't want any contact with Skye in the hospital. All she wanted (after living expenses) was pictures when the baby was a few days old. However, a few months later she was pregnant again and "ready to parent," she said. I have always felt that Christina regretted her decision at some level. My perception of these circumstances has led me to feel guilty that I have Christina's daughter.

Getting back to the present. I think my sadness has to do with missing an opportunity to make this right with Christina. That is, my thinking is that if I do a good job taking care of her boys, she will come to appreciate me as a mother. Maybe she will even "give me permission" in some intangible way, to be Skye's mother. Does that make any sense at all? I don't know if you have to be an adoptive parent to understand the issue of "entitlement." I have spoken with other adoptive parents, and many of us seem to struggle with whether or not we deserve to be parents.

§ § §

In March 2002, I received a very enthusiastic and complimentary call from *Adoptive Families, Inc.* regarding an essay that I had submitted. They were going to publish it in their 10th Anniversary Anthology. *[That article, "All Things Considered," is included as Appendix C.]*

By April 15th, John and I had completed the MAPP class and home study requirements. We were now certified foster parents. Though we understood that Christina's boys would not be moved from their current homes, we decided to send a letter to DFCS explaining our position. In part, it read:

> We care about Christina and want her to succeed. She is our daughter's birthmother. Whatever happens with the boys, we will continue to have contact with her so long as it is not unsafe for Skye or her siblings. We will also continue to have contact with Skye's extended birth family.
>
> We can accept the plan for the boys to remain in their current foster care homes if the county, caseworkers, and panel believe that the boys are happy and healthy. We would like to be considered the "back-up" foster family. If Christina does not get her sons back, and if one or both of the foster families do not want to adopt either of the boys, we want to be considered as the next potential adoptive family.
>
> If Christina is not able to keep the baby she will give birth to this summer, we would like to be considered as the foster-adopt family for that child. *[By April 2002, DFCS had learned of Christina's pregnancy.]*

Becoming Foster Parents

May 2002 to March 2003

When summer swim team practice at our community pool began in May, we saw neighbors we had not seen since the previous summer. This year, I noticed that a neighbor's teenage daughter was pregnant, and I decided to send a letter to the teen's mother offering my support and help, if they needed it.

The teenager's mother, Roberta, did contact me. Although her daughter, Chelsea, had committed to work with a certain adoption agency, when the baby was born it became clear that the adoptive parents that she and James (the birth father) had selected were not willing to keep the adoption open. Chelsea brought the baby girl home from the hospital. I was asked to help the young couple find adoptive parents who had demonstrated a belief in open adoption. Chelsea emailed me with a list of specific requests regarding the parents.

Her requests included: that Faith (as the baby was named at that time) be brought up in the church, that the family already have another child, that the family plan to pay for college and other educational expenses, and that the couple be no older than 35 and married with no serious health problems. As I had learned through past experience, every birthmother has certain criteria for choosing adoptive parents. Sometimes, she (or they, if the father is involved), don't know what the criteria are until they meet the "perfect couple." I believed it was important to present Chelsea and James with as many choices as possible.

I sent out an email with a description of the situation and the specific requests. I asked each couple who was interested to send me a "profile letter" with pictures. Fifteen families responded and the review process began.

While I was in the midst of helping Chelsea and James sort through their options, I received a call from DFCS, on Monday, June 17th, requesting to place Isaac with us as his foster parents the following Saturday. The social worker explained that though Christina was *missing* for six months, she had contacted DFCS in February and began meeting the requirements to get her children back. Isaac's foster parents, among others, thought that Christina would have her children back by summer. Accordingly, they made plans to move to Virginia in July. However, it was now looking like Christina would not get the children back by July. DFCS needed a new foster home for Isaac. Would we take him? We said, "Yes."

On June 19th, Christina left a note on our door that she had "cussed-out" the DFCS worker and needed to talk. I tried to call, but her phone had stopped working.

On June 21st, Christina called in tears, stating that she was being evicted on Sunday and had no place to store her furniture and things. We agree to provide boxes and to assist her in storing what we could.

The next day, we picked-up Isaac and his belongings from the foster parents who were moving and drove him to our home. The same day, John helped Christina pack and store boxes. We had no room for the furniture.

On June 25th, Christina drove up to our house unexpectedly and asked to use our phone. She was homeless, jobless, without a working phone, and without gas money. She called several people, including her brother, her mother, and a friend who had given her all the furniture. She cursed at him for not bailing her out this time. Ultimately, she decided to go and stay with her mother, trusting that she'd figure out a way to get her furniture moved before the landlord put it on the street. She asked me for $10 for gas. I scraped together $5.00. Emily heard our conversation and volunteered to give Christina her only $3.00. Christina took it.

Two weeks later, Christina found someone with a truck to move her furniture to a storage unit. While she was in Atlanta, her mother called John and said, "If Christina calls, tell her that her stepfather says she can't stay with us anymore." Fortunately, John did not have to relay that message. We later learned that Christina had moved in with her grandmother.

Being Isaac's foster parents was harder than we imagined. Our house was full of young children: 2, 3, 4, 5, and 7 years old.

As we were adjusting to our new living arrangements, Chelsea and James chose adoptive parents for baby Faith, and I created an Open Adoption Agreement, which all parties signed, to reflect the intentions of the birth and adoptive parents. Though they were happy with their selection of new parents, the birth parents found it very difficult to let Faith go. In mid-July, I attended a special church service planned by the families for the physical transfer of custody from birth parents to adoptive parents. It was very moving, but also stressful and highly emotional. I wondered at how it had all gone so smoothly with the four Falco adoptions. Had I been so overwhelmed by my joy that I failed to truly *see* how painful it was for my children's birth parents? Or, was this a more difficult transition because the child had lived with her biological family for several weeks? They had held her and cared for and bonded with her.

This experience affected my perception of Christina as the custodial parent of Isaac for the first years of his life. I recognized it wasn't the same as placing Skye for adoption at birth, a child she had never held or bonded with. But how, exactly, did time spent with a child change what was best for a child in the long run? This was something I would puzzle over for months and years to come.

In early July, Christina called to tell me that she was having a baby girl in early August. She also said she had put her name on the list for government housing. She had applied to work at McDonalds where she would be trained as a manager.

On July 12, 2002, I attended a "Custody Extension/Judicial Review-In Lieu of Panel" hearing as Isaac's foster parent. Also in attendance were Christina, the Lewises (Jacob's foster parents), the attorney and representative from the Child Advocates Office, Sandy (the social worker assigned to the case), Sandy's supervisor, and the attorney for DFCS.

Prior to the hearing, as we were waiting outside the courtroom, I asked Christina what progress she had made. She said she would not be able to get the government housing, as the list of other people waiting was too long. However, a former landlord in her hometown was looking for a place for her. There was a shorter list there. She had started orientation at McDonalds.

At the hearing, Sandy reported that Christina was still working on her goals. Though she had completed the parenting class and alcohol assessment, she had not followed the recommendations. The county wanted a psychological evaluation done. The judge seemed alarmed that this had not been done already. The Child Advocates office offered that the children were doing well in their foster homes. The Lewises stated that they loved Jacob and wanted to adopt him. Christina told the court that she had met her goals, that she was living with her parents, that she had a job, that she would have housing next week, but that she could not provide an exact address today.

I felt very caught in the middle. When asked by the Court what I had to say, I talked about Isaac's progress. I did tell the judge that Christina had shown up unexpectedly, and that we probably needed to work on our boundaries now that we had Isaac as a foster child. I wrote notes to the Child Advocate every time Christina said something to the judge that was not true.

By the end of the hearing, Christina was sobbing and stating that she didn't understand what she had not done to get her kids back. She argued that the county was setting new hurdles for her. The judge suggested a "family conference"–a meeting of the interested parties, to talk through the goals and other issues. DFCS was directed to work with Polk County, where Christina currently lived, noting that the move would slow down the process. A Polk county worker would need to see the new home. A psychological evaluation would be done in the coming week. Christina protested that she could not do a drug screen that afternoon because her car barely made it to Atlanta, and she needed to get to a repair shop.

Nothing was said about the new baby coming. Nothing was said about how much money it takes to raise three kids, or how Christina was even going to make money with a new baby to care for. Nothing was said about childcare. Nothing was said about reliable transportation or a proven, steady income.

Afterward, while Christina was sobbing in the waiting area, the social workers and foster parents talked, noting that Christina had yet to take responsibility for anything. She always blamed someone else.

DFCS seemed to want the psychological evaluation done to justify beginning the process to terminate her parental rights. I didn't understand the process or criteria, but no one seemed to have much faith in Christina. A new reality was setting in: It was going to take a long time before we knew who Isaac would call his forever family.

The baby was due soon. The supervisor said to me, "When she calls you to say that the baby is here, call us. We will send someone out to do an assessment and maybe take the baby." It sucked being caught in the middle!

§ § §

With two children on the swim team and three more who enjoyed the water, we spent a lot of time at the community pool. Our neighbors, Russ and Naomi Griffin, also frequented the pool with their daughter, Jordan, a close friend of Skye's. The Griffins were very taken with Isaac–particularly Russ. The couple had wanted to have another child, but secondary infertility interfered with that plan. The Falcos were not having an easy time with Isaac. There were too many young children with too many needs in our home. It had already become clear to John and to me early in our stint as foster parents that, if Isaac became eligible for adoption, it would be hard for us to give him all the attention he needed and deserved. But, as I watched Russ interact with Isaac at the pool, an idea began to emerge: What if Russ and Naomi adopted Isaac?

I discussed my idea with John and we both decided to approach Russ and Naomi about becoming trained as foster parents in the event that Isaac, one day, might move to their home. I knew, at some level, that it was *crazy* and far-fetched to think that DFCS would play along with my scheme. After all, I had failed to get both boys, Isaac and Jacob, in my home, as was my original plan. But, it just felt *right* to me. I found myself dreaming the impossible dream in spite of the odds.

There was a family conference with Christina on July 16, 2002. At the conference, it was established that Christina still needed to: (1) have stable and consistent employment for six months; (2) find licensed childcare; (3) establish a safe home; (4) provide food every day; (5) show the ability to pay bills and utilities; and (6) provide for transportation, car insurance, car seats, diapers, and clothing.

Meanwhile, fulfilling my promise to K.J. that he could have a birthday with his Nebraska brothers, I took my older two and my baby on a trip. We left John with Skye and Isaac in Atlanta.

As time wore on, I realized that my motivation to become a foster parent for Christina's boys had been selfish. I had wanted to either win points with her *or* adopt again. Now that I was living the *reality* of foster parenthood, I knew there was no way to win points with Christina. I had not seen that clearly until she matter-of-factly took my 7-year-old's only $3.00 for gas money. She wasn't capable of appreciating what we did. To protect Isaac, I had to reveal his mother's ongoing lies to DFCS and take the chance of destroying our relationship. Without intending to, I had potentially jeopardized Skye's relationship with her birthmother.

God was getting a good laugh over my foolishness regarding the adoption motivation as well. Sure, there are some good times with

Isaac. But my other children also fought with him and picked on him because he didn't know all our ways of doing things. John and I found ourselves getting exasperated because he was different. When he would hurt Journey, I felt angry instead of compassionate. And when my children would tell me they wanted him to leave, I felt ashamed about having created this difficult situation.

I sent invitations to Skye's 5th birthday party. These included invitations to Christina, to her extended family, and to Jacob and his foster family. Christina's baby girl, Claire, was born on August 6, 2002, and Christina brought her to the party too.

Christina and her family believed I was supporting them. After all, we were storing Christina's boxes from her Decatur apartment and taking care of her boy. Jacob's foster family and many of our neighbors believed that Christina did not deserve to get her boys back. I really wanted to do the *right thing*–if I could just figure out what that was.

In mid-August, we took a vacation to the beach. Isaac loved the ocean. We had gotten him potty-trained. He could ride a two-wheel bike with training wheels, and he was swimming in the big pool. The older children started back to school in mid-August. Skye was in

Kindergarten. K.J. was in first grade. Emily was in third grade. In September, Isaac started a 3-year-old preschool class at University Heights UMC where Journey also attended the 2-year-old class. I also managed to get him a scholarship to take gymnastics at the YMCA. We received word from the Court Appointed Special Advocate ("CASA") that Christina was no longer living with her grandmother. However, no one seemed quite sure where she was living.

I kept a journal about our time together. This is an example I entitled, *Afternoons Here*:

> The children arrive home from school shortly after 3 p.m. K.J., chin on chest, informs me that he was not allowed to play on the playground today because he didn't take his homework and agenda to school–the very homework we had worked on diligently the day before. Of course, I had asked him to pack the work in his backpack after we finished and he told me that he had done so Emily has somehow managed to come home without homework for the third straight day. This has something to do with the partially-formed relationship between her homeroom teacher and her special education teacher. I hope this doesn't come back to haunt us. Emily can't find anything to do! When I suggest reading, she scoffs. She really wants to watch television–forbidden by her parents during the school week.
>
> Skip ahead. The chosen snack is candy. Foolishly, I agree, thinking this will help me de-clutter one of the kitchen cabinets. The older kids have tortured Isaac and Journey awake from their naps. K.J. is protesting the homework: five sentences with his spelling words. Says he can't do it. It's too hard. Homework isn't fair.... We spend an hour on the damn five sentences. Meanwhile, I'm orchestrating the candy eating, prepping dinner, and breaking up fights. Isaac wants constant companionship. Journey wants to paint. Where is Skye?

We haven't heard from John. He is on a company retreat. Do I plan to feed the children soon or wait for him? Will the children even eat the food I'm preparing? Why do I spend so much time preparing the week's menu and the grocery-shopping list, trying to provide variety, and the right amount of protein, vegetables, fruits, and dairy? At 5:30, knowing I'll never get dinner ready before Skye appears and starts tearing apart the cabinets looking for anything edible, I give in: "You can watch TV until suppertime, downstairs, in the playroom." Off go Emily, K.J., and Skye. Isaac is my constant companion and Journey wants to paint. I set them both up in the carport with a small set of watercolors, water cups, and small brushes. I'm outside every 5 minutes breaking up a fight because Isaac is painting on Journey's side of the paper. We've been over the rules dozens of times: Only paint on the paper–not your skin, not the carport, not each other. Even Journey can repeat the rules to me, and often does before asked.

I'm cooking and working on a framing a picture John took of me with Journey on our recent trip to the beach. By the time I reemerge from the basement with my picture framing supplies, Skye has made several trips to the playroom, walking in front of Emily and K.J., to retrieve materials and join the painters in the garage. I walk outside and the children are covered in red paint and water. Sponges, a large bottle of paint, a running hose, and soggy children fill the scene. I go crazy. "You know better than this! Take off those clothes, bring them here, and go inside to the bathtub!" After I start the tub, I run off to tell Emily and K.J. what a lousy job they did of monitoring what was going on before their very eyes. "You know Skye isn't supposed to take off with bottles of paint unsupervised! What were you thinking?! Turn off the TV and come be helpful!"

By the time I'm done yelling at the elders, Skye has dumped the entire bottle of baby wash into the bathtub–another known no-

> no. I tell Skye we will simply skip her birthday tomorrow. She is clearly not mature enough to be a 5-year-old. Suddenly, she is willing to take responsibility for making sure that Isaac and Journey get clean.

§ § §

By October 2002, I was ready to forge productive relationships with Jacob's foster family. We had a common goal of wanting what was best for each boy. Lisa Lewis and I started exchanging emails about play-dates and information regarding the DFCS case.

I also began promoting my plan to get Isaac into the Griffins' home with DFCS. I told the social worker about our relationship with the Griffins and theirs with Isaac. I continued:

> Russ and Naomi have begun the foster care training process with DFCS and are about halfway through the course. I think they should be certified by mid-November.
>
> John and I really hope that the Griffins will have an opportunity to foster parent and, possibly, adopt Isaac if Christina does not put forth the effort to get her boys back. In some ways, it would be ideal. We would see Isaac all the time because of our friendship with the Griffins and the fact that our children attend the same school. Jacob is just down the road; and the Lewises are very agreeable to contact. Each of the children would be able to command more of the attention and resources of their parents: both Isaac and Jacob would be in homes where they were one of two children with two parents to look after them. It would be an "open adoption" among siblings–Skye, Isaac, and Jacob–who would still know each other as they grew up. That is our dream.
>
> I realize that there is still a long road ahead before it is known whether Christina will reclaim her sons. On the other hand, we want to be proactive about creating an alternative family for him

where he can thrive. We want you to meet the Griffin family as soon as it is convenient to do so, and to discuss this further. Russ and Naomi are anxious to assume foster parenting Isaac as soon as they complete their course, if that is possible.

§ § §

The social worker responded three days later with a brief message: "Isaac is not up for adoption, and probably will never be available for adoption."

On October 8th, I got a call from Christina after sending a letter to her mother, Eve, to find out what was happening on her end of things. Christina asked to speak to Isaac who gave her about 5 seconds on the phone before handing it to me saying, "I don't know what to say to her."

Christina asked if I knew about her "sweetie." I said I'd heard she had moved in with a new boyfriend, Billy. Christina said he was going to adopt Isaac, Jacob, and Claire.

I asked when she planned to visit the boys. She said she didn't understand why it had not been set up. I told her that she needed to request it. I asked if she had talked to the Court Appointed Special Advocate (CASA). Christina said she had never heard of her. "Why do these people act like they can't find me? It's not like I'm unavailable." She gave me her phone number at work as a way to reach her.

In late October, the CASA met with Christina and Claire. She reported to me that she found Christina to be articulate and polite. She told the CASA about her dream of opening a French restaurant and of having a big white wedding. Christina had decorated one of the bedrooms in Billy's house with children's beds and toys, and told the CASA that the room was for the boys when they eventually came home.

Christina told the CASA she was desperate to have the boys back, and wanted to have more regular visitation with them. The CASA asked her why she had not turned up for last Tuesday's visitation. She looked surprised and was adamant that she did not receive notification of the visitation schedule from DFCS.

Christina said she was getting a lot of support from family members now that she was living back in her hometown. When she worked evenings, either her mom or Billy collected Claire from daycare and baby-sat her. Christina said that Billy's parents were also willing to help out with Claire.

Billy arrived toward the end of the visit. The CASA asked him about adopting the boys and he said he would. Christina said that she and Billy wanted to have a child together, but that she had no intention of getting pregnant until they were married.

In the CASA's view, Christina had made a good start. The test would be to see if she could maintain this newfound stability. More frequent visitation with the children was needed. However, it was a two-hour drive between DFCS and Christina's home, so the logistics were challenging.

I didn't believe that Christina could maintain the stability she demonstrated to the CASA. The compassionate part of me, however, quarreled with my anger at her. I saw what was happening to Isaac. Christina had made it to only half a dozen visits with her children in sixteen months! On October 22nd, the Lewises and I had taken our kids out of school to see their mother. Isaac had a photo album to show her. For the first 45 minutes he waited, he kept hearing noises and saying, "That's her. She's here now." But after 45 minutes, all he could say was, "I want to go home. Just take me home." Later, this 3-year-old boy told John, "Christina doesn't want me in her home anymore."

I kept the Griffins informed of progress in the case. They seemed to have a realistic grasp of the situation. In an email sent November 5, 2002, Russ wrote to me:

> Right now, I want Isaac to come here and be with us so that he can have permanent placement for the duration of his foster

care, wherever that may lead, and allow you guys to move to a safe distance from the case so you do not feel in any way manipulated by or compelled to enable Christina. She must be allowed to sink or swim on her own.

Also, we want you to know that we understand your relationship and feeling of indebtedness to Christina. She did provide you with a child who is beautiful and a joy to behold. You owe her plenty for that, but please don't lose sight of Isaac. He too is beautiful and a joy and needs the best that life can offer.

We, in many ways, are indebted to you for bringing us this close to Isaac and helping us come to the realization that this boy would be a wonderful addition to our household, no matter what the final outcome. I believe Deb and I are ready and willing to take whatever result then follows.

§ § §

On November 6, 2002, I took Isaac to another scheduled visit with his mother. This time, she came. On many occasions I had coached Isaac, saying, "Christina wants you to call her 'Mommy'." But, at the visit, initially, he kept calling her 'Christina.' She turned to me and gave me a nasty look, saying, "He never used to do this before he came to your house." I explained that there were a number of people in our house who called her Christina and called me "Mama," and that I was doing the best I could.

The good news was that Sandy had talked with the instructor of the Griffins' MAPP class and she had approved Isaac moving to their house as soon as the paperwork was done. Isaac was spending more and more time with the Griffins to make this as smooth a transition as possible.

In mid-November, Christina's counselor of many months, met with me. She believed that Christina had met all of her goals with DFCS and should have Isaac returned to her *immediately*. A flurry of emails followed between different persons associated with DFCS and the foster parents, full of conflicting information. We seemed to be waiting for some input from Polk County to make a final decision.

Email to close friends and family dated December 4, 2002

> Today, Isaac and his brother Jacob had a visit with their mother, Christina, at the DFCS offices. After the visit, my dad took Isaac back to school, and I stayed for a meeting between Christina, the CASA, Christina's counselor, the caseworker, and the foster parents. The caseworker started the meeting with the announcement that Isaac would be transitioning back to his mother by way of weekend visits–two a month for approximately two months (December and January). If that was successful, he would begin visiting for a week at a time–one week in foster care, one week with Christina, one week in foster care, one with Christina, etc. This would go on for two or so months. In the meantime, there will be some sort of hearing before a citizen review board or judge. Jacob, who is more significantly bonded to his foster family, will have a more gradual transition.
>
> The caseworker also announced that since the transition will take time, Isaac will be moving to a new foster home. The Falcos had thought this arrangement would be temporary, but Isaac is now in his sixth month in their home, and they need to focus on the needs of their four children. The new foster family is a family that Isaac and the Falcos know, love, and respect, who live in their neighborhood, who adore Isaac and have been visiting regularly with him, and who would be willing to adopt him should Christina not be reunited with him. The CASA made it very clear that it was important for Isaac to be in a "pre-adoptive home," that is, with a family who would adopt him, if that becomes an option.
>
> There was more to this discussion, lots more. Christina did what she usually does at these sorts of meetings: she blamed everyone but herself for the present predicament: "Nobody

gives a damn about me. I had these babies all by myself and raised them by myself, and where were you? One time in my life, in my 29 years, I made a mistake! You treat children like pieces of meat."

The counselor said she had not been able to reach Christina in three weeks. She leaves messages with relatives that Christina never receives. Christina doesn't have a phone at home. That is an issue. Christina said Billy won't get one; and she can't get one because of her credit problems. DFCS can't leave children in a home without a phone for liability reasons.

There was talk about how needy Isaac is, and how the new foster family is situated to provide for those needs. I've forgotten exactly how this came up, but at some point, Christina began to explode at me. She said I had changed. I had turned into a different person. When she came to visit at Halloween, I walked "a mile" ahead of her. She didn't mention that I was chasing four other children and allowing her to walk with slow-going Isaac. She said she didn't call our house because I was so "cold." (Oh, that would explain why Isaac has not heard a word from her in the last month.) And, John "eavesdropped" on Billy's conversation with Isaac. John was helping Billy move the boxes that we allowed Christina to store in our house for several months. She said her mother thought I was a "snob" at Skye's birthday party. I had dozens of guests. This was the first time in four years that Grandma Eve had come to Atlanta to see Skye or Isaac, though she had many, many invitations, and we had made the drive to her home numerous times.

Even when the counselor tried to calm her down, Christina kept coming back to how angry she was at me. "I gave you my child!" And this is where it really started to hurt: "I could have changed my mind, but I didn't because I kept my word and gave you my baby! Now I have to see Skye growing up and want her in my home and know I'll never have her in my home. She is a constant reminder of a child I can't have. And now you throw MY child out on the street!"

When the others tried to explain again how this move was in Isaac's best interests, that it was "a blessing that Rebecca and John stepped up to take Isaac when the last foster home closed," Christina responded: "It was a blessing that I didn't change my mind, that I gave her my baby." She went on to say that we would never have the relationship we had before, and "You got a beautiful little girl for free." She even announced to the others: "Skye even calls me 'Christina' instead of 'Mommy,'" as if there was something wrong about that.

My rational mind kept telling me that she was saying these things just to hurt me, that she was rewriting history, that it was another manipulation... but my heart was wounded, so I couldn't help but cry and feel a deep, deep sadness. Our relationship has changed. I am worried about the future relationship for Skye, for us. Time will tell, I suppose. I do know that Christina's words reaffirmed for me that we must get out of this position as Isaac's foster parents. It looks like that is going to happen this month. Could you keep us all in your prayers?

Isaac moved to the Griffins' house and began intensive visiting with his mother, Christina. I got reports from Russ and Naomi about how he was doing. He had ups and downs. But that was to be expected.

§ § §

I started the New Year with an attempt to find Journey's biological father by letter to his last known address. Like my attempt to locate Skye's biological father–we received no response.

On January 10th, Lisa Lewis emailed to tell me that Christina had visited with Jacob and Isaac that day at the DFCS offices. Christina told them that she was engaged to Billy. However, Billy did not come to the visit. Isaac had become upset, but Chuck had been able to calm him down. Lisa felt that Chuck was a good influence on Isaac.

A Citizen Review Panel was scheduled to discuss Christina's case on January 29th. The CASA asked me to go and to provide information on how Isaac had faired in our home, as well as information on our long-term relationship with Christina. I prepared a 12-page report for the panel that included our history from the time of her pregnancy with Skye to the present.

I received an email from Christina on January 27th, which, I'm sure, she intended to be a note of apology. However, she went on to say, for the second time, that she regretted placing Skye for adoption because she "looks so much like me." She also said she was "scared that God was going to punish me in the future" for making the placement, and that she couldn't stand to hear Skye call her Christina instead of "Mommy." I knew it was crazy thinking, but it still hurt.

I suspected there were a number of reasons Christina might be saying these things, including unresolved feelings of loss that stemmed from the original placement, anger and other emotions directed at me/us as Isaac's foster parents, and her new persona as "mother working hard to regain her children from the clutches of DFCS." The bottom line was that I had to protect Skye from these comments. Our open adoption would have to be closed, for the time being.

I was trying to understand *why* this hurt so much. I knew the adoption couldn't be undone, legally. I still believed that Christina wasn't ready to be a parent to Skye when she was born. Was it my staunch advocacy of open adoption turned on its head? Was it unresolved infertility issues that left me wondering if I *deserved* to be a mother? Was it feeling betrayed after all the hard work I/we had put into this relationship?

When I looked at Skye, I knew that *no one* could love her more than I did. But I was not her only mother. She was who she was because of what *both* her mothers (and fathers) had given her, genetically and environmentally.

A few days later, I received a well-timed phone call from Emily's birthmother, Michelle. I had sent her an email briefly describing the rift in my relationship with Christina. Michelle called to respond to that email. She said that she had been very worried about me. My email reminded her of our early conversations, of all that John and I went through to try to have a child, and how much we wanted to be parents. She said we deserved to be parents, and that she chose us because she knew we would be the best parents for her baby. She said that both she and Tessa and Kyle (K.J.'s birth parents) *still* believed we were the best parents, that we loved our children and gave them what they needed and more. They had no regrets. If Christina had regrets, that was her problem. Michelle said she didn't want to judge, but, "You create your own problems. And you have to take responsibility for them."

I was so touched and moved that I thought my heart would burst. It meant *everything* to me to hear those feelings expressed by the woman who made me a mother! I told Michelle that I loved her, and I appreciated her taking the time to share her thoughts and to give me that kind of support.

This was (and is) the "up" side of doing an open adoption. This was why we chose to love and trust someone we hardly knew. It was about faith and hope. And then, lo and behold, the love came back in ways we never imagined.

Michelle also reported the good news that she and her husband, Mike, were expecting a baby in just about two weeks! This would be Emily's first brother (on her birthmother's side). It had been a physically difficult pregnancy, but they really wanted to have a child together.

On February 24, 2003, we learned that K.J. also had a new brother, Tyler. He now had three brothers in Nebraska and three sisters in Georgia.

By Spring, Isaac had returned to Christina, and Christina continued to visit with Jacob at DFCS. In an email, dated March 8, 2003, Lisa

Lewis reported to me about a recent visit. She said that Christina came with Claire and Isaac. She told Sherry that Isaac's babysitter had quit, stating that he was too disruptive and hard to keep. Christina thought he needed counseling because he had a terrible temper. She told everyone at the visit that she planned to quit work, stay at home with the children, and open a small daycare center in her home with an additional four to five children. The social worker responded that it was a *really* bad idea and would slow down her case to get Jacob back.

Jacob had known Sherry as his mother since he was an infant. During the visits, he did not want to be left alone with Christina. This upset Christina and strained her relationship with Sherry. Sherry, understanding that reunification appeared inevitable, offered Christina the opportunity to visit Jacob in their home at her convenience. Christina chose never to take that opportunity.

A Utah Birth Story

March to July 2003

Email to family and friends dated March 17, 2003

We go to a church whose membership is mostly gay and lesbian. There were several reasons we chose this church. One of the principle reasons was to place our children in an environment where they could experience that families are created through love, not just biology.

Well, the other day, Emily and I were delivering the Girl Scout cookies in our neighborhood. As we walked up to one house, two cars pulled in the driveway. There was a woman in one and a man in the other. Neither person was the woman from whom Emily had taken the cookie order. When we explained why we were there, the woman in the car offered to pay for the cookies "because she lived there too." As we were walking away, I wondered aloud to Emily, "Who do you think those people were?" Emily replied, "Well, the woman was probably the partner of the woman who ordered the cookies."

I was delighted. I gave her a hug and said, "You may be right." I was so proud of Emily–and of John and myself. To Emily, a man loving another man or a woman loving another woman or a man and woman loving each other, is "natural." Having parents who are the same sex or one parent or parents with different color skin–it's all normal. Diversity in families is taken for granted by Emily. This is part of the legacy we want to give our children.

I look back fondly on my childhood. My parents were not racists or bigots, but I lived in a protected community of mostly white, upper-middle class, heterosexual folks, where I wasn't exposed to "differences" the way my children are today. I learned lessons from my family about treating others fairly, about justice, about all of us being God's children. But I also absorbed the racist, bigoted messages in the general culture I inhabited. It seeps in like water seeps into a sponge. Even today, I sometimes think in stereotypes; and I have to remind myself that I know a different reality.

There are mornings when I wake up thinking, "Our church is too far away. It kills most of a Sunday to be involved there. Wouldn't it be simpler to find a church nearby?" or "Our neighborhood public school is so diverse economically and in terms of special needs that my children may not be getting the best education. Perhaps we should put them in private school. Am I sacrificing them to support the ideal of a diverse learning environment?"

But then I think, "What kind of people does the world need?" In my mind, the world needs peacemakers, bridge-builders, and compassionate and thoughtful lovers of life, the environment, and humanity. Am I doing my part to help each of my children become that kind of person? I hope so. And I intend to keep trying so that my little sponges will be better equipped to stand up to racism and bigotry in all its forms.

§ § §

In mid-April, we drove the van to Nebraska to meet Emily's new brother, Clay, and K.J.'s new brother, Tyler. It was a mostly joyful time spent with dozens of relatives. The only sad part of the trip was discovering that Tessa had been suffering from serious postpartum depression. Kyle had quit work to take care of their boys. Our children were oblivious to this new development. For K.J., the most memorable moments were snowball fights with his birth father and other relatives in Columbus.

In May, Journey would be three years old. From the time she started to speak, she had pointed out the differences between my skin color and hers. Her birthmother, Grace, was fair skinned. But Grace had indicated that her father was Spanish and Cherokee Indian. We didn't know the race or ethnicity of Journey's biological father. It was clear that Journey carried a set of genes for darker skin. In the summer months, she was a beautiful toasty brown.

Journey's skin color would not have been an issue that John or I thought much about except for the fact that *Journey* made it one. By the time she was three, she was talking about wanting to trade skin with me. It broke my heart. She was so beautiful! Why would anyone want my pasty-white skin? But I knew it wasn't really my skin she wanted. She felt different from the rest of the family. And I wanted to take her pain away. I wanted to give her a sibling who looked like her.

Adopt again? How had I so quickly forgotten the stress of having five young children in my home? I can't completely explain it. I reasoned that the *stress* could mostly be attributed to my eroding relationship with Christina and the neediness of Isaac. On the other hand, my child, my Journey, needed this other member of the family to help her feel less different, and more like she belonged with us.

I still had part-time work doing Georgia home studies for couples or individuals who were working with out-of-state adoption agencies and attorneys. I had recently completed a home study for a couple who was adopting a child from the Marshall Islands through a Hawaiian adoption agency. Their baby was a beautiful darker-skinned little girl. I decided to contact the agency for information about adopting a fifth Falco child. Did I discuss this with John? Well, no, not really. The attorney from the agency wrote back with specifics about their procedures and costs. The total costs were estimated at $25,000 to $35,000! That was way out of our price range, even *if* John agreed to pursue another adoption.

On May 21st, I received more news about Isaac. Christina had quit her job at McDonalds to be home with Isaac and Claire. A few days ago, Billy, Christina's fiancé, kicked her out of his house. Christina, the baby, and Isaac were now living in a shelter. Apparently, she had burned some bridges at McDonalds and could not go back to work there....

I talked with John about adopting a fifth child. He said, "No." We went to see a counselor to talk it out. We still could not resolve the issue. John, always the peacemaker, seeing how adamant I was, proposed a compromise. He suggested we foster parent again. I knew he was hoping it would be too much work to get re-certified or that we'd never see a child who met my specifications. I was hoping he'd fall in love with whoever came to live in our home and became available for adoption.

We scheduled our interviews and finished our paperwork for DFCS. Around this same time, I did a home study for a family that had adopted a child with medical needs *very quickly* through an adoption facilitator in South Carolina, called Special Link, Inc. I also spent hours on the computer searching for adoption agencies and adoption situations that might meet our needs, as I defined them. John tolerated my searching, hoping I would eventually give up.

I shared some of my research with John. I told him that for a *mere* $50 donation to Special Link, Inc., we could have our names added to the list of potential adoptive parents for "harder to place" children as they were defined by the facilitator. These included African-American children, biracial or mixed race children, or children with medical or other special needs.

In conjunction with another home study I was completing, I interviewed a couple who told me about an adoption agency in Utah (hereinafter "Utah Agency"). I looked them up on the Internet and discovered two intriguing features about their services. They required no money up-front. Adoptive parents were not financially responsible until they were matched with a birthmother. Secondly, the Utah Agency listed "available situations" on their website by race, sex of child, cost, and due date. I checked the site every day. I was looking for a child whose racial or ethnic composition would "match" the color of my Journey.

We had been fortunate to have months to plan with each of our prior adoptions. Adoption doesn't always work that way. Sometimes adoption decisions must be made very quickly. I was about to experience that first-hand.

On May 30th, with John's go-ahead, I sent a profile letter to the Utah Agency with instructions not to show it without my prior approval.

On June 15, 2003, our minister challenged us to "do one courageous thing that week in pursuit of justice." The message stuck with me.

On June 19th, a DFCS worker visited our home to update our home study and approve us for another year of foster/adoptive care.

On July 1st, I noticed a listing by the Utah Agency for a Caucasian/African-American baby due July 14th. On July 3rd, the listing was updated to read: ½ Caucasian, ¼ Hispanic, ¼ African-American baby boy due July 14th. The cost for all services was listed at $18,000. I emailed the Utah Agency to learn more about this birthmother. The adoptive parent coordinator (hereinafter "APC") responded that the birthmother was 32-years-old, 5'4" tall, 140 lbs. She had two other children, ages 13 and 6. She denied substance abuse. She was looking for a Christian family and would like pictures and letters through the agency. She was already dilated to 2 cm. I asked John if he was willing to allow our profile to be shown to this birthmother. Much to my surprise, John said, "Go for it."

The July 4th holiday passed. On July 5th, the APC called to say that Marissa had chosen us to adopt her baby. It was shocking and exciting. The APC asked if we had a home study. I told her we had a home study through our county DFCS that had just been updated. John and I agreed that we could not go forward until I met Marissa. John made arrangements for me to fly to Salt Lake City the next day.

I arrived in Utah around 1 p.m. on July 6th. The APC met me at the airport and drove us to Marissa's apartment. Tamara, age 6, met us at the door. Marissa was finishing cleaning the apartment. Terrence (the birth father) stayed behind the bedroom door that afternoon because he did not want to be involved in the conversation.

During the course of the conversation, which lasted until approximately 8 p.m., I learned these things: Marissa's mother was ½ Mexican and ½ white. Her father was ½ Native American and ½ white. Terrence was a 38-year-old African-American male, and the father of Tamara. He was 6'1" and weighed 160 lbs. Tamara was six, with a birthday in October 1996. They were all from Jacksonville, Florida. Angela, Marissa's first child, who had a different father, lived with Marissa's parents in Jacksonville.

Marissa and Terrence met in 1989, and started dating in 1991. They were married in 1995. Tamara was born in 1996. They separated when Tamara was 4 months old. He didn't see Tamara for 2 years, and then started seeing her again. They divorced during the two-year separation. According to Marissa, he was a loving father to Tamara.

When they lived in Jacksonville, Terrence had a job in environmental testing, taking soil samples. Marissa got her GED and did office work–but not in the last two years. As the economy worsened she could not find work and Terrence's hours were cut back.

Initially, she was happy about getting pregnant. She figured they had nine months to make their relationship better. Instead, the relationship got worse. At four months pregnant, Terrence asked her if she was sure she should have the baby. She started thinking about adoption.

In May, she left Terrence and moved into a battered woman's shelter. She did not discuss what abuse prompted this move. A month later, she and Tamara moved again to the YWCA. They had their own room now, but they shared a bathroom and kitchen with about 50 families. When she talked about adoption with the staff at the YWCA, she didn't get any support. Marissa wanted her child to have the opportunities that she thought adoptive parents could give him. She read an advertisement from the Utah Agency and called them. They offered to pay her expenses to move to Utah where they would house her until her delivery.

Marissa had read in our profile that the Falcos liked sports and being outdoors. She wanted me to know that Terrence was a good athlete. He was particularly strong in tennis and basketball. Marissa said she didn't do organized sports, but she loved the outdoors.

Marissa thought she wanted to resettle in Utah and get a clean start. She planned to get a job doing office work and then go to college at night.

Marissa's first delivery was "rapid labor" and required an emergency C-section because Angela was coming out butt first. She said she delivered vaginally the second time. It was a 5-hour labor in a hospital, using a midwife. It had been suggested to her that she have labor induced this time, but she didn't want to. The only medical condition she anticipated that the baby might have was asthma.

Tamara was a beautiful, dark-skinned child, and I enjoyed talking with her. I felt very good about my conversation with Marissa. We had *connected.* I believed that she was a birthmother I could have a long-term relationship with.

The APC took me to my hotel, handed me a letter that announced I was "matched" with Marissa, and told me I would be hearing from their financial person regarding our first fee payment–about half the total cost of the adoption.

Back in Atlanta, on July 8th, I went to DFCS to sign a "Release of Information." Our worker instructed me to send the Release to the Utah Agency. When they faxed it back to DFCS requesting our home study, she would release it. She could not give me a copy of the study directly.

Between July 8th and July 13th, the Utah Agency and DFCS failed to communicate with each other, and the home study was not sent.

On July 9th, I talked to Marissa. She had been to her doctor. She was 3 cm. dilated and 70% effaced. The doctor had scheduled an appointment for next Monday (her due date), and would like to induce labor if she had not yet delivered.

Marissa remarked that she didn't have a bond with her Utah Agency counselor. The counselor brought her 5-month-old and 22-month-old children with her to appointments, and they distracted her. Marissa said she wanted me to be in the delivery room if I could get there in time. She was disappointed that the agency had not given her profiles sooner so that we could have had a longer time to get to know each other before the birth. Although she had requested the profiles as soon as she arrived in Utah, it took three weeks to get them.

On July 10th, I talked to Marissa again. Terrence had been into the office to sign a waiver of his parental rights so that he could go back to Jacksonville. He didn't like Utah where he perceived that he was one of very few dark-skinned people.

Marissa talked about her first child. She was 19 when Angela was born. She explained that she was too young to have a child. She had stayed home with Angela for a year and a half; but all her friends were going out, and she wanted to go out too. She started going to clubs. Her mom could see that she was in conflict. Marissa agreed to allow Angela, at age two, to move in with her parents. She said, "If I can survive separating from my daughter after having her for two years, I know I can do this adoption. With this child, I won't have the same attachment."

Interestingly, Marissa also said that if she was a millionaire and had a mansion with twenty rooms, she wouldn't leave them empty. She would fill them with children.

On July 11th, in frustration over the inability of the Utah Agency to secure a copy of our home study, I sent copies of all four previous home studies, an update, and all the back-up materials for the current study, excluding the fingerprint report, which I did not have.

On July 12th, Marissa told me that she and Terrence had had a good conversation. As he had gotten to know me through Marissa, he had come to believe that adoption was the right decision. We would offer their son opportunities that they could never offer. We discussed how things might change for the better for each of them because they were making an adoption plan. Marissa was also excited about being able to visit us in the future. I told her that John had found a flight for me on Monday at 1:15 p.m.

On the morning of Monday, July 14th, before my flight, I went to DFCS again to request a copy of my home study to take to Utah. I was unable to locate either of the caseworkers that knew me. However, the unit supervisor responded. She checked my file and came back to tell me that the Falcos had a "foster care home study," not an "adoptive home study." She gave me a copy. I ran it by John's office and he faxed it to the Utah Agency.

During the day, the Utah Agency ICPC (Interstate Compact on the Placement of Children) expert reviewed the study and informed us that she did not think it would pass the Utah ICPC review. I began to panic. I asked her if I should still come to Utah. "Oh, yes," was the answer.

Before, during, and after the flight, I made several calls concerning the study. I spoke with at least six county employees, a private adoption agency, and the Georgia ICPC office. Although I got several conflicting responses, it became clear to me that the home study we had was not sufficient as it was. It was unclear whether or not it could be *fixed* by someone at DFCS, by a retroactive study, or by providing other documents not currently in the possession of the Utah Agency. I felt ill. The Utah Agency said, "Let's just try using your home study as is. Maybe it will go through after all."

While I was dealing with the home study mess, the financial paperwork from the Utah Agency finally arrived at the Falco home in Decatur, Georgia. We were to sign and wire funds within five days.

I landed in Utah around 5:30 p.m. and rented a car. As I started the car, I called the APC to find out how Marissa's doctor's appointment had gone that afternoon. She told a story of a serious altercation between Marissa, Terrence, and two other people that had been set off that afternoon when Marissa encountered another pregnant woman at the doctor's office–a woman with whom Terrence had had an affair. This woman had also been brought to Utah by the agency to place her baby for adoption. When Marissa returned to her apartment, she started a fight with Terrence. Others joined in. Police and medical personnel were called. Terrence ran off before the police arrived and no one was sure where he was. Tamara had witnessed the scene and been taken away by another caseworker. Marissa began having hard contractions and was taken to the hospital by ambulance. The APC told me to proceed immediately to the hospital. She would meet me there.

When I arrived, Marissa's assigned caseworker, Beverly, was there with her. Marissa was only 4 cm. dilated, but her contractions were hard and constant. Marissa seemed broken to me. We awaited the doctor's call to find out if she would be admitted or sent home. The nurse wanted to take Marissa's medical history, so the rest of us were asked to leave. Outside in the hall, the APC and Beverly shared rumors about the afternoon's events and planned to plead "confidentiality" when asked about it by the other birthmothers. I was sickened by the paternalistic protectionism they expressed regarding the women they called their "girls."

The doctor decided to admit Marissa. The APC went home. Marissa was moved to a labor and delivery room where she was given an epidural. It helped her pain, and it helped her labor progress. By 8:30 p.m., she had dilated to 8 cm. The doctor arrived at 9:30, and at 9:32 p.m., Marissa's water broke. She quickly progressed to 10 cm. Marissa gave me permission to take pictures while she pushed and delivered her baby.

It was the smoothest delivery I have ever witnessed. At times, it was perfectly quiet in the room. With each push, a little more of the baby's hair appeared. He was born at 9:55 p.m., at 7 lbs., 8 oz., 19 inches long. His APGAR scores were 8 and 9. Marissa wanted me to cut the cord, and I did.

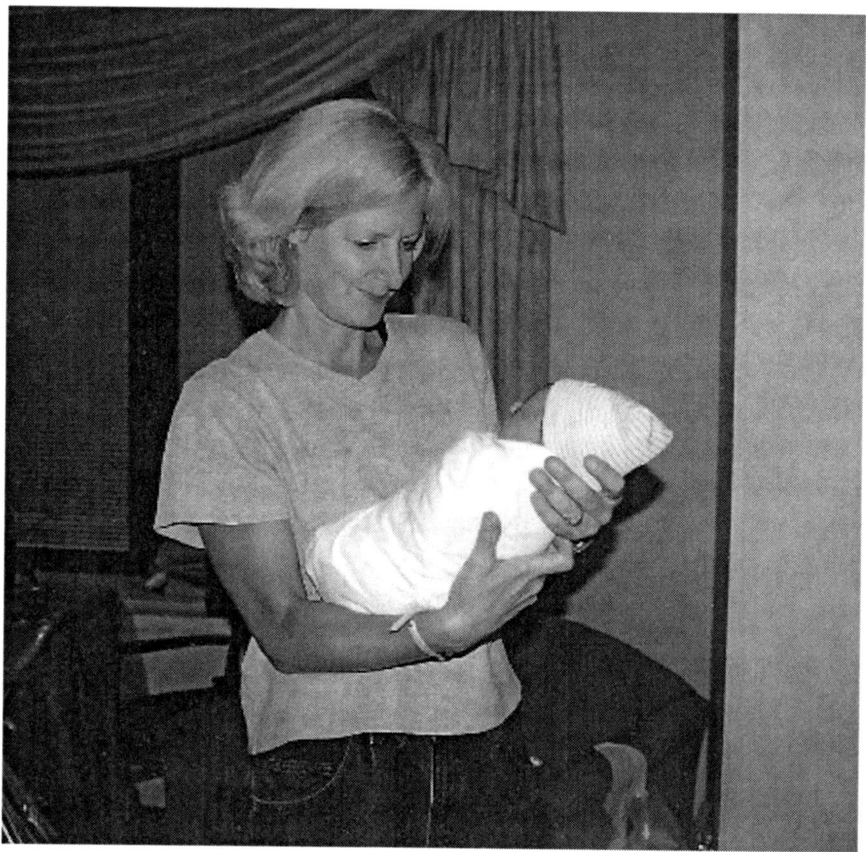

I stayed with Marissa and the baby until about 11 p.m. (1 a.m. on my biological clock) before leaving to find my hotel. I promised to be back by late morning. I called John to report on the baby. I was excited; and, yet, my stomach was in knots as I contemplated our legal dilemma and the possibility that we could not adopt him. As I tried to fall asleep, I decided that I would request an appointment with the Utah Agency's attorney in the morning.

Early on July 15th, I called the APC and requested an appointment with the attorney. She said, "Let's wait to call Greg. Let's talk to our

ICPC expert at the agency first." The "expert" reiterated that we should try the home study with ICPC first. "Get your county to fax your criminal reports. Get your doctor to fill out statements of good health for you and John. Get John to give his power of attorney to you so that you can sign all the documents."

Meanwhile, John had mailed, by overnight delivery, a copy of our home study and faxed the financial papers to me. My stomach would not settle down. What were we going to do? Who could give me a definitive answer? I knew we had completed the same requirements *plus much more* for our home study with the county; but it had the wrong label and it didn't look anything like the private adoption agency home studies we had for our other adoptions. I was overwhelmed by the thought that this agency had matched us without first reviewing our home study. Moreover, Marissa had relied on the Utah Agency's assurances that we were an approved family. I made up my mind that I would not sign any documents or pay any money without a commitment from the Utah Agency that they would make this adoption work.

I was so preoccupied with these thoughts that I could barely focus on my most important job: getting to know my new son and establishing a trusting relationship with his first mother.

When I arrived at the hospital, Marissa asked me if the baby had a name yet. I told her it was Justice Jeffrey. "Justice" had come to me as an appropriate name for a new son when our minister challenged us to do something courageous in pursuit of *justice* on June 15th. "Jeffrey" was the name of John's roommate and best friend at Duke University. Marissa told me that Jeffrey was the name of her 4-month-old brother who died. Her mother would be touched that the baby had his name.

Justice was adorable. His curly wet hair from the night before was now wispy and straight. He had perfect little lips that reminded me of Journey. He had Marissa's nose and the shape of Tamara's head. Marissa and I shared feeding and holding him.

Still, I was sick. I had made several calls to an attorney-friend who had agreed to help us with this adoption, but she had not returned any of my calls. I had to do something. I called another attorney who I knew was very familiar with adoption and ICPC issues. She was on the phone, but her assistant spoke with me and took careful notes. She promised to have the attorney return my call. It was midday.

Marissa and I discussed the pediatrician's visit earlier in the day, and how we would handle the circumcision that Medicaid did not cover. Another Utah Agency caseworker dropped off Tamara to meet the baby. Tamara was thrilled with him. She asked her mother if he was coming home with her tomorrow. Marissa reminded her that he was not. I took some more pictures.

Beverly arrived with her 5-month-old baby and chicken nuggets for Tamara. She wanted to know if Marissa was aware that she would be signing "her papers" tomorrow at 9:00 a.m. No, she was not aware. Beverly told me to come to the hospital at 9:00 a.m. too.

After two hours, I left to develop the birth pictures and to buy baby clothes, blankets, and diapers. I dropped off the film at Sam's Club and walked next door to Wal-Mart. When I found the infant section, I felt queasy and light-headed. I tried to compare prices of various items, but I could not. I felt so alone. I crumpled to the floor. Who could help me? Why didn't the lawyer call? After a few minutes of immobilization, I dialed John's number. Fortunately, he was there. What is wrong with me? Is it the home study problem that may result in lost money and no baby to bring home? Is it something about the Utah Agency? Do I not love the baby enough? Is it Marissa's love for the baby?

Talking to John helped because he knew how to listen and could acknowledge that my feelings were important without imposing his judgment on me. No resolution, but I could move again.

I selected the diapers and outfits and other baby items that would get me started. I returned to Sam's club for my 1-Hour photos. But before I headed out of the parking lot back to the hospital, I left another desperate message with the attorney about the ICPC situation and the impending signing of documents and transfer of money in the morning.

At the hospital, Tamara was preparing to leave with Beverly to be delivered to another babysitter. Marissa, Justice, and I were alone. I was aware that it was after 6 p.m. in Atlanta. I wasn't going to get a call from the attorney. I was on my own. Suddenly, I asked: "Has anyone talked to you about how you might handle raising the baby instead of placing him for adoption?" I can't explain exactly why I asked the question except to say that I sensed *no one* at the Utah Agency had explored this with her. I knew from my other experiences with adoption that this was a terribly important question. Marissa needed to reevaluate her decision now that the baby was here. Whatever she decided now, her conviction would be stronger and her grieving easier. It was a chance I was willing to take to help her.

Marissa said that no one had asked her that question. She knew it was the "best thing" for him to be adopted by us, but she felt pressure from the agency. They hovered around her, monitored her comings and goings–even her mail. But no one seemed to care how she felt. Just then, my cell phone rang. I apologized for the disruption and took the call outside the room. It was the attorney.

We had a lengthy conversation, for which I am eternally grateful. In short, she confirmed that I had the wrong home study. The adoption might be saved with retroactive ICPC compliance, but it could be very expensive–up to an additional $12,000 in attorneys' fees. She also shared some disturbing information she had obtained about the Utah Agency's business practices that left me feeling more distrustful of them. I told the attorney that I wasn't sure how to approach this with Marissa. We had "connected." I was the one she trusted. How could I not let her know what was going on? If she signed surrenders and we didn't get the baby, she would have no say about who did. The attorney suggested that I go back in the room and resume our talk about how Marissa was feeling about placement.

While I was out of the room, Marissa had called her aunt in Florida. The aunt had experience with both sides of adoption. She had placed a baby when she was young and later adopted a child. Marissa said my question about how she might raise the baby herself had prompted the call.

I told Marissa that I had been talking with an attorney because there were some things about the agency that made me uncomfortable too. Marissa launched back into her list of complaints about all the things the Utah Agency had promised and not delivered. The key missing element was any counseling for her or Tamara. As she shared her pain, it became clear to me that I needed to be honest with her. She needed to know about the home study mess. It also became clear to me that we were not going to pursue this adoption *this way*. I shared with Marissa what I thought was necessary for her to understand the predicament we were in. Marissa responded, "If you aren't going to get my baby, no one is."

A dark cloud over the room lifted. Marissa began to share her life story with me–the good and bad decisions, her hopes and dreams for her children. She wasn't sure how she would do it, but she was going to take her baby home. She had already been doing research on agencies and groups that might help her get started. I said, "You'll have to think of a name for him now."

Marissa responded, "I like his name."

She felt bad for me. I assured her that, though we could not adopt Justice through this agency at this time, we would be interested in adopting him if she later decided that it was the best decision for all of them. We would do it right then. We would have the right home study. Moreover, I wanted to continue to be her friend whatever she decided to do about adoption. She could call me just to talk. Marissa responded, "How could I ever forget you? We went through his labor and birth together. I didn't want any of those other people in the room. It's as if God put you here to support me and help me through this." It was an experience and conversation that I will never forget.

John had no knowledge of what I'd done, nor did the Utah Agency. It was getting late. I called John and he agreed to communicate with the agency. He wanted to do it that evening and get it over with. I gathered all the baby things I had purchased that day, along with the infant carseat I brought from Atlanta, and delivered them to Marissa.

A few minutes later the phone rang again. John yelled, "Run!" When he had spoken with the APC to tell her that we were not going to adopt Marissa's baby, she had concluded that we were trying to scam the agency. They were sending a caseworker to the hospital right away to confront me. Marissa and I said a quick good-bye. I had written my toll free number of the back of my "business card." Instead of a company name, it read, "Let my heart be broken by the things that break the heart of God." It seemed particularly appropriate at that moment.

I still felt sick… and sad… but better, in a way. I drove back to the hotel while John changed my flight home to the next day. I watched TV and tried to sleep. At midnight, my cell phone rang. I answered and a woman identified herself as director of the Utah Agency. There were no words of apology, such as, "I am so sorry that we screwed-up…." There were no words of comfort, such as, "I am so sorry for your loss…." Instead, she began: "I understand you had a conversation with Marissa tonight. Did you tell her that you had a home study that would not pass the ICPC process?" I told her that I did. Then came more questions about the home study. "Did you also tell her that you no longer wanted her baby?"

"No," I responded. I felt queasy again.

She was trying to trap me. She wasn't trying to help Marissa or me. She started, "Can you tell me…?"

"No. I can't. I can't tell you," I responded, and hung up the phone.

I pulled up the covers around me and hunched into a ball. I imagined thunderous footsteps coming down the hall and a battering ram crushing through the door, or glass shattering as they broke through the window. They were coming to get me. A few minutes later, my cell phone rang again. I listened to the ringing until it stopped. In the morning, I listened to the message. It was the director again, urging me to call and tell her exactly what I said to Marissa.

Maybe Marissa was right. Maybe God put me there with her because she didn't have any other support. Maybe God put me there to insure a just result–one that honors human relationships and connections above all else. I don't know. I do know I made a friend I will never forget. And I know I did the best I could in a situation where there were no perfect answers. I hoped it was enough.

I sent an email, telling my story, and I received many incredibly loving and life-affirming responses from friends and family members. One of the responses I received came from the director of Special Link, Inc., Carri Uram. She wrote (in part):

> Dearest Rebecca,
>
> What an incredible story! It is very sad and yet at the same time, completely uplifting because I know that God did not allow any of those circumstances to happen needlessly. If there is anything I've learned in my life, it's that God can turn the bleakest experience into the most glorious blessing ever!
>
> Because of your faithfulness and obedience, God has something very very special right around the corner for you. Something so wonderful that it'll be worth it all!

§ § §

On July 18th, I heard from Marissa. She said she was okay. They rushed her out of the hospital so quickly that she forgot her address book and didn't have my number. She was grilled and accused by the agency director the night I left her. The director brought in an affidavit and wanted her to sign it. It included such things as a statement that she owed them $4000 and that Marissa and I conspired to deprive the agency of its fee. She flatly refused. They actually told her, "You have a moral obligation to place your baby through our agency." They followed her back to the apartment and gave her one hour to collect her things and get out with her 6-year-old daughter and new baby. The agency told her they wanted her out so she wouldn't influence any of the other "girls."

Marissa and the kids went to a church collective. It was a group of churches that provided shelter to homeless families on a rotating basis–a week at each church. They would go to the church at 4:30 p.m. and leave at 6 a.m. the next morning. They were then taken to an office where they could use the phone or take care of other business.

Terrence had not been in contact with Marissa. She promised to stay in touch with me at least until she got settled somewhere. I was one of the only people she had to talk to. She said she really wished we lived closer so she could leave the baby with me to run errands. I was the only person she trusted with him.

Justice had a new name: Marcel Dakota. Tamara had Terrence's initials. Marcel had Marissa's initials.

Wrestling With Race and Special Needs

August to December 2003

It didn't take much encouragement for me to begin the search for a baby again. In late July, we hired a private adoption agency to update and give us the appropriate home study for an agency or private adoption. I was now sure there was a baby for us out there, somewhere.

After my experience in Utah, it was clear to me that if we were going to adopt again, not only would the child have darker skin, the child needed to be a boy. K.J. wanted a brother. And, if we were going to pursue adoption to benefit Journey, why not benefit K.J. too? He was surrounded by bossy females already. I had made a few contacts with adoption agencies and attorneys recently and over the years, so I sent a letter with the same basic information to each one: We were looking to adopt a biracial or mixed race male child (or twins), newborn to two years of age.

Email to family and friends dated August 11, 2003

> Yesterday, I said to John that "something about adoption" was going to happen today. Selfishly, I was hoping it would be an email or phone call about an adoption possibility. Our home study is complete. Now we wait. I was starting to feel sad about walking away from the adoption in Utah. When will I/we ever find another birthmother like Marissa? Will there be another healthy, beautiful baby…? It didn't happen. I didn't get a phone call or email. Instead, I got this letter:
>
> > Dear Rebecca,
> >
> > Thank you so much for the pictures; they turned out great! I am sending you a few pictures now, and I will send more soon. I want you to know that it has truly been a blessing to

> have you in our lives. Having you as a friend has changed my life and restored my faith in people (and God). I want to thank you for being there for me when I needed you most, and for your unselfish sacrifice. You and your family are in my thoughts and prayers every day. I hope to have you remain a part of our lives forever.
>
> With all our love, Marissa, Tamara & Marcel

I could not have received a better “something about adoption” today.

§ § §

On August 23, 2003, I received word from Lisa Lewis that Jacob had gone to his mother, Christina, with no provision for any visits from the Lewises after living with them for over two of the three years of his life. Lisa also noted that Christina was clearly pregnant again. At the court hearing, Christina had told the judge that she would be going to nursing school. I promised to stay in touch with them and to share any information about Jacob that I might receive from his birth family.

On the home front, ever since the Utah adoption failed, Carri Uram, from Special Link,Inc. had been my confidante. She had the experience and knowledge about black and bi-racial adoption that I needed, as well as many contacts with attorneys and agencies. Although I had spent many years dealing with adoption, both personally and professionally, there was something that felt different about adopting an African-American child. I couldn’t name it or explain it *yet*. Carri provided factual and practical advice. As time passed, I often asked Carri for her thoughts about different adoption situations. Here are a couple of example situations that I sent to Carri. For reasons I no longer remember, these situations did not work out:

August 22, 2003

I was doing some Internet searching this morning and got a response back from a New York (and Florida) attorney, *[name withheld]* Have you heard of her? She told us about a Hispanic-African American boy, born two weeks ago, with a heart defect that looks to be correctable. He has had one surgery, but needs another. The baby is in Texas. His adoptive family got scared and pulled out. Parental rights have been terminated. The baby is in private foster care through a Texas agency. The attorney says her initial consultation fee is $500. Her retainer is $1500. Her usual placement fee is $4500. She thought total costs might run $12,000. She said to talk to my husband first, but her fee was "negotiable" under the present circumstances.

September 16, 2003

Melanie *[from an agency recommended by Carri]* told me about another birthmother who is African-American and so is the father. She first contacted them in July, then disappeared, and recently called again, saying she wanted to place. They feel good about that. I do too. She is married, but not to the birthfather, and wants to save the marriage. She has a 2 1/2 year old son. This baby is a boy too. She is due 11/24. She is 5'8" and 135 lbs. The woman who has seen her says that she is "tall and beautiful and has pretty features." I asked about her complexion–medium to light. Birthfather is 5'10" and "muscular." He has moved "far away;" and in Arkansas they don't have to terminate his rights, just use the Putative Father Registry. *[The Putative Father Registry is a list of the names of men who have acknowledged paternity of a child by completing the Paternity Acknowledgment form or have indicated the possibility of paternity without acknowledging paternity of the child. The Registry allows possible biological fathers to provide identifying information about themselves, the mother, and the child so these registered men can be notified about adoption proceedings.]* The cost of the adoption would be $10,700. Expenses to her are $1000 (included in the $10k), but would not be paid until after the birth. So, there is little risk to us.

§ § §

I heard from Marissa again, and passed on an update by email.

Email to family and friends dated September 2, 2003

I am pleased to report that Marissa called again. She is still in a roving church shelter. Marcel has reached six weeks of age and is now eligible for daycare, which means that Marissa can now work harder at finding a job. Once she gets a job, she can get housing through a community organization. She says her resume is circulating.

Terrence is back on the scene. Though he does not have a job either, he is helping with money he has received in a legal settlement from a car accident. He has a car. He takes care of Tamara. He was able to pay for Marcel's circumcision and to buy a stroller and other things for the baby. Marissa says that they have had time to become friends for the sake of the children.

She passed on a tidbit, prefacing it with: "no offense." Terrence was in the park one day with them, holding the baby, when he said, "Marcel is too good for them [*the Falcos]*. Just think how close we came to losing him." Marissa shared this story, not to hurt my feelings, but to let me know that Terrence has attached to his son. And that's a good thing.

Boy, this is hard. I'm so happy for them; but I'm so down right now. The few opportunities that have presented themselves to us for another adoption have not been good options for our family. If I didn't want to adopt again, if I wasn't working for that,

I think I could receive Marissa's good news in the manner in which it was offered. But, it's hard not to feel the old infertility issue: "You're not good enough to be a parent. That's why you don't get pregnant. That's why you don't get picked. That's why...." I know it's crazy to be thinking like that. I have four children!

§ § §

Carri had a way of raising my spirits every time. She wrote:

As for not being "good enough," that's hogwash! Not only are you good enough, you WERE chosen by Marissa–but because of circumstances out of everyone's control–it did not happen. If that had been the baby that God meant for you to have, nothing could have stopped it from happening. That can only mean that He has an even better situation for you. God would not place it on your hearts to adopt again only to dash those hopes. When your family is through-you will know it deep in your heart, soul and mind.

Until then... I will look forward to the twists and turns in your journey.

§ § §

I was not a believer in God's orchestration of all life's events in the way that I perceived Carri to be. But her words were always uplifting and reassuring. I *wanted* to believe what she said.

As time passed and different adoption situations presented themselves, my thoughts about *race* were evolving. I had first wanted to adopt a biracial child because I thought: (1) he would more nearly "match" Journey; and (2) there would be a white parent with whom we could identify–probably the birthmother. Somewhere along the line, I had come to understand that more white women who become pregnant by black men placed their babies for adoption than the reverse: black woman impregnated by white man. But ever since I met Marissa and fell in love with her dark-skinned daughter, I had started asking myself: Isn't making the distinction between biracial and black just another form of racism? One could not control what the child would look like anyway. He might look black, like Tamara did, whether he was biracial or not. He might feel black because he was treated as black, regardless of his mixed heritage. If we were willing to deal with the African heritage of a biracial child, we ought to be willing to deal with "blackness" no matter what percent of his heritage could be labeled as such.

As I thought more about my expectation that I would be working with a white birthmother in a biracial adoption, I realized that I had been afraid I could not relate well to a black birthmother because we would be too different. But why did I think that? Michelle, Tessa, Christina, and Grace were all different than me. The birthmothers I related to best were the ones who had similar interests or temperaments or beliefs. Color might, and probably did, play a role in cementing a person's interests, temperament, or beliefs. However, I could not know through speculation whether or not I would *connect* with someone. It was something I would have to experience.

I suggested to John that we consider adopting a full African-American child if the following three conditions were met: First, the medical history would need to indicate no serious potential problems because our plates were already pretty full with the four children we had. Second, I needed to feel connected with the child's birthmother (or parents) for the sake of an open relationship. That is, we needed to know that she approved of our family's general child-rearing approach, our beliefs, the activities we intended to pursue (e.g. sports, a liberal church, education, travel, etc.) I also thought this approval was a good indicator of how I would connect to the child's personality when he arrived. Finally, I wanted a beautiful child. "I'll know it when I see it," was the way I felt about beauty. My children didn't look alike, but they were all beautiful. I knew they would be beautiful when I met their original mothers.

I shared similar thoughts with Carri, and she responded from her experience in an email:

> I've seen biracial kids who looked black and black ones who look biracial. I believe that people should be completely comfortable with "blackness" before adopting (even) biracially. If a biracial child feels that his parents find him/her acceptable because he's (at least) half white, he'll struggle with his racial makeup. I applaud you for thinking through the biracial baby versus black baby issue. Sadly some adoptive families only adopt biracially (initially) because they think they can't get a white one and biracial is the next best thing....
>
> Red flags always go off in my head when a new adoptive couple calls requesting a biracial child and asks if they can "get a light one?" What will happen if they don't? Or worse yet... what if they do get a light one? That poor child will get the clear message very early on that they can "pass" or that it's a good thing that they look so white. What does that say about how the parents feel about the other 50 percent of their child's heritage?
>
> As for the looks of the child, when it is the one that is meant for you, he will be beautiful in your eyes even if no one else thinks so.
>
> In addressing the concerns about a birthmother's compatibility with you, I just couldn't penalize an innocent baby who needed a loving home and family because her birthmother did not meet a certain expectation.

§ § §

I latched on to Carri's affirmation that we were ready to make ourselves available to adopt an African-American child if we were willing to accept and embrace his heritage. In late September 2003, I sent letters and profiles to all my contacts to update the description of the child we were looking for to include African-American. I told Carri about our decision and stated: if there is a black woman or couple who would choose our mostly white family, there must be a good reason for that. This time when Carri responded, I heard another piece of what she had tried to tell me earlier:

> What happens most of the time (tragically) is that black birth moms, or black birth couples, don't have the luxury of getting to pick a family. Usually, they are lucky if the agency or attorney can even find a great family who will want their babies. Rarely do black birth parents have the benefit of offering input into obtaining a special family for their baby.

§ § §

I asked Carri to clarify: Was she telling me that a black birthmother wouldn't have families to *choose* from because there were so few willing to adopt her baby *or* was she saying we wouldn't have the opportunity to make a *connection* to her as we had with our other children's birthmothers? Her answer was *both*:

> I get calls from adoption attorneys and agencies in urgent need, seeking a family–any family–for a black baby that is either already born or soon to be born. There is not a pool of adoptive couples from which to draw (or choose) for black babies.
>
> You may–or may not–get the opportunity to connect with a birthmother. Every situation is different and needs to be taken on a case-by-case basis. I would caution against making a connection with a birth mom an absolute "must." I urge you to let God lead. You don't want to miss out on the "right" one simply because it does not fit a certain mold. With that said, it is entirely possible that you will have all that you desire in your next placement, I would just stay open and flexible and see what the Lord brings you.

§ § §

It was a sobering response. But it helped prepare us for the next leg of our journey.

In early November 2003, I received a call from a woman, Julia, who worked as an assistant at an organization that provided adoption information and services. I had contacted the organization about our desire to adopt a fifth child in my networking efforts. Julia had recently been called by an attorney *[call him "JT"]* who was looking for parents to adopt a very premature African-American baby boy. Julia referred to him as "Baby Boo" because he was born right before Halloween. She wanted to know if we'd like to submit our home study and profile to the attorney and to be considered as possible adoptive parents. John and I were definitely interested, but we had questions. We could not help but remember our dramatic experience with the premature twins and our fears about ongoing or future medical problems. Would there be similar issues here?

Julia said the mother of the baby had given birth to him, signed surrender papers with the attorney on October 31st, and left. She did not want a relationship with the adoptive parents. I asked Julia:

- If the birthmother signed termination of parental rights papers on October 31st, does that mean the statutory period will end November 10th? *[In Georgia, once the legal birth parent of the child signs papers terminating his or her parental rights, she or he has ten days to change her or his mind for any reason. After the ten-day period, the surrender becomes irrevocable absent extenuating circumstances such as fraud or duress.]*
- Did she name a birthfather? How will his rights be dealt with?
- What kind of medical background information and social history will we get?
- When can we see the baby's medical records and have our pediatrician (or one referred by ours) check on the baby's current medical condition? We also want to learn about any potential future medical problems.

- At what point would the baby become our responsibility, financial and otherwise?
- Who pays the baby's medical bills? Is he on Medicaid? Has there been any problem in the past with this hospital trying to collect medical costs related to the birth from the adoptive parents?
- What are the likely legal or other fees? What are they for and when are they due?

Julia responded right away. She confirmed that the ten days would be up on November 10th. The birthmother had not named a birth father, so JT would contact the Putative Father Registry and then make a Motion to Terminate his parental rights.

Julia also said that because it was a "confidential" adoption, there would be no medical or social history of the birthmother available to us. It would be sealed. She could tell us that the 22-year-old was very healthy and had a good health history. No HIV. Julia described her as a very slender, very beautiful, medium height, light-skinned African-American woman who was well spoken and in the professional world.

We could get the baby's medical history, but not until the ten days were up. We would not even be allowed to *see* the baby until then. All our information about him would come through Julia. The attorney, JT, wanted to file the Petition for Adoption on November 12th. This was shocking to me. I asked for clarification: "Does that mean we have between the 10th and the 12th to decide if we want to adopt him?" The answer was: "Yes." The rush to file the petition had to do with DFCS. DFCS had to be notified quickly that there were adoptive parents for the baby or they would swoop in and take him into their custody.

The baby was eligible for Medicaid, but not on it. Julia said she would pursue it, but it would be more difficult because he didn't have a mother or a name. I told her to do so anyway. I thought that once custody of the baby was given to us, our insurance would pick-up the bills. But I asked John to check out how our insurance handled premature infants with large expenses.

Julia had been told that the baby would be in the hospital about three months–if his release coincided with his predicted due date. However, he was off oxygen already. Apparently, he had had an apnea episode on November 1st, so he would likely come home with an apnea monitor. The medical staff anticipated that he would have *no* long-term problems. In fact, he acted like a full-term newborn in terms of his responsiveness. Julia kept reiterating how beautiful he was. He came into the world screaming. He had APGAR scores of 7-8-9 at 1, 5, and 10 minutes.

Legal fees were estimated between $2500 and $3500. Once the 10 days were up, JT would ask for a $500 retainer and then bill us as services were used. It was clear from Julia's response that we had been "chosen" as Baby Boo's adoptive parents if we wanted him. The hospital and Julia were requesting that we give him a name. I told Julia that we didn't have a name yet. That was technically true. But the more important reason for not naming him yet was that John and I wanted to *see and hold* the baby before giving him a name. I told John to take a deep breath and blow it out slowly. We would need to be calm and focused to figure this out.

John said he was looking for a sign to direct us regarding Baby Boo. The next day, on November 5th, I got a call from an adoption agency in Sarasota, Florida about another African-American baby due in two weeks. They said they didn't have anybody in their database who was interested in adopting him, so they wanted to know if we were. I told John that the call from Florida seemed like a sign that we were needed. I emailed: "There are children–a particular child, in this case–who needs us. Where are the parents for African-American babies?"

Julia provided us with daily updates on the baby. On November 10th, I spoke with JT's legal secretary *[call her "SL"]*. She said that the letter declaring who the adoptive parents would be was not due until 15 days after the birthmother signed her surrender of parental rights. In this case, that would be November 15th. SL was going to be out of the office, so she wanted to send it the next day, November 11th! I told her I was not prepared to make the decision without first talking to the baby's doctor. She was not sure she could arrange that, but she said she would try to contact the social worker and arrange a meeting with the doctor. Then she said that JT would be in the office and *could* mail the letter as late as November 14th. That would give us a little more time.

I had also spoken with our pediatric nurse practitioner whose son had been born at 28 weeks and weighed 2 lbs., 10 oz. She thought the first two weeks were the most important in terms of predicting the baby's future. Higher levels of oxygen for long periods of time could be damaging, causing eye problems. An uneventful course in the hospital was the best. She was told by their doctor not to expect her son to go home before his due date. She said, if she were in our shoes, she would not make a decision until the baby had a cranial ultrasound which would show any minor and major bleeds or strokes. This would indicate any potential brain damage. If, like her son, this baby had no major setbacks, he should be perfectly normal.

The meetings with the social worker and doctor were arranged. John and I were able to see and touch him after all. He was so tiny, and without a speck of "baby fat." It was scary to think about being responsible for someone so small and, seemingly, fragile. But we knew he needed us–or someone. All we had to do was say "yes," and he was ours.

We had decided not to use the name "Justice Jeffrey" which we associated with the Utah baby. That left us with the difficult process of coming up with another name. I offered a dozen or more suggestions to John, but nothing quite felt right. I'm sure we were also hesitant to name him because giving him a name would finally indicate our commitment to adopt him.

In the midst of this intense discussion about adopting Baby Boo, Carri Uram contacted me with an opportunity to foster-to-adopt a little girl in Georgia. I told her we needed to stick with our original plan of adopting a boy.

Julia was anxious to get Baby Boo's adoption resolved. She had become very attached to him, and visited him every day. On November 13th, I summoned up the courage to tell Julia that despite having been reassured that Baby Boo's health risks were minimal, John and I were still worried about the "closed-ness" of the adoption. I emailed Julia:

> I kept thinking about this sweet child making trips to visit all his siblings' birth families while he had no one to visit. I thought of him walking through our house every day surrounded by pictures of birth families while he had no pictures of his own. It seems so unfair to him.

I spoke with SL to inquire as to whether or not there was a more appropriate family to adopt the baby. She and JT indicated that there might be. I reassured them that we did not want to leave him without a home, but that we did want what was *best* for him. JT had decided to wait until after the weekend to file the letter declaring the names of the adoptive parents. He was going to check into the possibility of another family (or families) and make a decision over the weekend.

The next day, JT emailed me to stop visiting the child if we were not going to adopt him. I sensed he was angry. I was trying to remain calm and rational. This baby didn't have anyone else, as far as we knew, and we didn't want to abandon him. But we were being rushed into a decision with lifetime consequences. There was so much we didn't know about his medical condition and how that would affect our other children. How would we sort this out in time?

If we had not adopted Emily the way we did–meeting her birth family, full disclosure about her medical history, the opportunity to update that information over time, and the like–would I feel this way about Baby Boo? If all my experience with adoption was this "confidential" one, would I be hesitating to take the baby? Carri had said not to hold the baby's circumstances against him. But, here we were doing just that.

On November 14th, I contacted Julia to get a status report. She emailed back that she was working with another family. That was good news. Two days later, Julia emailed in a panic because those parents had not worked out. I offered some suggestions and contacts. By November 18th, Julia had not heard back from any parents who were interested in adopting Baby Boo.

Around this same time, a call came in from a Colorado adoption agency with a birthmother due in February; and Carri contacted me about two other situations in South Carolina with pregnant women due to give birth to African-American baby boys. I took the opportunity to report to her about Baby Boo.

Email to Special Link, Inc. dated November 19, 2003

We are in quite a predicament here. Last night I learned that no one is willing to adopt Baby Boo and the time has run out to report who the parents will be to DFCS. Apparently, after we decided that our family might not be the best fit for the baby because we are so open and his adoption will be so closed, the doctor refused to talk to anyone else and no one is allowed to see the baby. Of course, that means no prospective adoptive parent is willing to go forward with an adoption of a baby they have never even seen. Some of this hinges on the arrogance of doctors and their ignorance about adoption. However, another element is the "privacy" of the baby. No one but the "parent" is supposed to be privy to the information about the baby. But no prospective parent is willing to agree to be the parent until he/she gets medical information about a premature baby.

My sense is that the attorney's office is pretty angry with John and me. Of course, we still feel like we made a decision that was in the best interest of the baby. No one seems to be able to see beyond his immediate needs as an infant. He is going to grow into a boy, a teenager, and a man. We were looking at the big picture. Meanwhile, I think the attorney wrote us off as soon as we explained our decision. I've heard nothing back from him regarding your offer of out-of-state families.

John and I decided this morning that we needed to offer to be his parents. I called and talked with the legal secretary and made our offer known. She said she would pass the information along to the attorney.

§ § §

We heard again from Julia, who thought the attorney's office had some other leads on possible adoptive families. Then there was silence.

Two days before Thanksgiving, I emailed Julia to find out if Baby Boo had a home. On December 2, 2003, she wrote back with good news. He had a name and a mother. He was growing and healthy. We breathed a sigh of relief. And, yet, we wondered: Did we do the right thing?

It wasn't long before I found another adoption possibility by searching the Internet. The birthmother was in Atlanta. Carri cautioned me about the fees that were proposed and about unlawful facilitators. Once we found out the birthmother did not want an open adoption, we decided it was not the right situation for us. Carri continued to be encouraging. But the roller coaster ride–up and down, up and down–was taking its toll on me.

As an eventful 2003 came to a close, it seemed we were no closer to adopting a fifth child. But we rejoiced in all the other accomplishments of our family. Emily, now in 4th grade, was a Girl Scout and a church acolyte. She was doing well in school now that she had an IEP (Individualized Education Program). She played basketball, soccer, and swam for two teams. She had started horseback riding lessons. K.J., a second grader, swam, played soccer, baseball, and basketball, and took keyboard and piano lessons. Skye, our individualist, delighted in anything creative, including the Halloween Pet Parade she had orchestrated this year. Journey enjoyed another year of Music Class, learned to swim, and had started gymnastics and a ballet-tap class. John and I were equally busy with work and volunteer activities. We had made trips to Disney World, Nebraska, and California. We had even purchased a deed to become co-owners of a ranch in Dahlonega, Georgia. Our latest building project was a deck and screen porch for our house.

I wrote in our annual letter to friends and family: "Despite all the busy-ness, we still made time to grow a small vegetable garden, to read, to ride bikes together, and to dance wildly to loud music."

The One We Were Waiting For

January to December 2004

The Adoption Agency asked me to speak at a program they sponsored at the end of January. I contacted the caseworker who completed our most recent home study for last minute instructions and to ask her about the agency's program for adoption of black and biracial children. I had become aware over the past year that many agencies separated their adoption programs not only into domestic versus international, but also into a Caucasian and mixed race *other than* African American program versus a Black and Biracial program. The programs were priced differently. It was less expensive to adopt a black or biracial child. The demand for these children, as Carri had explained, was not as high as it was for other children. Racism was at work. I found this disturbing, but it was the reality in the adoption world. From the caseworker I wanted to know: "How long is the typical wait to adopt a black or biracial child in your program?" The caseworker suggested I call the agency directly. On January 10th, I called and requested an application.

Two days later, on the afternoon of January 12, 2004, just as I was about to leave the house with the kids for their activities, I got a phone call from an employee of the Adoption Agency. She said, "We received a call from an African-American birthmother who wants to place her baby for adoption. She is currently in labor at Northside Hospital *[the local hospital where all of my sister's children had been born]*. Do you want the baby?"

I was surprised by the call. I had not even received an application for the adoption program yet. On the other hand, I had been down this road of anticipation and disappointment before. I responded, "We are interested, but we really have our hearts set on adopting a boy." The agency worker said she would call back later after the birth when they knew the sex of the baby. I gathered up my children and we went on our way to the sports' practices.

John came home from work while the rest of the family was gone. The phone rang. A voice on the other end exclaimed, "We have your son!" John, who had no idea what was going on, thanked the caller and proceeded to call me immediately for an explanation.

The African-American baby boy had been born at 6:57 p.m. His mother, Diana, had called the first adoption agency in the Yellow Pages when she arrived at the hospital. She wanted the agency to select parents for her child. She didn't care what race they were. Diana didn't want to meet the family. She had kept the pregnancy a secret. She later told the agency worker that if she kept the baby, she would be homeless. On the evening of January 12th, the Adoption Agency was still gathering information about the mother's and the baby's health.

This was exactly the kind of situation Carri had predicted. There was a baby in need of a family. It was a closed adoption. We would not be able to meet, see, or make that "connection" I cherished with other birthmothers. We had been "chosen" by default. That is, as we later learned, we were the only Georgia couple on the Adoption Agency's list with an approved home study who was also willing to adopt an African American baby. The adoption was rushed. We would have to decide now, in the next day or so, based on sketchy, perhaps inaccurate, background information.

By the end of the next day, all the information from the agency about the mother and child sounded good. I contacted my immediate family to let them know what was going on. Just weeks before, we had said "no" to adopting an African American boy that would have been a closed adoption like this one. Was this situation any different? It felt different to us. This was a full-term baby with no known health issues who would not come to us with special medical equipment. And, even though this was a closed adoption, we were provided with some medical and other background. I sensed that one day, maybe, we would be able to find this child's biological family members.

My father asked: "Why do you need to adopt a fifth child?" My brother asked: "Why do you need to adopt a non-white child?"

I tried to put into words what I was feeling when I wrote back to my parents:

> There are lots of little reasons, and a whole history or evolution that I will someday have to put on paper. But the simplest or most direct answer I can give you right now is: it's my calling. This feels like what I'm supposed to do–even though it may not make rational sense, even though I am creating new issues and challenges for us. I am following my heart, a path that I believe I am supposed to follow. I love you. I hope you can continue to tolerate, or even love, me too.

§ § §

Ten minutes later, my dad emailed back:

> I continue both to tolerate and love, and that will go on as long as I do. Just be sure of your feelings when you see the baby, that John is with you, that both of you stay in good health or all of us will have more than we can handle.

John and I knew that seeing the baby was going to make a difference, but we didn't know what kind of difference. On January 15th, we met the caseworker at Northside Hospital at 11:30 a.m. We sat in a small room, separated from the birthmother, and waited. At noon, a nurse pushed the baby bassinet into our waiting area. In an instant, I knew *this* baby was the one. I looked at John. No veto. He, too, seemed at peace with this decision. We signed papers, paid a fee, received instructions, and by mid-afternoon we were on the way home with a new baby.

Emily would not put him down. K.J. was extremely excited about having a brother. Skye organized his meager belongings and diaper bag, and assisted John in assembling a crib. Journey was a little perturbed at her big sisters for telling her how to hold the baby. John and I were still in shock!

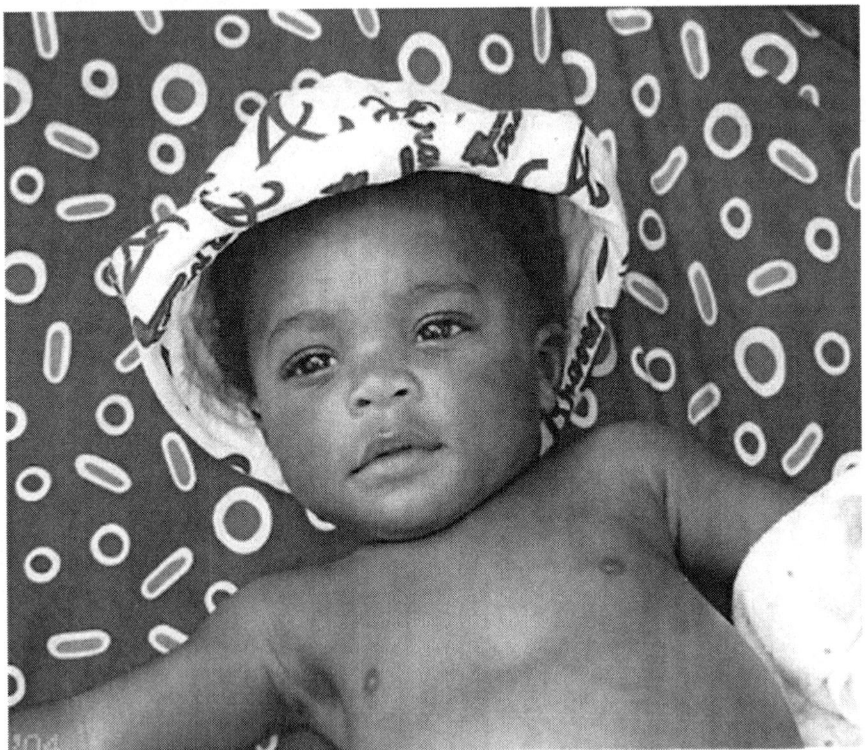

He had a name, this beautiful baby boy. The name had come to me back in the Fall when we were trying to find a name for Baby Boo. Our son's name would be Becton. Our birth announcement provided an explanation for the name: *Meet our new little boy, Becton Justice-Mahari Falco, born January 12, 2004, 6 lbs. 7 oz. 19.5. Becton is named for Rebecca's trial practice instructor at Duke Law School. Charles Becton is a former North Carolina Court of Appeals Judge, a well-respected trial lawyer, and a renowned trial advocacy skills teacher. We wanted Becton to have an intelligent, talented, successful, and compassionate African-American man as a role model. The name "Justice" is linked with "Mahari," an African name for "forgiver." We believe that any solution to racial inequality and prejudice in our*

country and other nations requires both real justice and a willingness to forgive.

§ § §

On January 19th, when Becton was only a week old, I took all five children to march downtown for Martin Luther King, Jr. day. I kept Becton in a cocoon under my coat. I wouldn't say it was a "rude awakening," but I was acutely aware that I still had a lot to learn about African-American culture to raise this new son of mine.

I also received an email that day from Michelle, Emily's birthmother. She wrote:

> "I just wanted to say congratulations! Y'all deserve at least 9 more for that little league team John needs to coach. We just wanted to send our love and let y'all know we are very proud to have you as an extended family."

Ironically, four days after Becton came home with us, I got a call from an attorney looking for adoptive parents for an African-American baby boy who wanted a *fully* open adoption–that is, an adoption with ongoing contact after the placement. When I told the attorney that we had just brought home a baby, she replied that she thought the birth family would be fine with us having two babies. For a split second, I considered the possibility. Then I remembered the man I married and referred the attorney to Carri.

Though I had said our family was *complete* before, I was even more convinced this time. I wasn't sure I would ever stop wanting babies, but I knew I was getting too old, chronologically, to continue adding newborns to our family. It just wouldn't be fair to the child. Now that Becton was here, I could give myself completely to the raising of these young Falcos. As our children grew, we were discovering more and more about their unique learning styles, medical issues, and personality characteristics. With each passing year, we saw more of their genetic "programming" displayed in the individuals they were becoming.

The key for us as parents seemed to be in learning how to direct these predispositions so that our children could be as successful as possible in their chosen pursuits, whether in school, in sports, in music or dance, in social interactions, or in any creative or other ventures. It was and continues to be challenging. And every day I am grateful to have such a devoted partner and father in John.

In April, a friend asked me if I had told Marissa, the mother of the Utah baby, about our adoption of Becton. No, I had not told her. I had certainly thought about her. But I wasn't sure I could find her. Last I knew she was living in a church shelter with her baby and older daughter. Surely, by now, she had moved on. However, the question spurred me to take action. I looked up the shelter number and called. The person I spoke with told me that she would look for a forwarding address or number. I left a number that Marissa could call and the message: "We adopted a baby."

Two days later, Marissa called. She sounded great. She, Tamara, and Marcel had moved out of the shelter after a few weeks and into an apartment. A couple of months ago, they had moved again to a better apartment in a better neighborhood. Marissa had a job with an insurance company and the children were in a wonderful daycare. Terrence had moved back to Utah a few weeks earlier. Although she wasn't sure where their relationship would go, she said he was a great help with the children. He had also given her a car. She said she was "very happy."

We talked about Becton's adoption. Marissa said that she had carried around a lot of guilt about what happened. She loved Marcel, but she felt bad for us. I told her that was part of the reason I wanted her to know we had a baby now. It felt like we both had the babies we were supposed to have. She went on to say that she still valued my presence in her life. When people ask, "So, why did you move to Utah?" she can't tell them about the original adoption plan. She has to make something up. It was nice to know there was someone she could be honest with. We ended by promising we'd be sending each other pictures of our children and would try to stay in touch over time.

At the end of April 2004, I took Emily, Skye, and Becton to Washington, D.C. for the *March for Women's Lives*. A number of people asked me about our weekend, so I wrote an email with the subject title: pro-adoption *and* pro-choice. I knew that some of my friends and former clients would be shocked to hear that I supported "choice." I went on:

> "Don't all adoption advocates believe that life begins at conception, and that abortion is the equivalent of killing?" I have wrestled with that question much of my adult life. The "Baby Killer" signs are so powerful. Believe me, I had a hard time explaining the signs to two young girls who do not yet fully understand sex or baby making. "Why are they saying we want to kill babies, Mama?"
>
> For a long time I tried to come up with a rationalization that eliminated the need for referring to the fertilized egg, the cluster of cells, or the embryo as a potential life. But it is a potential human being. The truth is that making the choice to terminate a pregnancy is a huge decision. I do not know a person who has made that choice who found it easy. In the cases I know about, it wasn't easy, but it was necessary for as many different reasons as there are women who make that decision. People get into these situations because of failed birth control. The withdrawal, the condom, the pill, and so forth didn't work. There was never an intention to be pregnant. Having a baby would have damaged the woman's life in some irreparable way. And not everyone can carry a baby to term and place him/her for adoption. There is a cost there too.
>
> Look at all the un-parented children there are already in the world. Look at all the children we refuse to acknowledge, to feed, to house, and to nurture into productive adulthood. Look at

all the women dying and crippled from illegal abortions or pregnancies and births that they would have chosen not to have had conditions been otherwise. It is very scary to me to think about governments, men, or anyone other than the woman herself making the decision to endure nine months of pregnancy, labor and delivery, and the responsibility of raising a happy, healthy child. I just can't imagine a world in which half of its citizens do not have the right to make choices that concern their own bodies.

It was a memorable trip in many ways. Of particular note is that we stopped in Durham, North Carolina for Becton to meet Charles Becton, his wife, and daughter.

In May, I was contacted by a birth grandmother about her 14-year-old pregnant daughter who was currently living in a maternity home. The young woman, Nicole, wanted an open adoption with on-going contact after the birth. She also wanted to pick the name that the child would use. I was asked to help locate possible parents for the baby who was due in late July or early August. The baby was thought to be a full Caucasian boy.

By June 1st, I had collected profile letters to send to Nicole and her mother. Along with the profiles, I enclosed a cover letter that read, in part:

> In my experience with other birth families, this is a very personal journey. I would never be able to predict who you ought to 'match' with. You will begin to know what feels right for you as you read the letters. Having said that, I am certainly willing to get other information about the couples who interest you before you make contact with them–if that is something you want.

Nicole and I corresponded. She had lots of questions about the process that I was able to answer. She also wanted to know if her requests regarding the adoptive parents were "reasonable." I explained:

> Different birth parents have different requests. If naming the baby is very important to you, then you have every right to hold out until you find a family that can honor your request. I will say, however, that sometimes, when adoptive parents and birth parents really click, they discover that they can be more flexible than they thought before they met each other. For example, you and the adoptive parents might agree to each give him a name (first or middle), and then compromise on what he will be called. Again, it is like any human relationship–you don't really know

what it's like until you are in the middle of it. Having said that, you have every right to stick with the stuff that is of utmost importance to you. Just ask yourself: Why is this so important to me?

Nicole chose parents that she thought would give her child a good home and a good life. I facilitated a match meeting. The name issue was resolved by giving Nicole's chosen name for the baby as one of his middle names. Her baby was born on August 5, 2004, in Savannah, Georgia.

Nicole wanted to spend the time in the hospital with just her family and the baby, but I was invited to be there and to act as eyes and ears for the adoptive parents. I flew down on the 6th and stayed with them until they were discharged from the hospital on the 7th. Nicole, her mother, and stepfather drove with the baby to the Atlanta area to deliver him to his adoptive parents. The idea was to be able to see her son's new home, room, and environment, and to continue to develop the relationship with the adoptive family. It was too painful for Nicole to go into the house that night, but the baby was delivered.

The next day, I met the birth family at the attorney's office to handle the paperwork. We were able to talk about her feelings before the signing began. Nicole had recovered enough to want to go back to the adoptive parents' home for a *real* visit. According to the adoptive parents, that visit went very well. Nicole planned to come back again in two weeks.

Nicole was a remarkable young woman who was genuinely in love with her baby and genuinely interested in only what was best for him. I felt privileged to have been part of this blending of families.

The timing of these requests to help others find homes for their babies was thought provoking to me. In 2002, when Chelsea and Jack were looking for parents for Faith, I knew I would have wanted to adopt her *but for* having just taken Isaac into our home as a foster child. In January 2004, when the adoption attorney asked us to take an

African-American baby boy whose family wanted a fully open adoption, I know I would have said "yes" *but for* having just adopted Becton. Later in 2004, when Nicole needed help finding parents for her baby boy who wanted a fully open relationship, I would have offered the Falcos as ideal candidates *but for* our full house. Each of these aforementioned situations offered specifics that I had on my mental list of what goes into a perfect adoption for me.

I don't have the kind of faith that would allow me to say these events were divinely ordered. What I do believe is that with all the complications in their adoptions and the less-than-perfect circumstances, Emily, K.J., Skye, Journey, and Becton are my perfect children. They are by no means always easy. Sometimes I feel like we are a group of seven completely different species living under the same roof! But that is part of what makes being their parent rewarding. No two days are alike. When I think about my job history and my personality, I have to acknowledge that I hate repetition. I have always been on the move, looking for the next challenge or adventure. Here it is. Here *they* are.

I also believe that the circumstances that prevented me from adopting those other children gave me the opportunity to do something good for *others*. That was my wedding pledge after all. As I was a participant and facilitator in those adoptions, I hoped–and I continue to hope now–that I would have other opportunities to facilitate the creation of families.

On November 18, 2004, I heard from Eve, Skye's birth grandmother. I asked about Christina. She confirmed that Christina had given birth to another daughter in late October 2003, named Caroline. Eve said that about the time Christina got both boys back from DFCS, she had managed to find Christina a 4-bedroom apartment where she and the kids lived for awhile. Then Christina got another boyfriend who lived in Atlanta and she started staying with him at his place, taking the kids with her. The boyfriend also had four kids. Because Christina was spending so little time at her apartment, she had to give it up. Then she and the boyfriend broke up. Now Christina is living with a friend in Marietta with her four children. Eve was worried about Isaac's behavior. She even worried that Christina might "give up" the children. I relayed this information to the Griffins, but I kept it from the Lewises. John and I thought this news would upset them too much.

By the end of 2004, my pursuit of adoption had become a thing of the past, and we had relaxed into our roles in the family. I created a "favorite things" matching test for the readers of our annual holiday letter. John's favorite things included "TiVo, power tools, business travel, and a place for everything and everything in its place." Emily loved "riding horses, talking to friends at school, TV & computer, and exerting control over small people." K.J. could be found "playing piano, playing soccer, reading, and zoning out in front of *any* screen: TV, computer, movie, etc." Skye would be "playing soccer, creating art, exploring nature, making huge messes, and refusing to clean them up." Journey's favorite things were "dressing up in fancy clothes and jewelry, playing Princesses, drawing letters and pictures, gymnastics and dance." Becton loved "electrical cords, toilet water splashing, plastic bottles, vanilla cereal snackin' squares, and sucking his two middle fingers." And I was especially fond of "taking pictures, time to write, running with friends, and our nanny Sherry!"

Never a Dull Moment

January to December 2005

I had been told that one does not cut an African-American child's hair in the first year of their life. I honored that tradition. As Becton's hair got longer, we used braids. Of course, I didn't know how to make the braids. I could barely get my other children to brush their hair, let alone style it. But one of the nurses at our pediatrician's office graciously agreed to braid Becton's hair for me. It was a lengthy process and somewhat painful to him; but she said that children get used to it. The second time she braided his hair, she had agreed to braid my hair too. I had this great idea that Becton and I would get our picture made in black and white with our braids, a striking contrast. Becton's hair almost knitted itself into braids. My hair was a different story. The nurse cautioned me to get the pictures made "soon," because my braids might not last more than a day. She was right.

I had never been a girly-girl. I probably spent ten minutes each day on my own hair and make-up–just enough mascara to make my blond eyelashes visible. So, when it came to keeping Becton's hair appropriately groomed, I was ill prepared. Dozens of African-American women offered unsolicited advice about how to care for his skin and hair over the course of his first year. I was never offended. I appreciated the help.

On Becton's first birthday, it was time of his first haircut. I had been taking the older Falco children to get haircuts at a kid-friendly salon near our home. However, when the owner told me that they "don't do black hair," I realized I would be looking for a new hair cutting establishment for all of us.

As I had done for the other children, I saved a "lock" of hair from the first haircut for Becton's baby book. I had to laugh. It wasn't a curl I could neatly store in a baggy and lay flat in his book. It was a puffball. I was in unchartered territory–for *me*–and I had better pay attention and learn everything I could.

With Becton's first year behind us, I was ready to write the story of his adoption. I titled it: "Confessions of a Southern White 'Mama'." It was published by *Adoption Today* magazine in its October/November 2005 edition. Although I have already shared most of the details that comprised the series of events leading up to Becton's adoption, it was only with hindsight that I thought I understood the process and its effects on me. I ended the article with this:

> In the process of adopting Becton, I came to understand myself better. I also became more sensitized to racism. I started with the simple idea that I would find a male child whose skin tone would match our other not-fully-Caucasian child, and he would fill the last puzzle piece of our family portrait. In the end, I have chosen something far more complicated. I have made the commitment to be a parent to Becton, a child who will always be perceived as different from me on the outside and whose ancestry honors traditions I have only begun to learn. Moreover, the historical and on-going oppression of African-Americans will affect Becton in ways I must strive to understand. Our family must learn to live with the closed nature of Becton's adoption that is one side effect of the role that race plays in adoption in this country.
>
> I hope Becton grows up knowing he is loved for who he is, being proud of his family and his ancestry, and feeling as beautiful as he is to me. It is also my heartfelt hope that being Becton's parent will encourage me to help build bridges between races and cultures, and to confront and tear down prejudices that are destructive to human lives.

§ § §

Tessa, K.J.'s birthmother, was good about keeping us up to date on developments in our Nebraska family. In April 2005, she wrote with news about a divorce, a marriage, and a baby in the extended family. I wrote back about planning a trip to Nebraska and to ask for some advice. One of the things we knew about Kyle, K.J.'s birth father, was that he had played baseball and, reportedly, was a third baseman with a "good arm." K.J. was playing baseball too, but he got discouraged easily when his team didn't win. Could Kyle offer some advice? He wrote back on April 21, 2005:

> All I can say is practice, practice, practice. It doesn't matter how good or bad one person on a team is. The team wins together and loses together. There is no need to be discouraged. Everyone will get better with time and practice. Even if your team doesn't win you have to look at how you played in the game. Did I do well at my part in the game? What do I need to work on to be better in the next game? Just work on getting your game at the best that you can make it and don't worry about wins and loses. At this point the win/lose record means nothing; it's all about improving yourself for the future. Good luck and play hard.
>
> Love, Kyle

§ § §

One of the things I loved about open adoption was the ability to have just this kind of exchange with family members. K.J. could feel supported by all of his relatives, biological and adopted.

Now that I wasn't writing to facilitate an adoption, I had more time to write about the daily life of the Falcos. Writing helped me cope when I felt inadequate and out-of-control. It was therapy. This is one example of the reporting I did about our days:

Email to family and friends dated May 7, 2005

At my children's school, I'd been given the job of taking black & white photos of all the fifth-graders for graduation. I still can't believe my baby is going to Middle School next year! I went to school in the afternoon, carrying Becton in the backpack, with my camera and a bag of costumes for Emily and K.J. for drama practice that day. After taking some pictures and delivering the costumes, I picked up Journey who had decided that she needed to go to the house of her friend, Jack. When I explained how that would not fit in the day's schedule, she fell apart. On the way home, she kicked the van window and squealed. As a consolation prize, I offered her the Krispy Kreme chocolate-iced donuts I was hiding in the basement refrigerator. She screamed that she only wanted crullers. She insisted that I go to Publix grocery store immediately and get them for her.

When I agreed, stupidly, to do that, she said: "No. I really want to get ice cream at Brusters. Then I want you to go to the grocery store for the crullers." I made it home and ran into the house, expecting to find Sherry to save me from hysterical Journey.

No Sherry. There was a message on the answering machine that she had a family emergency and would not be able to make it today. I went back to the van and announced that we were leaving to go across town to pick up Skye from her private school while Emily and K.J. were at drama practice. I knew there would be more screaming, so I promised ice cream for good behavior on the ride to and from Skye's school.

With Skye in tow, we bought the ice cream and raced home. I had 20 minutes to get Skye's soccer gear collected, Emily's and K.J.'s swimming stuff and changes of clothes, as well as snacks and a supper for 5 kids that would be eaten in the van between swimming and the church choir skating party that night. I asked

Skye to gather her things. She got most of it, but forgot shorts. When I asked her to go back for them, she yelled, "No. You do it. I'm busy." Meanwhile, Journey is screaming for the movie 'Anastasia' to watch in the car. "You find it, Mom!"

I did not have time to impose the discipline that was called for. Emily and K.J. had to be picked-up at a certain time at school or I would be in trouble with the drama teacher. I was already ten minutes late, having taken five loads of stuff to the van, when I slammed the door shut. It was then that I realized I had film canisters, not van keys, in my pocket.

Now, usually, when this happens, I send K.J. through the dog door in the basement to retrieve the keys. We call him our "rescue hero." Since he wasn't available, I asked Skye to help me. "No! I'm not doing it."

"You have to. I can't get through the door. It's too small for me. My shoulders won't go through."

"No!"

This went on for a few minutes as I walked her around the house to the dog door and pleaded with her for help. Eventually, she agreed. But as soon as she looked through the door, she yelled: "I'm not going! It's dark in there."

"Look! The light switch is two feet in front of you. All you have to do is crawl through and flip the switch."

"No. No. I'm not going!"

Ten minutes more had passed. In desperation, I said, "I'll have to do it myself. But you will pay for this!" (John later said he would have tossed Skye through the dog door at this point. I approach Skye differently. She is so 'street smart' that I was imagining her calling DFCS to report child abuse if I pushed the matter further.)

I stuck my head through. But when I got to the shoulders, I had to twist and turn, scraping myself. Now my torso was dangling in the air over the flight of stairs that John built for the dogs to reach the window. It runs perpendicular to the door, against the wall, with a landing about 18" wide. I was going to have to wrench myself around to reach the stairs. Then a new problem surfaced. Perhaps, until this time, I was in denial about the width of my hips. They were not going through. I was stuck like Winnie the Pooh trying to leave Rabbit's house after eating all the honey. I could not go back. I could not move forward.

Time was ticking away… "Skye! Take off my pants!"

"What?"

"Undo the button and zipper of these jeans and wiggle me out. That's the only way I can get unstuck."

She complied. Now the bottom half of my body was sticking out in the backyard, covered in only underwear and socks.

But–it worked. I cursed and rubbed bruises on my hips and legs, but I got into the house!

Minutes later, we were racing to pick up the kids from drama practice and hurtle onward to swim practice. As Emily and K.J. climbed in the van, I cautioned them to eat a quick snack and then get right to their homework because of our tight schedule. As we approached Agnes Scott College, where swim practice was being held, I asked the two how much homework they had left to do. "Homework? Oh, I'll get it out." Right.

Emily and K.J. ran for the pool. Journey said, "I need to pee real bad. Can I go here?" "Here" being the two-foot strip of grass between the parking lot and the tennis courts.

"Can't you wait to get inside?"

"I can't!"

"All right, then."

A minute later, Skye did the exact same thing.

Becton had taken a short nap in the car. As I picked him up, I could tell he was about to burst his diaper. While the girls were peeing in the UN-woods, I kept encouraging them to speed things up so I could get to the bathroom to change Becton. Once in the building, I successfully wrestled him out of the very wet diaper and into a dry one. I turned my back to put up the supplies. Journey comes running over: "Becton just sat in a puddle and he is soaked!"

John left work early to take Skye to soccer practice and Journey to Nanna's for transportation to choir practice at church while I stayed at the pool. From swimming, Emily left with her cousins for the skating party. I waited for K.J. As K.J., Becton, and I were driving to the church, K.J. said, "Oh, I just remembered I have three other homework assignments." I changed directions and dropped him off with his father and sister, who were nearly ready to go home from the soccer field, so that K.J. could complete his assignments before midnight.

Becton and I made it the rest of the way to church without incident. By now, there was only 20 minutes left of choir practice. I sat, stunned, for the duration. Then I collected Journey and Becton and headed for home. We stopped for gas. Becton had not been eating well that day. (Is it any wonder? What is he going to say about this crazy family when he is older?) I opened a cup of yogurt to feed him while the gas ran into the tank. Journey insisted on taking over while I finished the process and paid. When I returned to the car, Becton was covered in peach yogurt and Journey was laughing. I mean it was down his shirt and behind his ears. It was everywhere. There would be an unplanned bath to administer when we got home.

Well, that was my day. I suppose, someday, I will laugh about it. Right now, however, as I write this, I hear Skye and one of her friends crawling back and forth through the dog door. How do you think I feel about that?!

§ § §

In the summer of 2005, we bought an older home in the historic Druid Hills neighborhood of Atlanta where I had grown up. This charming home had a back staircase, solid plaster walls, an unconventional floor plan, beautiful molding, and a carriage house, but it had fewer bedrooms than our current home. We believed our children would quickly adjust. Emily would have her own room, but the boys would share a room and Journey and Skye would share a room.

In our Decatur home, Journey's room was decorated with stars, moons, and princesses, while Skye's room was animal-print linens and posters of creatures. I knew the girls would need to compromise about how to decorate and use their room, so I began the discussion with 5-year-old Journey as I put her to bed:

Email to family and friends dated August 24, 2005

Skye uses a white-noise maker to help her sleep. Journey plays Disney princess songs. I asked Journey how she thought we might handle this–after explaining what compromise is and why it is important. She said, "Well, either I get to take my princess songs and Skye has to leave her noisemaker here, or she gets to take her noisemaker and I have to leave my princess songs here." I responded: "That's one way to handle it. But what if Skye had her noisemaker on low on her side of the room and you had your princess songs on low on your side of the room? Then both of you would have something you want."

"Or, think about this: you never want the ceiling fan on. Skye wants it on high. What do we do about that? Perhaps, you could compromise and set the ceiling fan on low." Sure that I had made my point, I gave her a new scenario: "What do we do about the night light situation? You have a bunny light and a flower light. Skye's night light is an animal lamp."

Journey responded: "We use my lights. And if Skye has a fit because we don't use her animal light, then we do it my way anyway. Okay?"

§ § §

In November 2005, I wrote to inform our family members about some significant changes going on with our birth families in Nebraska. Michelle, Emily's birthmother, and Jason, Emily's birth father, had reunited after eleven years apart, other marriages and more children. Tessa and Kyle, K.J.'s birth parents who had stayed together, married and had three more boys, were getting divorced. Tessa and her boys were now living with Michelle and Jason. Without open adoption, we would have missed so much drama!

Finally a Happy Ending

January to April 2006

In early 2006, I talked to Marissa, the Utah birthmother, again. Over time, we had communicated sporadically, exchanging letters, pictures, and phone calls. A few months earlier, Marissa went through a horrific experience with Terrence. She was kidnapped, raped, and brutalized. Ultimately, he was tried and sentenced to 20 years to life in prison. For many years, Marissa had had ups and downs. She suffered from depression and a cyclical pattern of being involved with violent men. I still believed that she was smart, good-hearted, and that she cared deeply about her children. I also identified with her. I remembered being in an abusive relationship, not knowing how to get out, and all the while trying to do what was right and most loving.

The night before, Marissa's mother had called me from Jacksonville, Florida. She had said that Marissa and her two kids–Tamara, age 9, and Marcel, age 2 1/2–were homeless. She was paying for them to stay in an Intown Suites for a week, but she couldn't do any more. She was already raising Marissa's older daughter. She thought that both Marissa and Tamara needed professional counseling. She had promised Marissa, who didn't have her own phone, that she would call me.

I called back and spoke with Marissa, who told me that all the shelters in Salt Lake City were full. We talked at length about her options. Ultimately, I suggested we find a way to get her to Georgia where I could better help her. She agreed that sounded like a good plan.

When I got off the phone, Emily asked me what was going on and I filled her in. I reflected, "I know I can't save the whole world..." Emily responded, "But you can do something about this."

I contacted our church and others in the community whom I thought might be able to help. The response to my email regarding Marissa's emergency situation was heart-warming. Friends offered frequent flyer miles, clothes and toys, a bed and kitchen table, kitchen appliances, money, babysitting and homework help, meal preparation, and contacts with folks in Salt Lake City who might help. The Partnership Against Domestic Violence offered their services as well. One of our ministers set up a method for sending monetary donations through the church. I waited for Marissa to make definitive plans.

A few days later, Marissa called and told me that she had found housing in Utah. She had also found some kind of work. I told her there was money from others who were also concerned about her, if she needed it. She was very, very appreciative. I did not hear from her again.

Later, I emailed the people who had offered to help Marissa to thank them for their generosity. It had not gone unnoticed by Marissa. I believe that knowing she had options, knowing there was a way out or a way through her predicament, made the psychological difference that kept her going. I continued to be grateful that our lives had intersected even if it didn't turn out exactly as I had originally planned.

This must have been the year to finish old business with birthmothers because on April 1, 2006, I received a call from Skye's birth grandmother, Eve. She brought shocking news about Christina and her children, which I was quick to share with the children's former foster parents and a few others by email:

Email dated April 1, 2006

> Christina, birthmother of our daughter, Skye, has had seven children with seven fathers. The first boy was left with his father. Number two, Skye, was adopted by us. Christina tried to parent the third and fourth, Isaac (born 4/99) and Jacob (born 8/00). In 2001, DFCS in DeKalb County took custody. The children spent time in separate, loving foster homes. Christina had another

baby, Claire (born 8/02). Ultimately, the boys were reunited with Christina in the spring of 2003. By then, she was pregnant with the sixth, Caroline (born 10/03). A continuing tumultuous life followed: different men, different homes and schools.

A few months ago, Christina took the kids to Florida, gave birth to another baby girl and placed her for adoption through an agency. She returned to Atlanta, leaving the four other children in Florida with a family she met through the adoption agency. Eventually, the Florida family agreed to bring the children to Christina's mother, Eve, in northwest Georgia. Eve and her husband love the children, but they are not physically and financially able to keep them. The children were with their grandparents for three months before Eve asked Christina to take them back. She didn't want them. They were turned over to DeKalb County DFCS–I presume because the original custody of the boys was there.

It is my understanding that there is a hearing at juvenile court on Monday, April 3, to determine what happens next. If I can find out when and where the hearing will be, I plan to be there to stand up for the grandparents, to let the court know that they love the children, but that they aren't able to take care of them full-time. They would love an open relationship with whoever receives them. Christina's younger brother, and his wife seem interested in taking the younger child, Caroline. If that arrangement is approved, that leaves three other children needing loving homes: Isaac (almost 7), Jacob (who will be 6 in August), and Claire (who will be 4 in August).

Whether you have foster parent status or not, I think it may be persuasive to say to a judge that you have interest in one or more of these particular children and that you would maintain an open arrangement with the extended family. Let me know if you have any interest and what that interest may be. Thanks–
Rebecca

§ § §

I got an immediate response from Lisa and Wesley Lewis, Jacob's previous foster parents. Of course they were interested in adopting Jacob! I did not hear from the Griffins, Isaac's previous foster parents.

I went to the juvenile court hearing on April 3rd, and reported what I saw and heard there:

> The judge in juvenile court ruled that Christina's children are "deprived"– which means they stay in foster care for now. Christina was there, along with others (including myself) who care about the future of these children. Christina states that she does not want them back. She wants them in stable situations "where they have the opportunity to go to college." She was appointed an attorney, and a group of us met with him and Christina after the hearing. In short, we plan to go back to court on April 17th with a permanency plan for the children. Christina's brother and sister-in-law want to adopt Caroline. The Lewises, Jacob's foster parents for two years, want to adopt him. We are exploring adoption options for Isaac and Claire–and have some leads, but could use others. Christina is in agreement with this plan and intends to tell the judge on April 17th that she is ready to surrender her rights.
>
> A deprivation determination means that Christina will be assigned a caseworker who creates a plan for her to complete in order to get her kids back. This is not what she wants. Christina's attorney and the DFCS attorney think that if we come prepared with an adoption plan on the 17th, there is a good chance that the judge will dismiss the case and allow Christina to voluntarily choose homes for her children. If he does not dismiss the case, DFCS will have the say over who gets them.

§ § §

The Lewises, the Florida family, and I had all been at the hearing with an emotional Christina. After the hearing, the children met informally with those of us who had been in attendance. Etched in my mind is the initial encounter between Wesley Lewis and Jacob. Jacob ran to him; and Wesley, with tears in his eyes, embraced Jacob, saying, "I missed you *so* much!" I was so sorry that the children had had to endure such instability during the past few years, but I was certain in that moment that Jacob had found his way home.

I was feeling a little desperate about what would happen to Isaac and Claire. Could the Falcos adopt them? Each child really needed more time and attention than I thought we could give them in our family. But I just couldn't leave the situation alone. I felt like I *had* to find homes for them. I hoped the children would have adoptive homes in or near Atlanta, so they could see each other. Christina had agreed that Russ and Naomi Griffin could have Isaac. Why hadn't I heard from the Griffins?

I stepped away from the gathering at the courthouse to call them. I reached Naomi on the phone and reported what had happened in court. "He's yours if you want him," I remember saying. Naomi seemed confused. After talking with her for a few more minutes, I discovered that the email address I had for her was no longer working. She had not received any of the prior information and had no idea what I was talking about. I filled her in; and she hung up to talk with Russ. The Griffin family had some fast thinking *and praying* to do. Within a few minutes, Russ and Naomi called back to say. "Yes. We want to adopt Isaac."

In response to my April 1st email about the children, I had heard from neighbors and friends, Rachel and Steven, who were very interested in adopting Claire, though they had no prior relationship with the young girl. The family from Florida had also expressed an interest in taking both Isaac and Claire home with them before the Griffins resurfaced. The judge had seemed hesitant to send the children out of state. Though tearful and distraught, Christina seemed anxious to get the arrangements worked out so that she could move on. I feared that unless we came up with a clear and effective plan soon, Christina might waver in her spoken commitment to placing these children for adoption.

The Falcos went to Nebraska for Spring Break week. But while I was away and when I returned, I was heavily involved in working out the details of the children's adoptions.

On April 11, 2006, I talked with the attorney who had come to my aid in Utah. She had a very clear plan about what needed to happen legally. She said that Christina had a right to choose parents for her children regardless of the pending deprivation action. She recommended that Christina hire *her* and have *her* draft all the documents. The respective adoptive parents would be responsible for the legal costs. The attorney said that she could get started right away and be in court on Monday.

I relayed this information to the Griffins, Lewises, Christina's brother and sister-in-law, and Rachel and Steven. The families agreed to this plan. I set up a meeting with the attorney for them and Christina on April 13th at 3:30 p.m. The attorney planned to spend some time with each adoptive couple separately and with Christina. She was hoping to set the stage for Christina to sign surrender documents that very afternoon! If it didn't seem appropriate, she was prepared to take the surrenders in conjunction with the court hearing on April 17th.

DFCS had arranged for Christina to visit with the children at their office on the *morning* of April 13th. The prospective adoptive parents were also welcome to come. Sherry was going to warn Christina that a group of people might be at the visit. We all thought this would be a good opportunity to reassure her that all the children would have loving homes.

The prospective adoptive parents came to the visit at DFCS. Isaac, Jacob, and Caroline–all having prior relationships with their chosen adoptive parents, were happy to see them. Claire, on the other hand, was meeting a stranger, Rachel. Christina was uncomfortable with that arrangement. At the attorney's office that afternoon, Christina surrendered her parental rights to Isaac, Jacob, and Caroline in favor of the Griffins, Lewises, and her brother and sister-in-law, respectively. Rachel and Steven were disappointed, but they understood. Christina held onto her parental rights to Claire. In ten days, the surrenders would become final and the families would be free to file their petitions for adoption of their child.

The Griffins were still certified foster parents with DFCS. With a little coaxing, they agreed to take Claire as a foster child while Christina worked toward reunification with her–or not. It just made sense to keep the siblings together, if possible.

The attorneys did their jobs; and children left court with their new families. It was a joyous occasion for the new families, but understandably difficult for Christina. I stayed behind another few minutes to console her and to reassure her that she had done the right thing for them.

The Falco family was off to Durham for a Duke reunion; but we returned in time to host an "11th Day" party to celebrate the passing of the 10-surrender period. The Griffins, the Lewises, Christina's brother and sister-in-law, the Falcos, and all our children were there to celebrate. Naomi Griffin joked that she and I were related now. She just couldn't figure out what to call me: "half/sister non-bio-mom twin, maybe?"

It was a very good ending to a long and difficult journey that had begun with my desire to adopt Isaac even before he was born. Claire would ultimately be adopted by the Lewises, too. I could not have predicted this "end," nor would I have wanted it years before. But time, experience, and circumstances had changed my "wanting." This *was* the right ending, and a new beginning for these beautiful children and their new families–who were now my relatives–even though we didn't have a name for it.

Biological Difference–or Not?

May 2006 to January 2007

I wrote stories to family and friends over the coming years to share parenting issues, adventures, and amusing events. In this final part of my book, I share with you some of the stories that reflect my on-going thoughts about being an adoptive parent.

There are big events in life, like the legal drama related to Christina's children, that boldly announce change. But there are also small things that signal big changes. For example, going to the grocery store, a weekly event, with a new baby solicits strangers to ooh, ahh, and comment. I thought I understood this until Journey came along. Instead of hearing, "Oh, what a beautiful baby," as I had heard with my first three children, I also heard, "What country did you get her from?" I was confused at first; but I quickly realized that others perceived her as different-looking than me. To strangers she had an exotic look that prompted them to assume she came from another land.

When Becton came along, there was no mistaking that he was not my biological offspring–though I did get a few questions about his paternal origins. To my surprise, the question I most often heard in the grocery store was, "Are you a foster parent?" The assumption was that he couldn't possibly be *mine*. Why would a white woman have a black child unless he was "on loan?" I was glad Becton was too young to understand what was being said. I proudly claimed him, but I knew I was at the beginning of a different kind of journey.

Another routine experience, like grocery shopping, is exercise. All of my children had endured the Play Center at the YMCA so that their mother could attempt to stay in shape. Here, again, I discovered that being Becton's mother prompted a different kind of response.

Email to family and friends, dated May 6, 2006

I went to the YMCA to swim today. I put Becton in the Play Center, as usual. When I returned, one of the childcare workers had the children sitting in a circle. Each child seemed to be holding a book or toy. Another parent and I watched for a minute before the worker said, "Does anybody see anyone they know over there?" One child jumped up and ran to her mother. Becton looked up at me, a big grin covered his face, his hands went up, and he called loudly, "Mama!"

Just as he was getting up, the worker said, "That's not your Mama." I felt a little sick, but kept a big grin on my face. Becton looked puzzled. Then he started to come toward me again. The woman repeated, "That's not your mother. Come back and sit down." His head fell, but he turned and walked back to the circle.

As I called out, "I am his mother," with a smile still frozen on my face, Becton again turned toward me.

The worker looked at a little white girl who had risen from her place in the circle and was wandering aimlessly–not looking at me, and said, "Not the mother of this little boy," and she said again to Becton, "Sit down." He did. Sadness and fear covered his face as he began to suck his two middle fingers.

I reiterated, "But I AM his mother. Come here Becton." He glanced at the worker and then ran to me, smiling again.

I've been prepared for things to be different, parenting Becton. This is small potatoes. But it is still hard to see my precious child hurt because someone denied his reality.

§ § §

Though my family was complete, I still struggled with some of the issues that plague infertile couples. What sort of children would I have had if I had been able to conceive? I confessed my turmoil to close friends and family.

Email dated July 7, 2006

> Our children's swim team coach just announced which kids have made the finals for the county swim meet. My children were not among them. Yesterday, I was with K.J. and Emily for most of the day at the preliminaries. I experienced an array of emotions related to my children and competition–none of which I shared with them. I am always careful to encourage them to work to their abilities and to praise them for the hard work they do. Sometimes, I also nudge them to try new things, and to look past or conquer their fears. But I will not be a parent who tries to live out her athletic dreams through her children.
>
> I watched other mothers with their children. Interestingly, and not surprisingly, I am attracted to competitive, strong-willed women as friends. What I observe, for the most part, is that these women have competitive, driven children. Is it genetic or learned? My experience would suggest that it is mostly genetic. My children are not competitive. They are happy to be here, to socialize, to receive ribbons, to be part of a team–but they are not "fighters." They have no idea what their race times are, and they don't care.
>
> There is a part of me that is sad when my children are left behind. They are not sad. It is my sadness. I also find myself feeling jealous of friends who have children who compete strongly. But then I feel ashamed to have these feelings.
>
> I wonder: Would a non-athletic adoptive mother of a child with the potential to be an Olympic gold medalist notice that child's talent? Or would she enroll him or her in painting and pottery classes?
>
> Being an adoptive parent ought to force one to think outside

one's "box" of experience. I try to ask myself on a regular basis: What am I missing? What else might this child get excited about doing or learning or being?

I know that not all competitive parents produce competitive children. I remember how my dad enrolled my artistic brother in one sport or another, but he never took a real interest. Meanwhile, his daughters were playing basketball, volleyball, softball, and soccer.

When I think about adoption, I try to appreciate the struggles and sadness that comes with being an adoptee or birth parent. But there are also times that I feel sadness in my identity as an adoptive parent. It is a kind of sadness that I don't think I would feel as a biological parent. Every time I hear someone mention a physical or personality trait that is shared by parent and child, I feel a twinge of jealousy.

The other day, Skye was looking at a picture of my parents with their three oldest children at ages 3 to 6. Skye asked, "Which one is you? Oh, wait, it's that one *[indicating me]*. I can tell because she looks like me." I felt pure joy at hearing those words.

Now, I love my children. And I would not trade them for aspiring Olympic athletes or carbon copies of John and me for anything. But, today, on my baby Emily's 12th birthday, I just wanted to acknowledge that these feelings I've mentioned exist–in flashes and sporadically–still and perhaps for always.

§ § §

There were other times when not being a genetic parent was irrelevant. I share one example of that kind of experience.

Email to family and friends, dated August 20, 2006

K.J. would be classified as a "shy kid." He was the kind of small child that hid behind my legs when introduced to someone new, the kind of child who would not make eye contact or volunteer an answer in a group. Having some familiarity with those feelings of shyness myself, I have always pushed K.J. to work through his shyness so that he doesn't miss out on events and people and the positive feelings that come from having overcome your "weaknesses."

K.J. is also a child who has been involved in our church all his life. He seems to have accepted the existence of God and the moral example of Jesus. (Contrast this with his sister Skye who will tell you that God is something adults made up.) All of this is background to the following story:

Yesterday, we received a call from our Children's Minister asking if K.J. would read the Gospel lesson in church today–Promotion Sunday. K.J. quickly agreed to do so. Yesterday was also the day of Skye's birthday party. Some of K.J.'s friends were in attendance as well. Toward the end of the party, K.J.'s friend, Jake, invited him to spend the night. I reminded him that he had already made a commitment to read scripture in church the next morning. With that, he began to moan, complain, and say he didn't want to do it. After some discussion with Jake's mother and John, I offered him the option of going to Jake's house, but being picked-up in the morning in time to get to church. K.J. agreed and apologized for his behavior.

When I arrived at Jake's house to get K.J., he was already grumpy. On the way to church, I had him read the verses aloud to me. Each time he did it, his head sunk lower on his chest. He insisted he couldn't do it. He insisted that he was too shy, that nothing could help him, that no reward or consequence could persuade him to follow through on his commitment. I tried every angle I could think of, but he dug-in his heels. When we got to church, I took him to the sanctuary to practice. He stood with the Bible open and hung his head. It seemed pointless. I got other adults involved in persuading him and trying to build his confidence. They were not successful either. As church began, I took him to sit on the front row with the rest of his family. Skye's helpful remark: "I wouldn't do it either."

I reminded K.J. that this was a safe place for him, that people here loved him, that no one would laugh if he fumbled a word, that he was articulate, and that he would feel good after he had spoken. Useless. It all seemed useless.

Fortunately, the service was focused on children and youth. K.J. seemed to begin to forget about some of his misery as we sang hymns that he knew and as children received their Bibles. When it came time for his part, he stood, I held the microphone, and he read. He did a beautiful job. When it was over and he sat down, K.J. let out a sigh of relief, followed by a huge grin.

As the service moved on, I wrote this note to K.J. and handed it to him. It said:

> You may not believe this, but I am like you on the inside. I was so shy when I was young that I was afraid to say anything–even in Sunday school–unless I rehearsed it in my head to make sure it sounded "smart." If I had to do what you did today, I would have a stomach full of "butterflies." In other words, I'd feel like I was going to throw-up! But if I did speak up or speak to a group, I felt so good afterward. And it built my confidence that I could do that sort of thing. So, I believe I know something about how you feel. And I am so, so proud of you!
>
> Love, Mama

After K.J. read the note, he smiled at me and leaned his head against my shoulder.

On the way downstairs to pick-up the younger children, K.J. made this unsolicited remark to me, "I don't think all that whining

I did was really worth it." Then, on the drive home with John, he said, "You know, all that fussing I did was for no reason. And I feel good now."

§ § §

K.J. and I shared shyness. Skye and I shared an enthusiasm about life and learning. The problem with Skye, as her father and I saw it, was her insistence about obtaining the "stuff" that would, in her mind, increase her learning and enthusiasm about life. I shared this story with my family and friends.

Email dated December 19, 2006

Skye is out of school this week, though the other kids are still in. We decided to go to the Atlanta Botanical Gardens. Skye was amazing. Although she has not been there since she was a toddler, she took charge of the map and led us on a tour of the place, seeking out areas that interested her and helping me keep Becton interested and occupied. She knows so much more about plants than I do. She seems to be a sponge when it comes to botanical and "creature" information.

But all good things must come to an end. As I predicted, she did not want to leave without a trip to the gift shop. Now, mind you, before, during, and after our trip, I cautioned Skye that this trip would not include buying anything other than the tickets to get in and, perhaps, some nourishment. She offered to trade her lunch for stuff, but I declined to go along.

Skye homed-in on a Venus flytrap. It was only $5.00. She told me all about their habits and nature. Surely I could buy that for her. "No," I said. Skye pledged her "Christmas money" to me. I reminded her that she did not yet have any Christmas money, and that she already owed me money from this empty fund. She began to cry. Soon she hated me and blamed her brother for my unwillingness to yield because his misbehavior in the store stole my attention away from pleading her case.

Years ago, I was the girlfriend of a recovering alcoholic. I went to some AA meetings, and I learned about the 12-step program. During this painful gift store experience, I kept thinking, "She's like an addict, and 'stuff' is her drug. I brought her into the bar. I'm an enabler! Can I just offer her some coffee and a cigarette to get her mind off of this? Should I ask her to turn her misery over to a 'higher power'?"

Okay, so my analogy may not be perfect. There are probably other issues going on here. But when I finally put my foot down about leaving the store without the plant, she begged, "Then you have to take me to the Dollar Store." Again, my mind drifts to: "If she can't get the good stuff, Boones Farm will do."

As we walked to the car, I suggested that Skye work for the money. Maybe she could do some chores. Her response was: "I'll do one chore for $5.00, not one chore for every dollar." As a parent, you have to wonder: Where is this child headed in her life?

Once Skye has switched out of that "addictive" gimme-gimme mode, she becomes creative, insightful, and delightful again.

Meanwhile, I turn around to pay attention to Becton and he has invented a game of "falling down." Instead of running forward and faking a trip or fall that tumbles him forward, he is running forward and then arching his back so that he throws himself backwards, head-first, onto the ground. Over and over again he does this. I think, "Maybe Becton has come up with the metaphor for my parenting life."

§ § §

It was a good thing I was no longer trying to appear spunky and young to entice birthmothers to place their babies with me. In early

February 2007, I received the call from a nurse who announced, "You are definitely menopausal."

Sherry responded, "No kidding," after seeing me take articles of clothing off, only to reapply them a few minutes later, several times a day for months. John's comment at the end of the day was more like: "Why don't you go take your first 45 minute nap?" He recognized that I spend the other 15 minutes of each hour flinging off the covers and my clothes and fanning myself.

Emily said to me, "My friends can't believe you are 40 *[I wish!]*. They think you are 20 when they see you from behind. It's only when you turn around and they see your face that they know you are older." Should I be flattered? At my age, my mother was the parent of a twenty-five-year-old. She was beautiful. (She still is.) But I imagined she could begin to enjoy some of the empty-nesting advantages of middle age. I, on the other hand, was the mother of a 3-year-old. I still had a long way to go raising children. I was very resistant to looking and feeling "old."

Being menopausal also marked the official end to my fertility. This was something of a joke since I was never fertile. But since my official medical label was "unexplained infertility," I fantasized for years about the unexpected pregnancy. Lately, with the demands of five children, I'd fantasized about getting pregnant, having a biological child, and placing the baby for adoption. Wouldn't that be a twist?

A few weeks later, when I was explaining the hormone replacement patch to John, he said, "I always thought we would eventually get you pregnant."

The comment caught me off guard. I asked, "Do you feel sad about that?"

He responded, "Well, not any more. But I did."

Obviously, I was not alone in trying to conceive a child. John was there to administer fertility drugs, supply specimens, and to support me in those uncomfortable positions that were supposed to make pregnancy more likely. But as time wore on, and it was *I* who experienced the monthly bleeding, *I* who counted the days and watched the calendar for optimal fertile times, *I* who listened to labor and delivery stories of other mothers in my circle of friends and acquaintances–it began to feel more like *my* private journey and loss. I knew that John also endured conversations from co-workers and clients about their pregnancies and families, but I was mostly aware of his efforts to be a good father and provider to the children that we had through adoption. At some level, I must have assumed that he had moved on.

What is it about the "biological child" that is so compelling? I have told the story before of my father's comment at my own birth: "I knew you were mine because you looked like me." Those were words of love and belonging. And, as a child grows, there are more of those kinds of comments: "She gets that *[name the characteristic/trait/talent]* from me." I made those comments myself about my brother's and my sister's children.

Skye and I were together recently when I remarked that a particular trait I have comes from my mother. Skye said, "I have that, too. I got it from you." Then she paused and said, "I wonder if Christina has that too." She knew, as soon as she made the first remark, that it was more complicated, less seamless, for us.

The connections we have with our family members, whether positive or negative, are still *connections.* Some of those connections–our looks, our mannerisms, our abilities, our personalities–are connected to our biology. And, yes, sure, I believe that being loved and feeling loved is principally what belonging to a family is about. But biological differences make our connections more complicated.

Couples are often in different places regarding how long to pursue fertility treatments and whether or not to pursue adoption. One of the ways that I measured the success of my own marriage to John is that each time we have been at different places on this journey, we have found common ground, and been able to more forward. When I thought about his recent comments, it was actually reassuring that we both experienced a similar feeling of loss.

Maybe that was the way I should look at these biological differences between the members of our family created through adoption. We may experience life differently at times because of our innate differences. And each of us experiences the loss of something biological–the biological child, the original parents, the biological siblings…. But I truly believe that through our love for one another, we will always find some common ground and be able to move forward.

Extended Family in Adoption

February 2007 to February 2009

Email to family and friends, dated February 13, 2007

I try to be so organized about upcoming holidays and events. I am constantly writing appointments, ideas, and errands in an oversized calendar that travels everywhere with me. I look for sales on toys and clothes and other items for birthdays that are months away and babies that have not yet been born. When it comes to special days that are celebrated at school, I try to contribute something to everyone's party whether I can physically be there or not. When it comes to Valentine's Day, I am prepared with an array of commercially produced valentines from which my children can pick the "perfect" cards for their list of friends. In the event they want to create homemade cards, I have craft supplies labeled and boxed for their use.

Over the weekend, I was able to convince Journey and K.J. to complete their valentine cards and attach candy. I worked on Becton's cards, and Skye began hers. Emily spent her time doing other things. This afternoon–the afternoon before Valentine's Day–I found Emily in our carriage house watching TV. I had just returned from taking K.J. to his cartooning class. Ignoring the fact that Emily is not supposed to be watching TV without my permission, I asked her if she was ready to do her valentine cards for friends and teachers. She responded, "Well, my friends and I have decided just to bring cupcakes and cookies and other sweets to share. It's a group of six of us. Can you make something?"

Emily is calmly sitting on the sofa. In the room behind me,

Journey and Skye are surrounded by the craft boxes, cutting and pasting and drawing. Becton has arrived with me and is busy cutting and tearing paper. In the next minute, he dashes to the bathroom, announcing loudly: “I need to go potty!” I rush after him. He turns and smiles as he puddles on the floor. After cleaning him and gathering the wet clothes and rug for the laundry, I return to Emily. “What exactly do you have in mind, and why are you telling me this now?!” It is 5:15 p.m. The beef stew is in the crockpot. The biscuits are in the oven. The broccoli is cut and waiting to go into the steamer. Sherry is out of town and John is at work.

Essentially, Emily doesn’t really want to be involved in this project for her at all. But Journey, Skye, and Becton have ideas about what kinds of cookies they want to make. I end up taking the three youngest to the grocery store to gather the supplies. Now, I’m not Betty Crocker. The preformed, pop-in-the-oven variety of cookies is fine with me. Add sprinkles or chocolate kisses and we’re done. But I’m feeling stressed. This is one of Becton’s days home from school. And Skye stayed home sick as well. I’ve washed all the clothes and folded them. I’ve cleaned up the kitchen a million times. I’ve been at someone’s beck and call all day. I haven’t exercised in days, but I’ve eaten every scrap of leftover food. I’m feeling fat and ugly.

We are standing in the check-out line at the grocery store, and my “sick child” asks me to buy more candy for her. I’ve had enough. I say, “I have got to get a job!”

Journey asks, “Why, Mommy?”

I diplomatically respond, “I need to contribute financially to the family, the way Daddy does.”

Journey asks, “What does that mean, Mommy?”

Rebecca: “That means, I need to make money for the family.”

Journey: "Please don't get a job, Mommy. I'll give you my tooth fairy money."

It didn't matter that there was more chaos and conflict surrounding the cookie-making and clean-up of craft supplies later. This was my "valentine"–being valued by one of my angels for the job I try to do, no matter how badly I do it some days.

§ § §

Email to family and friends dated March 21, 2007

As parents, we try to teach our children important lessons to shape their character and sensibilities. Most of the time, I fear, my words are heard as "yabber yabber yabber…" One of my attempts at "shaping" involved putting framed posters about sportsmanship, charity, diversity, and so forth on a wall in the bathroom that the children most often use.

Today, when Skye came home from school, she hurried over to

tell me this story: "We had a new boy visiting the school today and I was playing with him. Another student said to me in a nasty voice, 'You are playing with a black boy.' I said to him," 'The hand of friendship has no color'" You guessed it: it was a direct quote of the caption to one of my posters. Skye was clearly proud of herself and so was I!

P.S. If you happen to see Skye, please don't mention this. She knows I've written an email about it, but she says she will "die" if people start "congratulating" her. She could hardly stand it when Emily said, "Way to go!"

§ § §

By the summer of 2008, we had lost touch with Emily's birthmother; and Emily and I were struggling–as mothers and teenage daughters do. Spending time with her relatives over the years had given Emily a partial view of their lives, but it had not shown her their day-to-day struggles. In a recent confrontation between Emily and me, she shouted: "You should have left me in Nebraska. I would have been better off there!" Though I made many mistakes as a parent, I knew that Emily's romantic view of life in Nebraska contributed to her assessment that I was an imperfect mother. So careful not to disparage Emily's birth family, had we done her a disservice by not telling the whole story?

Skye's relationship with her birthmother had been much more complicated. Not long ago, when Skye and I were talking about her behavior, she commented: "I better watch myself or I'll end up like my birthmother." Skye was forced, at a young age, to confront Christina's weaknesses as our family became entangled with the foster care system in an effort to help her younger siblings. The drama had been intense at times. Was this good for Skye?

Journey, a sensitive child by nature, was very sad. Her birthmother had disappeared when she was 15 months old. Often, when Journey was upset with John or me, she cried for Grace. Recently, I took

Journey to get her ears re-pierced because the holes had closed over. She froze and couldn't go through with it. Later, Journey cried, remembering that the first time she had her ears pierced, she had held "Grace-Teddy," a bear given to her by her birthmother, and now lost. Journey asked, "Why did Grace give me away?" Although I could answer her question factually, I knew it wasn't the same as hearing the words directly from Grace. I asked Journey if she wanted to search for Grace, and told her that I would help her find her birthmother.

Grace's story was complicated as well. She did not tell her family of origin about her pregnancy. Searching for her now meant potentially opening doors that Grace might want to remain closed. Whose rights or needs should have priority–Journey's or Grace's? And what will Journey find at the end of this search? Is she too young? Is there a "right age" to search?

Becton called himself a "song and dance man." He was full of life, laughter and love. His birthmother had chosen a closed adoption. We did not even have a picture of her to share with him. Right now, it didn't matter to Becton. Color didn't matter. His family was his family. But, someday, I imagined, that would change. We prepare for that day as best we can with the friendships we cultivate, the schools and activities we choose, and the artwork in our home. We had hesitated before agreeing to a closed adoption, but Becton was the right child for our family.

Open adoptions are not created equally. Even ideal open relationships could change over time, as ours had, as the individuals involved changed and grew. Moreover, the inequalities could create hardships for the children involved, even when we, as parents, had the best intentions. My father used to tell me with regularity: "Life is not fair." That is an understatement in a family created through multiple adoptions.

I asked myself: *Would we do it differently?* Absolutely not.

As I looked forward, I imagined that we would find Emily's birthmother and that Emily would spend more time with her half-sisters and younger brother. K.J. would meet his new half-sister and continue to enjoy his role as big brother to three younger full-siblings. We would continue to help Skye nurture relationships with her biological half-siblings and their families–both biological and adoptive. And, one day, she would have a relationship with her birthmother again. We would search for Journey's birthmother. Whatever we found, we would support Journey in dealing with it. Becton would realize that he is "black," and as he established his identity in this race-conscious world, we would stand with him and for him. When he was ready, we would search for his biological parents as well.

These post-adoption, growing-up years were mysterious. But many of the most rewarding experiences in life begin on paths to destinations unknown. At the very least, we had the truth on our side. We had shared or would share–at the proper ages of our children–all the information we had about our children's origins. The philosophy of open adoption had given us a foundation. If we continued to keep our children's best interests as our guiding light, I trusted we would all survive this adventure and be better off for having made the journey.

§ § §

We were struggling with how best to parent K.J. He had been diagnosed with attention deficit disorder and anxiety issues. We sought professional help. Open adoption is touted as a great way to get medical history for your child, to learn something about their potential strengths and weaknesses, and to learn something about how there personalities might develop. It's easy to use the "good" information to bolster your children: "You have great ball-handling skills just like your birth father" or "You are so graceful, just like your birthmother who was a dancer." But what do you do with the "bad" information? If your child's biological relative goes to jail for writing bad checks, do you worry about his future when he develops a habit of lying and sneakiness? If you know your child's biological relative was manipulative and self-centered, do you worry about your child's future when she demonstrates similar traits? How do you know what comes from *nature* and what comes from *nurture*–especially when you hear people say things like: "You are just like your mother/father!"–and you know it to be true in a particular case?

Looking back, I think I crossed the line whenever, in a fit of anger or frustration, I suggested to my child that he or she could end up doing some bad act like a biological relative. I meant it as a warning, much as a parent would say: "If you don't bring your bike in, someone may steal it and then you won't have a bike to ride." Instead, my words were more like "labels," forecasts of inevitable doom and gloom. I have tried not to repeat this mistake.

But I still question how much of the *bad* information to share and when. How much and what kind is helpful? When does it become hurtful to share the truth? Is it better to be honest about a person's origins even if there is *some* hurt involved?

In December 2008, we reconnected with Michelle, Emily's birthmother. Emily, K.J., and I flew to Nebraska to spend four days with birth family members. Emily and K.J. were celebrated like rock stars. It was a time of love, laughter, and reunions that they will not soon forget.

These are some notes from my journal as the adoptive mother who witnessed this joyful weekend:

> I am sitting in our motel room, which has been "Grand Central Station" for a stream of visitors of all ages. As I reflect on these past two and a half days, I am not sure my presence is even necessary–other than the fact that I brought these people together. I sit back and, mostly, watch. Emily and K.J. were both born here in Columbus, Nebraska. And we have had contact and visits with their birth families from the beginning. But the kids are now old enough to hold their own with their relatives. Emily is visiting three older half-sisters (the oldest to whom is now married and pregnant with her first child), as well as a younger half-brother and her birthmother. Emily has also seen two grandmothers, an aunt, a great aunt and uncle, and many cousins. K.J. is visiting with three younger brothers, a half-sister, his birthmother and her mother, his birth father and his wife, another grandmother, aunts and multiple cousins. The boys wrestle and chase each other. The girls laugh, exchange clothes, and hang out together as if they do it every day.
>
> This biological or genetic connection is more than eye color, body shape, or even mannerisms. There is an intangible something that brings them together like they have never been apart. It's what I hoped for – but it is scary at the same time. My head knows that my presence has mattered and continues to matter. I am "Mom." Their other mothers are called by first names. But in my heart, I am jealous. They will never be exclusively MY children….

As we said our "good-byes" this morning, Tessa and Michelle were crying. Observing the pain on my face, Tessa remarked, "Don't worry. These are happy tears." Michelle followed: "It's hard. But it's what we wanted. We have this time because of you." I am reminded that my children's birthmothers and I are more similar than different. They too feel "jealousy." It's different than what other mothers experience, I suspect. But between us, together, we hope to give our children what they need. My additional hope for them is that they get something extra: a perspective on the unfairness of life and the magnitude of love to accomplish amazing things.

§ § §

The day after Christmas, my sister called to tell me that a package to me had been delivered to her house–the Falcos' "old" house. It was a package from Grace, Journey's birthmother! Journey and I were overjoyed! The package contained some gift items for Journey, a letter to her, and a longer letter to me. Grace's letter to Journey was loving and kind. Her letter to me spoke more about the difficulties in her life. It was clear that she was hurting, but he source of the pain was not clear to me.

There was no return address, only the address of the UPS store that sent the package. I did an Internet "white pages" search for "Grace *[Last Name]*" near that UPS location and made my best guess about where she lived. Journey and I wrote letters and included items in a box that I then sent to Grace. My letter said:

> What a shock and pleasure it was to receive a phone call from my sister, Joanna, the day after Christmas, telling me that there was a package from you to me at her house–which is our old address/house. I'm so glad my sister and her family bought our house. Needless to say, John and I went rushing over to retrieve the box. Journey had sent a letter to Santa wishing for the "best Christmas ever," and your gift and letter made it so for her. She has been longing to hear from you. Thank you for making her dream–and mine–a reality.
>
> I hope you don't mind that I am sending you this box at this address. I didn't know if your failure to send a return address meant that you didn't want to be contacted or if it was an oversight. I'm not trying to put any pressure on you about contact. I realize that I don't know enough about your situation. Obviously, you are in a lot of pain. I don't know who in your family, if anyone, knows about Journey. I don't know what being in contact with us would mean for your life. But, please know, that all of us want to stay connected to you, if that is possible. You will need to let us know what the next step would be.
>
> In the meantime, I have sent you several things. One is a set of crafts that Journey created from craft-kits over the holidays. She wanted you to have them. Journey also wrote you a letter. I am also sending along our annual Holiday letter and picture. It will give you a little insight into what has been going on in our family

this past year. Finally, I have sent you a book of recent pictures of Journey and other members of the family. I can provide you with other pictures of Journey over the years when you are ready to receive them. I trust that you will let me know when that time is.

I probably don't need to say this, but, just in case, I want to make sure that you know how much we love you, that you have nothing to apologize for, and that you have given us the greatest joy in life by allowing us to be Journey's parents.

As you will surmise from my "holiday letter," one of the things that I keep learning over and over again as a parent to many children through adoption: the biological connection runs deep. It affects so many things. Frankly, I don't know how people in closed adoptions can ignore it. Last night, Journey said to me: "I know where I get my sensitivity from. It's from Grace...." You see, she is always processing the connection even when you aren't here.

If you do decide to contact us again–and we hope you will–please use the information provided above. That is our new address and phone number. I don't know if you have access to a computer, but you can email me from home or the library or anywhere at the address above.

We love you. We think about you every day. You are part of our family too.

The post office was unable to deliver the package after several attempts. It was returned to us and sits in my closet waiting.

§ § §

In early 2009, I joined Facebook to track the behavior of my 'tweens and teen. Right away, Skye's birthmother, Christina, found me. I shared some information with her about Skye and she wrote back at length to tell all the ways that she and Skye were alike. For instance, both played clarinet in school. Both enjoyed piano playing. Both struggled with ADHD in school–although Christina did not have medication as a child. She said that being smart was very important to her, but that she was too stubborn to ask for help when she was not able to learn as fast as other students. She wondered how things might have turned out differently if she had been willing to ask for help and/or medicine.

Especially interesting to me, as the adoptive mother who struggled to get through Skye's defenses, were Christina's comments about "control." She wrote that whenever she was made to do something, she fought it. But if she was left on her own, it usually got done. She remembered sitting up for hours at night trying to get her schoolwork right so she'd be like the other kids at school. Now that she was on medicine for ADHD as an adult, she could focus better and feel successful. Christina wanted Skye to know that she thought Skye was a "super smart person."

Christina also resonated with Skye regarding stage fright. She said she was outgoing around people, but if thrust in the spotlight or asked to perform around strangers, she was scared to death. This was exactly what I had experienced with Skye.

Another trait that seemed to have passed from mother to daughter regarded "touch." Christina remarked that she was guarded or put up walls, no matter how close she was to someone. She got uncomfortable or stiff when people tried to hug her, though she knew she craved the affection. She thought this, too, might have to do with "control" because she was okay with being the initiator of hugs or other demonstrations of affection.

I was grateful to have this information. When a child displays characteristics like stubbornness in family relationships or terror regarding public performance or resistance to affection, it is natural, as a parent, to wonder what you've done to create these obstacles to your child's happiness. Knowing that there might be a biological component didn't solve the issues, but it allowed me (and John) to be less hard on ourselves *and* to be less hard on Skye. As difficult as it had been over the years to deal with Christina at certain points, I found myself again being appreciative of this open relationship. None of us had to be stuck at a particular point in our lives. We were all capable of continued growth. This was as true of me as it was of Christina or Skye.

Parenting Dilemmas and Blessings

March 2009 to February 2010

Email to family and friends, dated March 31, 2009

How complicated is life in a family created through adoption? Let me count the ways....

Yesterday, Emily became an aunt. Her oldest biological half-sister (on her mother's side of the family) gave birth to a baby boy. Today, Emily received pictures of her nephew. She was obviously very proud to be included. She had spent two days texting back and forth with another bio-sister, Bella, in anticipation of this event.

A few minutes later, Emily sees her sister, Skye, with her hair, newly straightened, by Sherry. Emily makes some kind of disparaging remark. Sherry reprimands her to speak more kindly to her sister. Emily responds: "She's not my sister. We are nothing alike. We have nothing in common." Okay, so Emily is 14, but that doesn't excuse her behavior. But does being adopted excuse her? Every time that Emily has contact with her birth family, she gets good vibes. She is currently basking in the glory of being a distant, but not forgotten Aunt, when along comes her tedious, younger Falco siblings.

So, how do I respond? Is she working out some grief related to her birth family that I should respect and encourage? Do I punish her for being disrespectful to members of her family? I don't always know the answer to those questions–especially when I'm being told by Emily that I don't understand her particular adolescent situation of the moment.

Then there's K.J. He and I went to a parent-teacher conference today because he is failing language arts. I won't bore you with all the gory details. But the questions that plague me, on and off, again and again, are: Would his birth parents understand this better than I do? Would Tessa and Kyle know what to do? I wonder if I'm missing something because K.J. and I do not share the same genetics.

Skye has traits of both her mothers. I could have given birth to Skye's impassioned outrage. My mother reminds me that when I lived at home, my dad and I would go into his study and yell at each other, leaving her still shaking, when we ended our disagreement and walked away, ready to move on to other things. But with Skye, there is a hysterical, unknown factor at work as well. Yesterday, she was so mad at me about enforcing discipline with her that she shouted: "I want to go live with foster parents! Anything is better than living with you!" Does she mean that? John and I were foster parents to her brother. She has a worldliness about her that I never had as a child. But I also know her birthmother's history and temperament. She and Skye are cut from the same cloth. What do I do with that knowledge? The answers are not easy to come by.

I don't have a pithy, tear-jerking end to this. It is what it is. I do the best I can; and I keep learning from them. My prayer to God each day is that I can continue to do so.

§ § §

With my ex-sister-in-law's permission, I am including her response to the foregoing email:

Here's what would happen if all of these kids were your biological children: Emily would still find something "out there" that seemed better than "at home" and flaunt it as part of her becoming a young woman with independent thoughts and ways. KJ would still do things that only God understands. Skye would still throw fits and she would say "I wish someone would adopt me so I could get away from YOU!" when she was angry. She will, under any circumstances, find your button and push it when she's mad. That's what Leos do. Journey would be upset and hurt that she wasn't either an only child or wasn't given favorite status in everything. She's going to take everything personally until she's at least 28. Becton would have been the result of some wild mid-life crisis where you ran off with a rap singer and John had to come fetch you and you two still wouldn't be the same color.

So, in short, you'd have exactly the same complications, just a bunch of bio children and stretch marks. Instead, you have these great kids and wonderful abs. You're doing fantastic, both with parenting and keeping your body together. Wow. No kidding! I love your life!

§ § §

I had to laugh at myself. I could get so in-my-head, trying to be the conscientious parent and advocate of open adoption, that I sometimes lost my sense of humor and "blessing"–both very necessary in the parenting toolkit.

§ § §

Email dated March 2009:

Yesterday, Skye and I took Xavior, her 6-month-old puppy, to have his stitches removed, 10 days following surgery to neuter him. This young dog is almost 40 lbs, much larger than his 20-something lb. mother. According to DNA tests, his father was a very large dog. But we didn't know that when we adopted Xavior. For months, maybe years, Skye had been begging for her own dog, a small dog that she could sleep with and keep in her room. When Xavior was born to a foster dog down the street, he seemed to fit the bill, and Skye desperately wanted him.

As we waited for our turn at the vet, a family friend, appeared with her 4-month-old puppy, a beagle mix, a small dog. Skye and I went over to greet them. The puppy was one of a litter born to the dog of our friend shortly after we had committed to adopt Xavior.

As Skye and I were getting in the car later, I said, "You know–this is nothing bad about Xavior–and he's a member of our family–and I love him–but if we'd known about Melissa's puppies before..." Skye cut me off: "I know, Mom. I remember seeing pictures of the puppies. I would have wanted to adopt one of those puppies too."

More than five years ago, after two years of failed attempts to adopt a fifth child, we were suddenly presented with the opportunity to adopt Becton in a *closed* adoption–something we'd never done before and had reservations about doing. But we met Becton and fell in love with him. He was ours. The next week, I got a call from an attorney who wanted me to adopt an African-American baby boy in a fully *open* adoption.

"The one that got away." The thing, the person, the dreamed of and longed for ideal appears–and it's too late. There's a song from Disney's "Pocahontas" that says: "You can't step in the same river twice. The water's always changing, always flowing." One step, one decision changes the trajectory of the journey.

But what do you do with those feelings about "the one that got away"? It seems to me that if you don't acknowledge the loss and feel the sadness and *deal* with it, you limit yourself. I've known women who would not face the reality of their infertility and mourn the loss of their unborn children until it was too late to adopt or to celebrate the freedom that childlessness brings to some. The loss defined them.

The ideal man, the ideal dog, or the ideal child. isn't really "out there." Our dreams are part of us. *We* create them. We know their contours. They are predictable. We anticipate how they will make us feel once realized. There is less mystery there than we might assume.

On the other hand, to take a chance on something, on someone, who is *not* known, is more of an adventure. There's another song in "Pocahontas" that says: "If you walk the footsteps of a stranger, you'll learn things you never knew you never knew." How rich I feel to be given the opportunity to learn and experience so much from these unexpected treasures.

Email to family and friends, dated May 17, 2009

"Do you still have that black child?" was the question put to me at the photo counter at Sam's club Friday morning. My first thought was: "And where else would he be?" But that is not the way I responded. The question came from a young woman, African-American herself, that I have had a photo-printing relationship with since Journey was a baby. She knows me as the woman who "adopts all those babies." She is not ill-intentioned. But her question reminds me that I have opportunities almost every day to educate, or not–to be outraged, or not–or to simply keep moving. This kind of question is a reminder that we are not a "usual" family. We are different.

If Becton had been with me, she would not have asked that particular question. But she might have asked another question that referenced our relationship as adoptive parent and child. I am careful, now that my children are no longer babies, to think about how they will hear and judge my responses to questions that spotlight our relationship as legal, but not biological.

Emily, at 14, would like for me to stop talking about adoption. She wants things to be "normal." Meanwhile, she has phone and Facebook relationships with many of her biological family members. Thanks to open adoption, that IS "normal" for her.

K.J., shy as he is, could almost be an open adoption advocate himself. He knows the language. He appreciates the advantages. He will still sing the "Happy Adoption Day" song with me–well, maybe not in public anymore.

Skye is irritated with her birthmother for all her screw-ups. She tolerates adoption talk, but she doesn't want a lot of focus on it. Skye has a great relationship with one of her half-biological-brothers, and pleasant ones with many other relatives. And, she is beginning an email relationship with her birthmother.

Journey, as many of you know, carries around a lot of sadness about her birthmother's disappearance. If I begin to forget this, I will find little reminders like the book she brought home from school this week, written about Becton's birth, but dedicated to Grace.

Becton, for his part, has just learned that his original birth certificate states that his name is "Baby Boy Bell." He thinks it's funny. It has not yet settled in with him that his birthmother did not give him a name. Someday, I suspect, that fact will make him sad.

I like to tell the story of the day I went to K.J.'s Second Grade class at Laurel Ridge Elementary School to celebrate his adoption day: the anniversary of the day his adoption was finalized. His cousin, Kylie, was in his class. That was the day my older niece and nephew first really understood the concept of birthmothers. They ran home and asked their own mother, my sister: "Who is our birthmother?"–to which Joanna replied, "Well, I am." The way she reported the incident, the children were disappointed that they only had one mother. We all got a laugh out of that. I like the story because it is a reversal of the usual.

Being reminded that our family is created through adoption is not just an opportunity to educate others. It is an occasion for me (or my children) to revisit my/our grief. Almost 15 years later, I still ask myself: Am I a good enough parent? Am I entitled to be her or his mother? I know the logical answer: Of course, I am! Though I do not share the perspective of some adoptive parents who feel they "rescued" their child from an otherwise miserable existence, I have an inner confidence that these are my children. But the blemish of infertility and the inadequacies of my body to accomplish the whole matter undercut this. In some ways, it's like being a rape survivor, which I am also. I can tell the story over and over again. As the years have passed, it has become easier and easier to do. And I know that I have important things to share about safety and sexuality and recovery, etc. But the telling still reminds me that I am blemished.

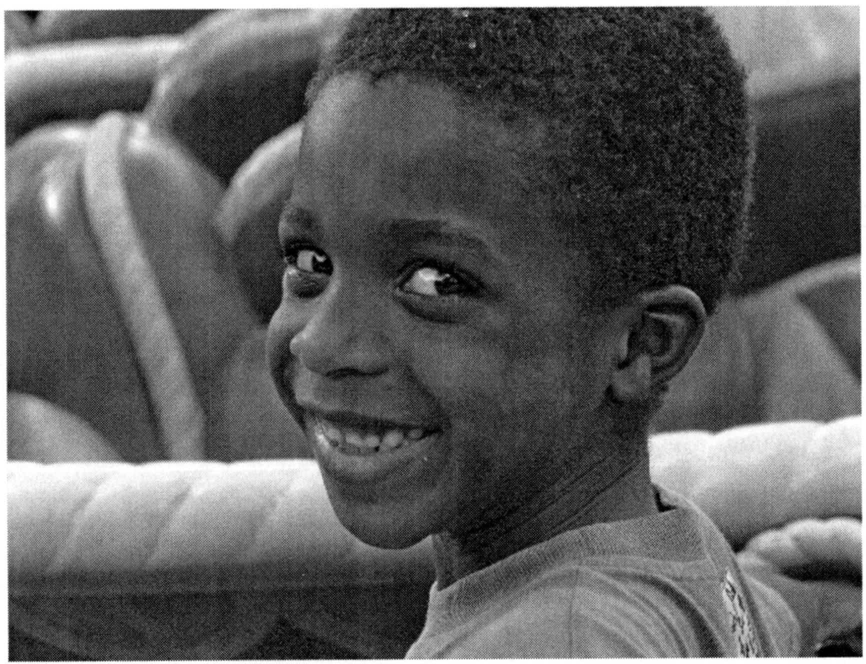

Yesterday, Becton and I sat down to watch Disney's "The Hunchback of Notre Dame," one of the few movies in our possession that he has not seen. It isn't an easy story for a 5-year-old to understand. He asked lots of questions: Why does Quasimodo look that way? How did he get that way? Will he change? Will his dead mother come back? Will the people stop laughing at him? With each question, I recognized the opportunity to teach him about difference, about beauty, about standards imposed by society, about biological versus adoptive parenting, about cruelty and discrimination and the power of love. It was almost overwhelming.

As I look back on this now, after my experience at Sam's Club, the word that comes to mind is "patience." It takes time, repeated education, personal experience with all sorts of people, being-in-the-right-place-at-the-right-time, and so much more, to change minds and hearts. Youthful, righteous indignation is powerful stuff, but it isn't all that is needed. I used to think it was: present a compelling argument and people would stand in line to vote for my cause. When I was younger, I thought my father was the role model in my family. After all, he went out into the world and made the money for our family. He had higher education and he helped people with his wisdom and compassion. It was not until years later that I realized my father could not have done what he did without all the work my mother did behind the scenes. But she did it with her elegant and compelling presence, not by argument or force.

> If I'm honest with myself, the decision to adopt my second son–"that black child"–did not come to me as a compelling argument. It became clear over time, with repeated education, through personal experience with all sorts of people, being-in-the-right-place-at-the-right-time–and so much more. I have no right to expect all other people to understand my motivations, my story. But I do have an obligation to protect my son, and all of my children, from harm, be it intentional or not. This I will do, for they had no choice about becoming "different." I chose to step outside the "usual" box and take them on this journey with me. And their judgment about how well I do matters.

§ § §

Oprah Winfrey has a column in her magazine "O" called, "What I Know For Sure." I like the sound of that. I'd like to believe that I could know certain things to be as inevitable as death and taxes. On occasion I have felt that I did. But most of the time, I discover exceptions to the rules. This has been particularly true with my children. Nevertheless, I'll take a stab at it because it seems like the logical way to end this story.

- What I know for sure is that we are all the same, but different.
- What I know for sure is that our personalities are entrenched, but their expression can be changed.
- What I know for sure is that honest expressions of love toward another person are mightier than any exertion of power.

As I write these last few pages of my story, I am waiting for a call from a pregnant woman–call her Kate–who wants to place her baby for adoption. I was introduced to her through a friend of a friend of a friend. I tried to educate Kate about the different types of adoption; I solicited profiles to meet her specifications from prospective adoptive parents; and I introduced her to an adoption attorney who could speak knowledgeably about her case and the law. She chose two moms with a young daughter to adopt her expected son. If Kate doesn't have the baby in the next two days, her labor will be induced mid-week, and I will meet her at the hospital.

Kate has been highly emotional, sometimes disturbingly so. She has stopped answering calls at times or been too eager to please at other times. Some people would call her "high risk for reclaim." But I am going to ride this out with her. Kate may disappear. She may place the baby and then reclaim him. But I trust the process. I trust her to make the best decision she can under the circumstances.

Truth is, I'm not that different now than I was in 1982 at 24 when I gave a ride to a stranger because he seemed to need help with his car. I trust people–some would say "to a fault." But I would rather err on the side of too much trust than not enough. I trust what a rape survivor says when she tells her story. And I trust what members of the adoption triad tell me as well. I think most people want to tell the truth. They lie when they believe they will not be accepted for their bad decisions or who they are. I don't know how to fix that except to keep offering a safe place for the truth and forgiveness when it isn't given.

Appendix A

Researching Adoption

Suggestions by Rebecca Patton Falco

The following are questions to ask yourself before you start doing research on adoption agencies or attorneys. Your answers may change over time, but preliminary answers will help you focus as you make your inquiries:

- Are you interested in adopting only an infant or is an older child acceptable? How much older?
- Would you be willing to adopt a child with special medical/physical or emotional needs? What kinds of "special needs" are acceptable to you?
- Is a child of either sex acceptable or do you have a strong preference about the sex of the child?
- Do you want a closed, semi-open, or open adoption? (E.g., do you want to meet the birth parents? Do you want on-going contact? Your position on this may change as you learn more about adoption.)
- Do you want a child who is full Caucasian or another race, or is a mixture of certain races? (Be aware that if you are Caucasian and want to adopt a full Caucasian child, it can take longer. It is important that you follow your heart. Ask yourself: would I be just as excited if a birthmother called me who was carrying a *[name of a race other than your own]* child as I would if a birthmother called me who was carrying a *[name of my race]* child?)
- Are you interested only in domestic adoption or are you open to foreign adoption? Which countries or regions of the world? (Whatever you choose, find out from the agency how much medical and social history will be available about your child.)

After you have an idea of what kind of child and what kind of relationship you want with birth parents, then make a list of questions to ask each agency. These would be some of mine:

- What are your requirements for adoptive parents? (E.g., some agencies require that you be in a certain age range, have a certain religious affiliation, provide proof of infertility, have been married for a certain length of time, etc.)
- Can a gay/lesbian person adopt through your agency? If so, are there any special conditions that an adoptive parent who is gay/lesbian must meet?
- How long does it take to adopt *[describe the type child you are looking for]* through your agency? Will it take longer for a gay/lesbian person to adopt? If so, how much longer?
- What age and race/ethnicity of children are available? Can an adoptive parent express a preference regarding the sex of the child he/she adopts?
- Does the time it takes to adopt differ depending on the age, sex, or race/ethnicity of the child? How does it differ?
- Please describe how your process works? (There may be an application process, a home study, educational workshops….)
- How do you match adoptive parents and birth parents or children? (E.g., is there a waiting list? Do you prepare a "resume"? Does the agency rep select who matches with who or does the birthmother, etc.?)
- How does your agency find birthmothers? (E.g., will the agency be advertising or will you or both?)
- What type of adoptions do you do–foreign or domestic? Open or closed? What do you mean by "open" or "closed"? (*Believe me*–the agencies mean very different things when they use this terminology.)
- How long does it take to terminate the parental rights of the birth parents? (E.g., Georgia has a 10 day waiting period; NC has a 21-day period; Nebraska's surrenders were irrevocable as soon as signed, etc. This question may help you find out where the birth parents are that the agency works with–which will also help you find out if it is likely you will be traveling to complete an adoption, or hiring another agency or attorney in another state to complete legal requirements on that end, etc.)
- Do you provide counseling for the birth parents? How does it work? Both before and after birth? Counseling for adoptive parents too? (I

highly recommend counseling for both birth parents and adoptive parents.)

- How much does an adoption through your agency cost? (It is important to find out how you pay their fee–up front, month by month, or as services are used, etc.–and what the fee covers. There are lots of "hidden costs" in adoption.)
- Does your fee cover the cost of finding a birthmother?
- Counseling? (For birth parents and adoptive parents?)
- Birth parent living expenses? (Some birth parents don't need these.)
- Medical expenses? (Many birth parents could qualify for government assistance.)
- Administration of surrender/termination of parental rights documents?
- Legal fees to finalize the adoption?
- Is the cost different for in-state versus interstate adoptions?
- What is an average total cost?
- What is the range of total costs?
- Can they refer you to some adoptive parents who have worked with their agency and completed an adoption and some clients who are currently working with their agency to adopt? If you are gay/lesbian, you will probably want to ask if the agency has gay or lesbian individuals or couples who have adopted through their organization and who would be willing to talk to you about their adoption experience?
- If the agency does not work with prospective adoptive parents who are gay, can they recommend agencies, organizations, or attorneys who do?
- Ask the agency to send you written information to review and ask if they offer information sessions. Is there a cost associated with these?

If the agency seems put out with you because you ask so many questions, take that into consideration in choosing or not choosing to work with the agency. If they can't be sensitive and understanding at this stage, what are the chances they can help and reassure you when you are in crisis? Don't let the agencies intimidate you! You may feel desperate and at their disposal, but they aren't all powerful entities. They need your money and the confidence of birth parents to exist. They ought to sound like they care about you, the birth parents and the child.

But also remember that the agency you are talking to is not responsible for the time and money you may have already spent trying to conceive a child or adopt one through other means. Many prospective adoptive parents, when they get to this point, dump their anger and grief on the agency worker. The anger and grief are important issues to work on either through the resources of the agency, your own therapist, or family and friends, but the cost of and emotions surrounding adoption should be dealt with separately, if at all possible.

Appendix B

Background Information Form

(Space between questions has been reduced from original form)

Due date ______________

Birthmother

Age _____ Date of birth __________

Address

Telephone ___________________

Race __________________ American Indian? ___

Marital status ___________ Ever married/divorced? ___

Birth father

Age _____ Date of birth __________

Address

Telephone ___________________

Race __________________ American Indian? ___

Marital status ___________ Ever married/divorced? ___

Pre-Birth Planning

Referral source to adoptive parents:

Birthfather's awareness of pregnancy and adoption plan/status of relationship:

Support system (family/friends) and their attitude toward adoption:

Living/financial situation:

Reasons for considering placing child for adoption:

Medical insurance? _____ Type? ________________

Prenatal care:

Will birthmother sign consent to release medical records to adoptive parents? ___

Prior counseling (psychiatric treatment; medication in past two years)? _____

Receiving SSI or disability? _____

Alcohol or drug use during pregnancy:

Previous pregnancies/medical problems:

Tentative Plans for Labor and Delivery

Birthmother's plans for childbirth preparation:

Birthmother's wishes for who she would like present for her labor:

Birthmother's wishes for who she would like present for actual birth:

Where will adoptive parents be?

After the birth, what are the birthmother's wishes for contact with baby and adoptive parents?

Who will take care of baby in hospital?

In the hospital, the birthmother would like to "room in" with baby OR room on obstetrics unit and have baby brought to her on request OR room on obstetrics unit and go to nursery for contact with baby OR room on non-maternity unit and not have baby in room at all?

Who will name the baby?

Does birthmother have concerns about confidentiality while in hospital?

Birthmother's plans with regard to transferring baby to adoptive parents and leaving hospital?

Contact, Communication, and Visits

The adoptive parents will mail to the birthparent(s) pictures of the baby at the following times:

What type of telephone contact do the adoptive parents and birthparents want with one another? How often will calls be made and who will initiate the calls?

During the first year after birth, visits will be arranged as follows:

How will the child's first birthday be handled?

After the first year of the child's life, visits will be arranged as follows:

Other specific requests for contact? (e.g. video tapes, etc.)

Background, Educational, and Health History Report

Name:

Information on you and your parents	Birth Parent	Mother	Father
Birth date/place			
Height/weight			
Hair color			
Eye color			
Skin shade			
Race			
Ethnic background			
Religion			
Years of education			
Diploma/degree			
Areas of study			
Interests/ Hobbies/ Talents/Interests			

Falco

School
Activities

Current occupation

Job & past
work Experience

Personal and
professional
goals

Marital status

General health

Other significant
information

About your family:
Brothers and sisters: names, ages, description (hair & eye color, etc.), education, occupation, general health, etc.

Children, if applicable: names, ages, description (hair & eye color, etc.), educational performance, general health

Describe your relationship with your parents:

Your parents' reaction to pregnancy and adoption:

About you:
Describe your personality (outgoing, shy, active, quiet, etc.)

Why have you chosen adoption rather than other alternatives?

Is there anything else you can add about yourself or your family that may be of interest to the adoptive parents in raising the child?

Is there anything else you would like your child to know about you?

Do you or close biological relatives have any special medical conditions?

Please list any major surgeries you have had and when:

Drug/alcohol/smoking history: please specify drugs, frequency of drug use, and if they were taken prior to or during pregnancy:

When did prenatal care begin? Name and address of doctor:

Any complications with this pregnancy or previous pregnancies?

Appendix C

All Things Considered

By Rebecca Patton Falco

Rarely a day passes when I am not aware that I am one of ten parents in my family. John and I are the day-to-day parents, the legal parents, of our children; but there are also four other sets of parents for our four children. These parents gave our children their "looks" and their aptitude for certain skills. And, because ours is a family created through open adoptions with continued contact and interaction, these other sets of parents also give our children experiences and memories and love.

In our children's birth stories and in their on-going relationships with their birth families, there have been some unhappy circumstances as well as some happy ones. These circumstances include divorce, remarriage, changes in significant others, child abuse, substance abuse, recovery from abuses, loss of employment, new employment, time spent in jail, serious physical illnesses, mental illnesses, deaths, and new births. Not all of these circumstances are ones that we can discuss candidly with our young children while they are young, but we do share as much as we can. Our expectation is that eventually they will know everything that we, as parents, know now.

In our family, we celebrate differences. Our families of origin are different. Our genetic make-up is different. We joined this family under differing circumstances. Whenever possible, we discuss those differences. We have many good things to discuss about our birth families. But we also have "bad acts" and "bad choices" to discuss. This gives us the opportunity to reinforce the point that a "bad act" or "bad choice" does not make a person bad. It also gives us the opportunity to explore when a person's circumstances are under that person's control and when they are not. John and I hope that all of this contributes to developing empathy and compassion in our children. We already know from their choice of friends that they do not see race and disability as “difference” that matters.

Shouldn’t our children be permitted to claim all of their heritage without feeling shame? If each of us led a perfect life, most children would not be placed for adoption. But the less-than-perfect circumstances that brought our children to us do not make them less than perfect children. Mine are my angels, my undeserved gifts from God and from their birth parents.

LaVergne, TN USA
02 August 2010
191660LV00003B/1/P